Budapest

Michael Jacobs is a freelance writer and senior honorary research fellow at Glasgow University. He has been a regular visitor to Hungary since 1980, when he went there to research *The Good and Simple Life: Artist Colonies in Europe and America* (1985). His many other books on art and travel include *Between Hopes and Memories: A Spanish Journey* (1994), *The Painted Voyage: Art, Travel and Exploration, 1564–1875* (1995), and *Madrid Observed* (1996).

Budapest

⊠ A Cultural Guide ⊠

Michael Jacobs

Oxford   New York
OXFORD UNIVERSITY PRESS
1998

Oxford University Press, Great Claredon Street, Oxford OX2 6DP

Oxford New York

Athens Auckland Bankok Bogota Bombay
Buenos Aires Calcutta CApe Town Dar es Salaam
Delhi Florence Hong Kong Istanbul Karachi
Kuala Lumpur Madras Madrid Melbourne
Mexico City Nairobi Paris Singapore
Taipei Tokyo Toronto Warsaw
and associated companies in
Berlin Ibadan

Oxford is a trade mark of Oxford University Press

British Library Cataloging in Publication Data
ISBN 0–19–210001–7

1 3 5 7 9 10 8 6 4 2

Typeset by Best-set Typesetter Ltd., Hong Kong
Printed in Great Britain by
Mackays of Chatham,
Chatham, Kent

To Ildikó, Árpád, and Réka

Preface and Acknowledgements

Budapest is a city that makes an immediate strong impression on the visitor, and not simply because of its dramatically beautiful situation on the Danube. When I came here for the first time eighteen years ago, after having spent a previous period in a then moribund Vienna, I was instantly enthralled by Budapest's gaiety and energy, and by the way it exuded all the scale, grandeur, and excitement of a major capital. My response was typical of that of generations of travellers to this city: as early as 1840, over thirty years before the joining together of Buda and Pest, an English visitor called Julia Pardoe wrote: 'there is such a constant variety and movement in [Pest's] streets, such a blending of the Oriental with the European, and such a holiday look about the whole population, that it is impossible to feel ennui in the chief city of the Magyars'. Nearly a century later, when the city was already in cultural and political decline, the Irish wanderer Walter Starkie found that 'life in Budapest moves to a more rapid rhythm than elsewhere in Europe, as though every moment of the day had unlimited possibilities of emotional excitement'. 'Budapest', summarized the contemporary Italian author Claudio Magris, 'is the loveliest city on the Danube. It has a crafty way of being its own stage-set, like Vienna, but also has a robust substance and a vitality unknown to its Austrian rival.'

But Budapest is also a city of paradoxes that has managed to combine a smiling, dynamic image with a reputation for nostalgic absorption in its past so great that a recent French guidebook to the place has been subtitled 'Danube Blues'. Even today, in this post-communist era of rapid change, the visitor will find here constant reminders of a largely vanished Europe—old-fashioned courtesies and customs (from the kissing of hands to the constant presentation of flowers), ancient trams rattling down broad boulevards, faded neo-baroque interiors, exteriors pockmarked with shrapnel, streets of granite cobblestones, smoke-filled restaurants with murky fish-tanks, grand turn-of-the-century apartment blocks whose elderly inhabitants spend their evenings slowly ascending the stairs that surround the blackened, balconied courtyards. As with the ageing bodies lingering in the steam of Budapest's Turkish baths, this is a city weighed down by memories and openly scarred by history.

In studying the way this city of blatant contradictions has been represented both by foreigners and by the Hungarians themselves, it is perhaps not surprising to find that a truly balanced portrait of Budapest has rarely been achieved. The most common prejudice this century has been to praise old Buda at the expense of modern Pest, with romantically inclined writers such as Patrick Leigh Fermor going even so far as to find the city's soul in the now over-restored fragments of Buda's medieval and Renaissance past. Romantics of an earlier generation had stressed instead the city's 'oriental' aspects, Budapest being generally considered in the nineteenth century as the frontier between Europe and the 'Orient': Johnathan Harker, the hero of Bram Stoker's *Dracula* (1897), wrote that in crossing from Buda to Pest he had the 'impression that we were leaving the West and entering the East; the most Western of splendid bridges over the Danube . . . took us among the traditions of Turkish rule' (Stoker, who had never been to Hungary, was probably unaware that all of Budapest's surviving Turkish monuments are on the city's western or 'Buda' side). The French writer Victor Tissot, the author in 1881 of the enormously successful *Unknown Hungary*, was another traveller of this period who came to Budapest under the influence of an orientalist daydream, obsessed by the city's Turkish baths and becoming enamoured of what is now the relatively neglected tomb of the Dervish mystic Gül Baba. As with his counterparts in the formerly Moorish town of Granada in Spain, Tissot consoled himself for the absence of pure oriental types in the Budapest of his day by taking an exaggerated interest in the local gypsy population, whom he seems to have regarded almost as modern successors to the Turks.

Budapest's serenading gypsy bands, so integral today to the stereotypical tourist vision of the place, have also supplied the city with a necessary folkloric element. For perhaps Budapest's most paradoxical feature is that it is a bustling metropolis that has often played down and even been ashamed of its urban status. During the interwar years, when Budapest first developed as an international tourist resort, it became unique among European capitals in promoting itself as a spa town, with an image based to a great extent on wooded parks, outdoor pools, and garden restaurants. More surprisingly, from the moment it emerged as a leading city it has rarely been treated as a subject by Hungarian artists and writers, who, like many of their architect contemporaries, have been drawn instead to the life and traditions of the Hungarian countryside.

The reservations shown towards Budapest by its own inhabitants, combined with the general Hungarian tendency to humorous self-deprecation (you need only read Örkény's *One Minute Stories*; see p. 102), has ensured that the place, for all the immediacy of its appeal, has not as yet become a cultural destination comparable, say, to Vienna or Prague. This continuing state of affairs justifies, I hope, the publication of the present book, which is underlined by a strong belief that Budapest has as much to offer the tourist as any of its city rivals, and that a fuller understanding of the place is dependent on a knowledge of Hungary's rich, idiosyncratic but undeservedly little-known culture.

It goes without saying that my own fascination with Budapest owes a vast debt to all the many friends I have made here over the years. Judit Polgár, who did so much to encourage my early interest in Hungarian culture, has been unfailingly helpful, as has Katalin Keserü, who has taught me much of what I know about Hungarian art and architecture. I have also fond memories of the many hours spent in the company of Károly Alexa, Ferenc Banga, Julia Borbély, Zsófia and Henry Copeland, Réka Kardkovács, Lia Rádocsay, Lajos Sváby, and Lászlo Szabados. Those who have made specific contributions to this book, ranging from driving me around the Uj koztemeto cemetery to answering questions about Hungarian literature and politics, include Bob Dent, Péter Esterhazy, Zsolt Kezdi-Kovacs, Attila Ledenyi, Ilona Planck, Andras Renyi, and Mihaly Szegedy-Maszak.

Several British friends, including Paul Stirton, Jim Urquhart, and Adam Yamey, have been invaluable companions during my wanderings around the city, nocturnal and otherwise; Alison and Helen Bell helped to make a visit to Budapest in the winter of 1993 a particularly memorable experience. Back in Britain I have received scholarly assistance from Alexander Fyjis-Walker, Juliet Kinchin, and Robert Gibbs, and much needed support from Jackie Rae. Particular patience and tolerance have been shown as well by my publishers at Oxford University Press, who have had to put up with numerous delays to the manuscript caused by my having been side-tracked to places as far away as Buenos Aires and Timbuktu: my thanks in particular to Simon Mason, George Miller, Rebecca Hunt, and Shelley Cox.

Finally, I have to confess that my love for Budapest is inseparable from my friendship with Ildikó Várnagy, Árpád Szabados, and their daughter

Réka. They have treated me like a member of their family from the time of my first visit to the city, and it is to them that I dedicate this book, remembering especially all our long conversations until the early hours of the morning.

Contents

Part One

1

At the Court of King Matthias

SHORTLY before the millennial celebrations of 1896, a young, tubercular sculptor called János Fadrusz began work on an ambitious equestrian statue of a monarch who had come to symbolize Hungarian greatness—Matthias Corvinus. This monumental bronze, portraying its armour-clad subject with the laurel crown and flowing cape of a Roman emperor, still stands in the main square of the Transylvanian capital of Kolozsvár, where Matthias was born. However, the context for which this stirring, patriotic work was created has significantly changed: Kolozsvár has become the Romanian town of Cluj, home to an increasingly beleaguered Hungarian minority, whose members are said secretly to be photographed every time they cross the square to enter the Hungarian consulate. Fadrusz's work has only survived thanks to the pedantic insistence that Matthias was not a Hungarian but a Transylvanian; and it is the name of the Romanian painter Nicolae Grigorescu, rather than that of Matthias, that has been given to the nearby art school marking the monarch's birthplace. The plight of Romania's Hungarians lends a certain conviction to the nationalist belief—ridiculed by the novelist Péter Esterházy—that justice died with Matthias's death, and that Hungarian history was reduced thereafter to 'nothing but a series of *oys*, *veys*, lamentations and defeats'.

The reign of Matthias Corvinus represented the culminating moments in Hungary's history as an independent kingdom—a history that would be greatly mythologized in later centuries, but which is preserved in present-day Hungary largely as fragments that are either tantalizingly small or else over-restored to the point of being a sham. The Turks, like the Mongols before them, devastated Hungary's medieval past, many of the remains of which were later hidden by the Habsburgs under a late baroque veneer. Rapid industrialization from the 1870s onwards, followed by the shattering consequences of the Second World War, contributed further to the wiping away of this past.

Visitors to Budapest itself need particular persistence and imagination to piece together a picture of its medieval townships. Virtually nothing survives from before the Mongol invasion of 1241–2 other than the ruins of the Roman settlements of Aquincum and Contra-Aquincum—ruins that are unlikely to inspire some latter-day Gibbon to extol the lost glories of ancient Pannonia.

The quest for Contra-Aquincum—the kernel of modern Pest—begins and ends in the unappealingly named March 15 Square, which is dwarfed by the underpass leading to a 1960s suspension bridge. The Allied bombs that destroyed so many of the buildings along the Pest bank of the Danube exposed the foundations of a Roman fortress built in AD 294 under Emperor Diocletian to protect the river crossing to Aquincum. The ruins are now the centrepiece of a small and sad garden, which has steps leading down to glass cases cowering under a concrete overhang. Crammed between the site and the underpass is the main surviving testimony to the bustling commercial settlement that grew up around the Roman fortress—the Inner City Parish Church.

This palimpsest of a building, so eloquent of Pest's troubled history, was probably founded in the eleventh century to house the body of the martyred bishop St Gerard. Around 1200, when the town thrived through receiving special privileges and attracting numerous German settlers, the church was turned into a three-aisled Romanesque basilica incorporating stones from the Roman *castrum*: it was here, in 1211, that the 4-year-old Princess Elizabeth of the House of Árpád (later St Elizabeth of Hungary) was betrothed to the scarcely much older Markgraf Ludwig von Thüringen. An ashlar wall and an indented cornice from this Romanesque structure survive in the south tower of the present building, which was rebuilt as a Gothic hall church in the fifteenth century. Used by the Turks as a mosque, damaged during the capture of the city in 1686, remodelled after a fire in 1723, and reconstructed after the Second World War, the church, when entered today from its baroque west façade, gives little hint of its being a repository of most of what remains of medieval and Renaissance Pest.

It is above all to the western side of the Danube that one must go to search out traces of Budapest's early history. The Roman ruins here, though barely more inspiring than those on the other side of the river, are remarkably extensive, and give an impressive indication of the size

4

of Roman Aquincum, which is estimated to have had a population of somewhere between 26,000 and 40,000. The ruins lie scattered over a large area of what is now known as 'Óbuda' or 'Old Buda'—a district that has become transformed in modern times into a heavily industrialized area criss-crossed with rows of enormous grey apartment blocks. It was in fact in the 1930s and 1940s, during the development of the area in this unprepossessing way, that a number of seventeenth- and eighteenth-century buildings were pulled down to reveal the remains of the second-century garrison town that had formed the basis of Aquincum. The most important discovery was of an amphitheatre that is thought to have held no fewer than 16,000 spectators: this figure is rather more startling than the actual ruin, which forms an oval of shallow blocks lying around like an unloved children's toy between speeding streams of traffic. More engaging are the remains of the civilian town, which are situated a good distance to the north, in rather more suburban surroundings. Much smaller than the garrison town, this part of Aquincum includes the foundations of an amphitheatre that accommodated a mere 8,000 people.

Evacuated with the coming of the Huns in the fifth century, Aquincum was soon reduced to a village living mainly off fishing. Though remaining a modest community right up to the end of the twelfth century, it appears none the less to have been favoured by the Magyars soon after their arrival in Hungary in about 896. In a north-western corner of Óbuda, below a brick factory off the main road to Vienna, the foundations have come to light of a late tenth-century church which has been identified as a royal chapel built over the tomb of Árpád, leader of the Magyar conquest. To the south of this, on a site near the garrison town amphitheatre, the scant remains have been found of a large royal palace built by Árpád's successors probably in the late twelfth century, when the first influx of French and German settlers had begun transforming the fishing village of Buda into an important mercantile port and artisan centre.

The Romanesque columns and other carvings discovered on the palace's site are elaborate works of Byzantine inspiration. However, an austere simplicity and total absence of decoration characterizes the early medieval structures that can be seen on the verdant Margaret Island, in between Óbuda and Pest. The island, first recorded as a hunting-ground for the early Magyar rulers (and today a massive recreational park), had emerged by the late twelfth century as a place of monastic retreat. Its oldest building, a tiny and recently reconstructed Premonstratensian chapel, can claim to be Budapest's only complete structure dating from before the Mongol invasion. Nearby, and comparably plain, are the ruins of a Dominican convent erected as part of the rebuilding campaign undertaken after 1242 by Béla IV, whose daughter, St Margaret of Hungary, spent much of her life here as a nun. The structure's austerity is in this case a reflection both of the monastic ideals of the Dominicans and of the impoverished state in which Hungary had been left by the Mongols.

The Mongols, after laying waste to Pest in 1241, had gone on to sack Buda in the following year, aided by an exceptionally severe winter that had led the Danube to freeze over. After their departure Pest seems to have been temporarily abandoned, its remaining citizens having moved over to Buda. In the meantime Béla IV, for obvious reasons of security, decided to relocate Buda at the top of the hill immediately to the south. The population of Buda was greatly boosted by the introduction of many more foreign settlers (Czech, Italian, and, above all, German) to safeguard the new town.

The new Buda was developed at considerable speed, and was ringed by defensive walls within a year or so of its foundation. Previously there had just been a couple of stone buildings on the 'Castle Hill': one of these was a huge square tower that would later be absorbed into the massive palace complex; the other was a private royal chapel which would soon be replaced by what is now popularly known as the Matthias Church. The latter, officially the Church of Our Lady, was built between 1255 and 1269, and had two towers, a nave, a transept, and a chancel terminating in a polygonal apse. Recalling in its ground-plan and decoration some of the Gothic churches of northern France, it had the distinction of being the first important Gothic building in Hungary. Some of the masonry and Gothic figural sculptures of the original church have managed to survive the centuries of alterations that climaxed in a late-nineteenth-century restoration intended to make the building more Gothic than ever. With its genuine Gothic elements mingling with its plethora of pseudo-Gothic paintings, decorations, and reconstructions, the present church is the perfect embodiment of the mythical transformation of Hungary's fragmentary medieval past.

Other major churches went up in the Castle district during Béla IV's rule. Because the Matthias Church became almost exclusively associated with Buda's German community, the Hungarians retaliated by the construction of the Church of St Mary Magdalene in the north-eastern corner of the district. After a typically complex history terminating in the building's near-total destruction during the Second World War, the church has now been left as a solitary late Gothic tower rising up alongside foundations and explanation panels that enable one to imagine the shape of the original Romanesque structure. Far more eloquent and extensive are the ruins of the Abbey of St Nicholas, which was erected in the early 1250s by the Dominicans, then the greatest landowners in Buda. Unfortunately, the visitor who comes to admire the soaring proportions of the abbey's transitional, Cistercian-style church has also to contend with the piped music and blandly futuristic setting of the Budapest Hilton.

Many other medieval remains, more appealingly situated than those of the Dominican abbey, lurk behind the pastel-coloured, stucco-faced houses that line the Castle district's quaintly variegated rows of houses. This showpiece area, with its streets that still respect the original medieval plan, is like a miniature version of central Prague—a late baroque façade shielding a medieval core. As you enter a restaurant, a wine bar, a gallery, or any other of this district's many establishments, you are likely to be confronted by Gothic arches, courtyards, vaults— traces of the intense building activity that was initiated in Buda in the middle decades of the thirteenth century.

For the next phase in the development of medieval Buda you must turn at last to the daunting bulk of the Royal Palace, which is like a mirror of Hungarian history from the Middle Ages right up to the communist period. Approaching it from the quaint, homely streets that take up the rest of the Castle district, you might find it difficult to believe that the pompous and heavily restored complex in front of you contains such a wealth of medieval masonry within: the crenellations and rounded bastions attached to the palace's southern side are from here hidden from sight, and all that you can see is a monstrous neo-baroque assemblage of giant columns, endless windows, and a crowning dome. Only after wearily crossing the first courtyard and being greeted at the end of this by the theatrical late-nineteenth-century Matthias fountain are you given any hint that you are nearing a medieval world of fabled reputation. But you have still to cross another large courtyard, enter the unpromisingly named Budapest History Museum, and descend into this museum's basement to penetrate finally into this domain—a domain now preserved as a maze of fourteenth- to sixteenth-century stone

fragments linked together by constantly ascending and descending concrete walkways.

The surprising extent of the medieval palace to have survived the
drastic remodellings of the Habsburg era would probably never have
been revealed had not bombs reduced much of the building to rubble
during the Second World War. The remains uncovered while the debris
was being removed and the complex painstakingly restored have now
enabled historians to reconstruct the original ground-plan and to iden-
tify the different stages in the palace's labyrinthine history. Though this
history goes back to the time when Béla IV built a small residential castle
on the southern, rockier half of the Buda Hill, the earliest parts of the
palace to have come down to us date from the early fourteenth century,
after the extinction of the House of Árpád and the advent to the Hungarian throne of the Italian-French Angevin kings.

The reigns of Charles Robert and Louis I (the Great) had many of the
Golden Age qualities that would come to be associated with the rule of
Matthias Corvinus. Hungary's standing in Europe was enormously
enhanced, and a fruitful alliance was entered into with both Bohemia
and Poland. The years of uncertainty before the establishment of
the Angevins had been a period of economic stagnation in which building work in Buda had come to a virtual halt; but now the economy
recovered to such a degree as to make the Hungarian florin one of
Europe's strongest currencies. Building activity was renewed in Buda, a
university (one of Europe's earliest) was founded in Pécs in 1367, and
the Hungarian court began attracting increasing numbers of artists from
abroad.

The new centrality of Hungary in European affairs was reflected in
the heterogeneous influences now affecting the country's arts. The heavy
German presence in the country inevitably resulted in strong cultural ties
with Germany, particularly in areas outside the ambit of the court such
as the mining towns of Upper Hungary (now Slovakia). The Angevins
meanwhile were more interested in Italian art and architecture, especially
during the first decades of the century, when their political aspirations
were largely centred on the south of Europe.

One of the Italians who appears to have been lured over to Hungary
was Niccolò di Tommaso, a north Italian artist who had worked for the
Angevins in Naples; to him has been ascribed the Giotto-inspired, mid-
fourteenth-century frescoes of apostles and scenes from the life of Jesus
and Mary that decorate the Romanesque castle chapel at Esztergom. But

it was above all through manuscript illumination—an art which would also be dear to the heart of Matthias Corvinus—that the achievements of *trecento* Italian painters came to be known in Angevin Hungary. Among the various Italian manuscripts that ended up in Hungarian collections during this period was a large group of works from the 1330s and 1340s which have been ascribed to the circle of Niccolò da Bologna, the leading limner of the Bolognese school of illuminators. The so-called Nekcsei Bible (which belonged to the Hungarian state treasurer Demeter Nekcsei) was one of these, as was the magnificent Legendarium now in the Vatican. Both these works suggest an artist who either worked in Hungary or else had been drawn into the Angevin orbit in Naples: the former manuscript is not written in the Bologna rotundo script but in the Hungarian-favoured Gothic minuscules, while the latter portrays the Hungarian saints with a thoroughness that indicates an artist steeped in Hungarian history and culture. A Hungarian artist (usually identified as Miklós Meggyesi, court painter to Louis I) might indeed have been responsible for the greatest manuscript from fourteenth-century Hungary, the Illuminated Chronicle (Hungarian National Library), which was produced between 1374 and 1376 to celebrate the engagement of one of Louis's daughters to the son of the king of France. The style of these miniatures is wholly Italian, but the costumes are clearly Hungarian, and there is even a scene featuring what is generally identified as Buda's Castle Hill.

Italian architecture also made an impact on Angevin Hungary, at least from the late 1320s, when work was probably begun on the Royal Palace at Buda. Whereas Hungarian workshops had played the leading role in the earlier Angevin residences—at Visegrád and Temesvár (now Timişoara in Romania)—Italian-trained craftsmen appear to have been brought in at Buda, and to have constructed a largely brick-built building reminiscent of the brick *palazzi* of northern Italy, complete with characteristically Italian twin and triple windows, and Gothic foliated ornaments of Byzantine/Sicilian-Islamic derivation. However, a reaction against Italian architectural models seems to have set in by the 1340s, apparently under the influence of one of medieval Hungary's most enthusiastic builders, Queen Elizabeth—the second wife of Charles Robert, and a princess of the royal house of Poland.

Angevin attitudes generally towards Italy took a turn for the worse in 1345, with the murder in Naples of Queen Elizabeth's son Andrew. This effectively signalled the failure of the Angevins' Neapolitan campaigns, and the abandonment of their Mediterranean policy in favour of one directed more towards Bohemia and Poland—a policy that would be greatly favoured by the annexation of the Polish throne by Louis I in 1370. This change of political orientation was mirrored in the architectural developments of mid-fourteenth-century Hungary. The Italianate brickwork used during the first constructional stage of the Buda Royal Palace gave way to limestone quarried near Buda and carved under the direction of Master János, a Hungarian stonemason much favoured by Queen Elizabeth. Described in contemporary documents as a 'paunchy' citizen of Buda, Master János headed a workshop that seems to have been in close contact with building workshops attached to the Czech and Polish royal courts. Sculptural figurative fragments associated with him and his circle have a noteworthy naturalism that brings to mind the art of Peter Parler, the great German mason who established himself in Prague.

But the apogee of Gothic naturalism in Buda was not reached until the reign of Louis I's successor, Sigismund of Luxemburg, under whom Hungary's cultural affiliations became more complex than ever. Sigismund, brother of King Wenceslas of Bohemia, came to the Hungarian throne in 1387, after Louis had died without leaving any male heirs. Known to many of the Hungarian aristocrats as 'the Czech swine', he was scarcely more loved by the Czechs themselves, thanks to his opposition to the teachings of Jan Hus. Though he managed to be crowned king of Bohemia in 1420 he was not able to take possession of his kingdom until 1436, three years after being made Holy Roman Emperor, and only one year before his death. For much of his fifty-year rule over Hungary he had been distracted by events abroad; and he had led an increasingly itinerant life, with long sojourns in Paris, Burgundy, South Germany, Switzerland, Constance, Vienna, and Italy. And yet, despite the relatively little time he devoted to Hungary, he did more for the cultural life of Buda than almost any other Hungarian monarch before Matthias Corvinus.

Artists and craftsmen whom Sigismund had met on his various European journeys were sent to Buda, thus greatly increasing the extent of foreign influences on the art and architecture produced in Hungary. There are a number of anonymous works of art in Hungarian collections whose authors' country of origin is difficult to determine. This is the case with the so-called 'Matthias Calvary', one of the most exquisite examples in Europe of the medieval goldsmith's art. Kept today in the

Cathedral Treasury at Esztergom, it was probably once in the possession of King Matthias, who must surely have commissioned its High Renaissance pedestal. The cross itself, dating from the first quarter of the fifteenth century, is an elaborate Gothic structure in which white, green, and blue enamel figures shine against a gold background. This type of work, known as 'ronde-bosse enamel', involved a complicated and costly technique that had been evolved at the beginning of the fifteenth century in workshops in Paris, Burgundy, Tuscany, and Lombardy. Whether the artist of this particular Calvary was French or Italian has been endlessly debated, the usual conclusion being a compromise one—he came from the papal territory of the Vaucluse in the south of France.

An equal amount of time has been spent discussing the cultural formation of Thomas de Coloswar, one of the earliest of the outstanding Hungarian panel painters whose works can be seen at Esztergom and the Hungarian National Gallery. Despite Thomas's Transylvanian name, he is thought to have been mainly active in Buda: his main surviving work, the magnificent Garamszentbenedek altar at Esztergom, not only was commissioned by someone in Sigismund's Buda entourage but also contains a predella scene in which a Danube barge has been tentatively identified. But the main argument in favour of a Buda-based artist is the fact that no other place in Hungary (and few in Europe) could have furnished him with as many influences as those that have been identified in the Garamszentbenedek altar—influences from Cologne, Austria, Bohemia, Poland, eastern Germany, Burgundy, the Netherlands, and Italy.

The convergence in Buda of so many diverse artists and artistic tendencies can be seen partly to reflect Sigismund's ambitious plans for the Royal Palace. Sigismund's energy as a builder matched that of his Angevin predecessor, Elizabeth; but his impact on the Buda palace was so great that the Angevin contribution to the building was soon forgotten. 'Before Sigismund's time,' commented the Italian humanist Bonfini in the late fifteenth century, 'nothing worth mentioning was built in Buda Castle.'

Sigismund's principal addition to the palace complex was a long northern wing known as the 'New Palace', much of which was taken up by a Great Hall partly built, it would seem, by French masons. Conferences and festive ceremonies were held within the hall, from the balconies and windows of which the courtiers could observe such further spectacles as pageants, tournaments, acrobatic performances, and even the occasional execution. Information derived from foundation walls, carved stones, and contemporary descriptions shows the hall to have been a pioneering late Gothic structure resplendent with turrets, flamboyant windows, and oriels. French in certain of the details but thoroughly original in its overall conception, the structure was lavishly praised by numerous foreign visitors, and was highly influential. Echoes of it can be felt in the extraordinary castle built at Vajdahunyad by János Hunyadi, father of Matthias Corvinus—a castle that would later be reconstructed as the centrepiece of Budapest's 1896 millennial celebrations.

Though the architecture of the Great Hall can only be seen today in the conjectural drawings of archaeologists, there have at least survived from the early fifteenth-century palace some superlative remains of the original decoration. Within the excavated Royal Palace is a reassembled stove made out of German-style tiles with jousting knights and other exuberant late medieval forms. But the Gothic high point of the surviving palace consists of the fragmentary busts of saints and courtiers that were discovered as recently as the mid-1970s. The saints had clearly been intended for the palace chapel; but they have now been united with the courtiers in a darkened, spotlit room that thrillingly accentuates the drama of these powerful heads. Were they executed by one of the French artists whom Sigismund contracted in Paris in 1416, or by one of the Germans whom he sent over from Augsburg two years later? Whoever carved them, these heads, with their lively postures and expressive features, are works of the highest quality that develop to an uncanny degree the naturalism of late medieval art. In terms of the artistic history of the Royal Palace, they stand out as a final powerful assertion of the Gothic style before the advent of the Renaissance under Matthias Corvinus.

Sigismund's reign, as well as encouraging this flowering of the Hungarian Gothic, also prepared the way for the spectacular arrival here of the Renaissance in the second half of the fifteenth century. Cultural and intellectual relations with Italy, recovering from the strain they had undergone during the last years of Angevin rule, were now closer than ever before. A number of prominent Italian intellectuals began working in Hungary, some of them occupying local bishoprics: both Giovanni da Buondelmonte and the future Cardinal Branda Castiglione invited Italian artists to work on their respective episcopal residences at Kalocsa and Veszprém. The most influential of the Italian bishops was Andrea Scolari, whose retinue of Florentine artists, scholars, and canons established the diocese at Nagyvárad (now Oradea in Romania) as Hungary's main intellectual centre outside Buda.

The importance of the Scolari name in the history of Hungarian culture was further strengthened by Andrea's brother Filippo, a leading military commander better known as Pippo Spano. Famous as the powerful striding figure painted by Castagno for the Florentine church of San Apollonia, Filippo Scolari spent much of his later life in Hungary, where he was entrusted with the defence of the country's southern border. As well as commissioning fortifications from the Florentine Matteo Ammanatini (a carpenter and architect in the circle of Brunelleschi), Filippo had numerous buildings erected or enlarged on his vast Hungarian estates: a castle at Simontornya, sumptuous palaces at Ozora and Temesvár (now Timişoara in Romania), a church and hospital at Lippa (now Lipova in Romania), and, finally, a burial chapel for himself at Temesvár. For the decoration of these buildings, he called over from Florence in 1427 the fresco painter Masolino da Panicale, who had just completed his pioneering collaboration with Masaccio on the Brancacci Chapel at Santa Maria del Carmine. Masolino would remain in Hungary for the next three years.

After Filippo Scolari's death, both Ammanatini and Masolini went on to work for Sigismund, who surrounded himself in his later years with Italian humanists. The eminent scholar Ciriaco da Ancona acted as Sigismund's mentor in Rome, while the no less distinguished Poggio Bracciolini penned verses to celebrate his coronation as emperor. In Buda, Sigismund's humanist circle comprised such luminaries as Ambrogio Traversari, Antonio Loschi, and Francesco Filelfo. Above all there was Pier Paolo Vergerio, who stayed on in Hungary until his death in 1444 and exercised an especially strong influence on Hungary's own humanists, such as Andrea Scolari's successor as Bishop of Nagyvárad, János Vitéz. The Croatian-born Vitéz acted in turn as a link between the intellectual worlds of Sigismund and Matthias Corvinus: he was both Matthias's childhood tutor and the uncle of another of the internationally acclaimed figures of Hungary's Renaissance—the poet Janus Pannonius.

Between Sigismund's death in 1445 and Matthias's accession to the throne in 1458 lay a period of political and economic confusion in which the patronage of the arts in Hungary reached a virtual standstill. Hungary, after having been ceded to the Habsburgs in a controversial treaty of succession drawn up by Sigismund, came into the barely more favourable hands of Wladislas I of the Jagiello dynasty of Poland. In the meantime the Turkish threat to Europe was increasing alarmingly: by 1453 the Turks had occupied Constantinople, and by 1456 they were on the threshold of Belgrade, the most important fortress on Hungary's southern border. Catastrophe was only narrowly averted by the man who had succeeded Pippo Spano as the defender of this border—János Hunyadi, the elected viceroy of Hungary. The greatly outnumbered forces of Hunyadi, after having lost to the Turks in previous conflicts, managed to score a victory at Belgrade that would hold back the Turkish advance on Europe for a good fifty years. The path was also laid for the accession to the Hungarian throne of Hunyadi's son, Matthias.

Matthias was an infant prodigy whose knowledge of Latin had been advanced enough for him to act as his father's interpreter in conversations with ambassadors. On his election to the throne, at the age of only 17, he would soon prove to be not only a wise diplomat and outstanding military leader but also a patron of the arts more energetic than almost any other in the history of medieval Europe. His passion for learning and the arts was, as we shall see, absolutely genuine. However, he would not have considered these activities as ends in themselves: he would also have appreciated their vital role in promoting the image both of a family risen suddenly to power and of a country maintaining a triumphant independence between the Habsburgs and the Turks.

The creation of this image was to a great extent the work of the court's ever more powerful humanists, who should not be seen simply as the purveyors of learning for learning's sake but also as the Renaissance equivalent of a present-day public relations company. To those contemporary critics of Matthias who found his expenditure on the arts to be excessive, self-indulgent, and ostentatious, the humanists responded by speaking of the 'glory of the kingdom' and invoking the virtue of magnificence—a virtue they considered essential to any noble monarch.

Some of the humanist myth-makers, led by the Italian Filippo Buonaccorsi and the Hungarian historian János Thuróczi, were keen to emphasize parallels between Matthias and Attila, who was now transformed from a savage Hun into the epitome of the ideal ruler. But it was essentially the world of ancient and specifically imperial Rome that provided the humanists with the imagery in which to cloak their king. This Hungarian of humble ancestry who had been born as Mátyás Hunyadi was given now the Latin name of Matthias Corvinus; portraits showed him as a Roman emperor, while works of art compared him in his wisdom to Athene and in his fortitude to Hercules. The Renaissance obsession with classical antiquity came immediately to affect all aspects of his court at Buda, down to the very lifestyle of the courtiers. Indeed, Matthias's very first summer as king had largely been spent watching chariot races, gladiator fights, lion hunts, and other spectacles that seem consciously to have recreated the activities of the Roman Colosseum.

The Renaissance took hold in Matthias's Buda earlier and more speedily than it did in any other European country. Moreover, this was the Renaissance in its purest Italian form, free of any local interpretation, untouched by the distinctively Hungarian spirit that romantic nationalists would later associate with Matthias's reign. This was Italian culture transplanted into Hungarian soil largely by the Italians themselves, whose presence in Hungary would become greater still following Matthias's marriage in 1476 to Beatrice of Aragon.

Matthias's political links were with Naples, Ferrara, and Milan; but his cultural ties were principally with Florence. The proud Florentine Vasari referred to the 'many Florentines' who took up residence at the court of Buda, and mentioned specifically the famous sculptor Benedetto da Maiano, who apparently executed here a number of works in *intarsia*. Another Florentine was the architect Chimenti Camiccia, a follower of Alberti and Michelozzi who directed all architectural work at the court after 1479; yet another was probably the anonymous author of the exquisite pedestal of the 'Matthias Calvary', a work previously attributed to the great Lombard goldsmith Caradosso. Apart from Caradosso and Camiccia's Bolognese predecessor, Fioravante, the only prominent artist at Buda to break the Florentine hegemony was Giovanni Dalmata, a sculptor of Dalmatian origin who had been active in the papal court at Rome before coming to Buda in 1485 or 1486. Though once thought to be the author of the beautiful portrait reliefs of Matthias and Beatrice now in Buda's Castle Museum, there is little today that can be confidently ascribed to Dalmata other than the two surviving fragments from the serenely grand, white marble Altar of the Madonna from Diósgyör Castle (a work divided between Budapest's Fine Arts Museum and the Museum at Miskolc). However, we know that Matthias's enthusiasm for Dalmata was so great that, in a characteristically Renaissance gesture, he had him raised to the nobility and granted a large estate and castle.

While not always successful in persuading some of the greatest

Italians of the day to come to Buda, Matthias managed often in compensation to obtain designs and other works by these masters. Mantegna
was approached, as was Filippo Lippi, who sent over a painted portrait of the king; Pollaiuolo designed drapery for the throne, while
Verrocchio, willing but unable to come to Buda, was said by Vasari
to have produced bronzes for the Royal Palace.

The fruitful cultural exchange between Hungary and Italy resulted also
in many Hungarian artists and intellectuals studying or even settling in
Italy itself. The Italian rooms of Budapest's Fine Arts Museum include a
painted *Allegory of Fertility* that could easily be mistaken for the work of
a Ferrarese artist such as Lorenzo Costa; in fact it is by a Hungarian who
changed his name to Michele Pannonio after becoming a court painter
at Ferrara.

To Ferrara went also Bishop Vitéz's celebrated poet nephew, Janus
Pannonius, who was drawn to this town, like several of his compatriots,
by the private school of the humanist Guarino da Verona. Entering this
school in 1447, when he was just 13, he stayed on in Italy almost unin-
terruptedly until 1458, writing during these years Latin poems that established him as the first writer of stature in Hungarian literature. One of
his poems, written on the occasion of his 17th birthday, describes with
an almost present-day directness the spiritual and physical tensions of
an adolescent torn between his sexual and intellectual desires; another
poem, *Farewell to Várad*, contains instead nostalgic memories of a visit to
his uncle's diocese. His feelings towards Hungary (where he returned to
serve as bishop of Pécs) were not in fact entirely straightforward, and
were latterly embittered by a conflict with Matthias Corvinus that would
hasten Pannonius' death from consumption at the age of 38. His years
in Italy had underlined for him the educational and cultural shortcom-
ings of his home country; at the same time, however, they had stirred
in him a patriotic longing to praise Hungary's own virtues and to
increase its intellectual standing in the eyes of Europe:

> The land of Italy was once the source of all my songs;
> To you, my fair Pannonia, that honour now belongs.
> Great glory have I won, indeed, but more on you be poured,
> My homeland, whose illustrious fame my spirit shares abroad.

The Florentine Neoplatonist Marsilio Ficino, whom Matthias unsuccessfully tried to woo to Buda, acknowledged Pannonius' greatness by
dedicating to him in 1469 his celebrated commentary on Plato's *Sympo-*

sium; and he might well have recalled Pannonius' praise of Hungary when, in 1477, he donated to Matthias's ever more renowned library at Buda a copy of his life of Plato. In the accompanying inscription, addressed to his humanist friend Bandini, Ficino wrote that he was sending his Plato, not to Athens, because that city was ruined, but to King Matthias, who 'with marvellous power and wisdom has restored in a few years the temple of the great and wise Pallas'.

By the late 1480s an Italian proverb had been coined: 'In all of Europe there were just three great jewels: Venice on the waters, Buda on the hills, and Florence in the plain.' The widespread fame that Matthias's court had brought to Buda was increased by the effusive foreign reactions to the architecture that had been built under Camiccia's supervision. Whereas Matthias, influenced perhaps by the views of Bishop Vitéz, had insisted that the Gothic style be employed for all ecclesiastical structures (from the cathedral at Kassa, now Košice, in Slovakia, to the lavish remodelling of Buda's Royal Palace chapel), he had strongly encouraged the use of a Renaissance style for his secular buildings. The hunting lodge at Nyék (in the Buda hills) as well as the enlarged Summer Palace at Visegrád (which had appeared as 'a terrestrial paradise' to the papal nuncio Bartolomeo de' Maraschi) were both thought of in terms of ancient villas such as those described by the Roman author Pliny; the transformed Royal Palace at Buda, meanwhile, appears to have been partly modelled on the near contemporary ducal palace at Urbino.

Detailed and encomiastic descriptions by the court chronicler Bonfini enable us to imagine what these places must have been like—descriptions that in the case of Visegrád can be echoed by some of the most eloquent ruins from late medieval Hungary. Beautifully situated on a steeply sloping site alongside the Danube bend, the reconstructed ruins of Visegrád reveal pure Renaissance elements arranged within a fourteenth-century Angevin structure: thus an octagonal fountain of Hercules sits in the middle of a Gothic courtyard crowned by a classical balustrade. That Matthias's architect was as yet reluctant to develop a wholly Renaissance style is proved by the presence at the top of the palace of the canopied 'Lion Well'—a characteristically late Gothic structure of playful and fantastical elaboration.

Matthias's remodelling and enlargement of Buda's Royal Palace was both later in date than his work at Visegrád and much bolder in its application of Renaissance forms. Bonfini's account suggests a place of fabled grandeur such as Italo Calvino might have evoked in his *Invisible Cities*.

A two-winged bronze gate portraying the Twelve Labours of Hercules marked the grandiose entrance to a complex hung with giant bronze candelabra, glazed with tiled floors, and divided into three main court-yards adorned respectively with Greek and Roman deities, portraits of János Hunyadi and his sons László and Matthias, and a marble fountain supporting a bronze representation of the palace's presiding goddess, Pallas Athene.

The fountain—reconstructed and minus the statue of Pallas Athene—can still be seen in an otherwise bare courtyard; elsewhere in the Castle Museum there are stove tiles from Matthias's palace, and a plethora of red marble fragments—pilasters, balustrades, capitals, door surrounds, window frames. Enough of these fragments' elegantly classical detailing has been preserved to remind us of the influence the palace must have had in expanding the decorative vocabulary of Central Europe. This influence is certainly felt in the work of the great Bohemian mason Bene-dict Reid, who was sent by Wladislav II to study classical architecture in Buda rather than in Italy: ornamental details from Buda's Royal Palace reappear bizarrely distorted in Reid's stunningly original late Gothic Wladislav Hall in Prague—an example of the kind of imaginative trans-formation of Italian influence that had yet to be achieved in Hungary.

Matthias's palace at Buda would have impressed visitors with its scale, its consistently high level of craftsmanship, and its novelty in the context of European architecture north of the Alps; however, it would not have seemed especially original to Italians who had closely followed the latest trends in their own country's architecture. Only with Matthias's extra-ordinary library—on which so much of his energies were expended—could it be said that Hungary offered something that was not only unique to Central Europe but also virtually unrivalled even in Renais-sance Italy. In 1489 the Florentine humanist Bartolomeo della Fonte com-mented on how Lorenzo de' Medici had been inspired by Matthias's example to found his own library of Greek and Latin works: Italy was at last emulating Hungary rather than Hungary Italy.

No Hungarian monarch before Matthias had displayed such a passion for books, not even Sigismund of Luxemburg, who had shown no par-ticular interest in the famous collection of illuminated manuscripts that he had inherited from his elder brother, Wenceslas IV of Bohemia. Matthias's love of books had probably been nurtured by Bishop Vitéz, who had created at Nagyvárad Hungary's first humanist library. Matthias himself seems to have begun amassing a library in about 1467, and was assisted by agents who travelled on his behalf around Italy, Germany, and Greece. His large collection of Greek works was further expanded following the fall from favour of Janus Pannonius in 1470 and the subsequent confiscation of the latter's belongings. He was also able to acquire, in 1478 and 1488 respectively, the extensive libraries left by the astronomer Johannes Regiomontanus and the distinguished Italian patron Galeotto Manfredi, prince of Faenza. During the last years of his life, when the Florentine Taddeo Ugoleto worked as his librarian, Matthias's collecting activities had taken on an almost obsessional fervour.

Matthias was not just someone interested in books as objects: he was also a voracious reader who built up a library intended to reflect all aspects of literature and science, from poetry and drama to philosophy, medicine, and mathematics. Much of his spare time was occupied in reading, which he found the perfect diversion from the pressures of kingship. However, he had little success in conveying the pleasures of reading to his courtiers, whom he once had to rebuke for criticizing a book-loving bishop who had been caught reading before a council meeting.

A high proportion of the books in Matthias's library, such as those of Pannonius, were plainly produced works that were clearly meant to be read rather than simply looked at. But the ones that made the library so famous were the 1,000 or so illuminated manuscripts that were mainly commissioned by him from workshops in both Florence and Buda. In Florence, four scribes and illuminators were working permanently for him from as early as the 1460s; its most outstanding artist was Attavante, the author of the naturalistically embellished Brussels Missal. The Buda workshop, active only from the 1480s, was referred to in the early sixteenth century by the leading Hungarian humanist Miklós Oláh: 'I have heard from old people that when Matthias was alive he engaged thirty copyists proficient in painting too . . . I used to know their leader Felix Ragusinus Dalmata myself; he knew Greek, Latin, Jewish and Arabic and was also well versed in painting.' Among the artists who worked under Felix Ragusinus was Giovanni Antonio Cattaneo de Mediolano, whose masterpiece is the famous Cassianus Codex now in the Bibliothèque Nationale in Paris. Another illuminator was Francesco di Castello, whose works were praised by Matthias (in a passage clearly indicative of the intense pleasure that art gave him): 'subtili artis pictoriae magisterio depicta sunt.'

The splendour of Matthias's illuminated manuscripts was matched by that of the setting in which they were housed. Bonfini vividly described the way in which light streamed in through stained-glass windows on either side of a seat draped in golden cloth, where the king would sit absorbed in his books. Around him were gilded shelves lined with manuscripts whose gilded leather spines were attached to brightly coloured silk or velvet boards bearing gilded silver studding and enamel clasps. Curtains woven with gold and coloured yarn protected the more precious volumes, while the others were kept below the shelves in richly carved chests.

Matthias's library was the ultimate symbol of his reign, and its gradual decay and dispersal after his death reflected the decline of Hungary itself after the 1490s. Despite all the dynastic imagery created by the humanists at Matthias's court, the king died heirless, leaving Hungary at the mercy of the unruly nobility, who chose another Bohemian, Wladislaw II, as their king. Both Wladislaw and his equally weak son, Louis II, proved incapable of maintaining Matthias's strong, centralized power; control of the country was left increasingly to the nobility, who turned to the German banking family of the Fuggers to look after the economy. The exploited and disillusioned peasantry, led by the Transylvanian captain György Dózsa, took it into their own hands in 1516 to defend the country from the continuing threat of the Turks. However, this peasant crusade was directed almost immediately against the nobles themselves. The rebellion was soon crushed, Dózsa was executed on a red-hot iron dais, and a law was passed effectively reducing the peasantry to serfdom and forbidding them to bear arms. This last measure was a particularly short-sighted one in view of the growing power of the Ottomans, who, at Mohács in 1526, managed to rout the Hungarians in just under two hours and to kill their king. The Ottoman army, under the leadership of Suleiman I, went on to raze Buda, which they would occupy after 1541. Hungary was divided into three parts, with Buda acting as the capital of the country's Turkish-ruled heartland (the northern and western extremities of Hungary were taken by the Habsburgs, while Transylvania became a nominally independent principality subservient to the Ottoman Turks).

During Hungary's last years as an independent country, no building of note was put up in Buda, and nothing remarkable was added to Buda's Royal Palace. The same Bonfini who had praised the lavishness of Matthias's expenditure on the arts now tried to please Wladislaw II by accusing his old patron of spending 'insane amounts of money' both on works of art and on inviting artists from abroad to come to Hungary. The Renaissance culture that Matthias had done so much to encourage in Buda lived on in Hungary principally in Esztergom, whence the widowed Queen Beatrice retired: it was at Esztergom that there was founded in 1506 the first centralized Renaissance chapel north of Italy (this remarkable structure, the Bakócz Chapel, survives in an altered state in the unappealing setting of the town's coldly neo-classical cathedral). But the great cultural achievements of the age were largely unconnected with the court, most notably the expressive late Gothic panel paintings of the Master M.S., whose masterpiece—disgracefully little known outside Hungary, but comparable in style and quality to the greatest works of the German sixteenth century—was an altarpiece for the mining town of Selmecbánya (now Banská Štavnica in Slovakia).

During Matthias's lifetime Bonfini had predicted that the glory of Matthias would live for ever, being guarded against oblivion by 'metal, marble, and writing'. The irony of this prediction is that within less than a century of the king's death the metal had all gone (some of the bronzes were last heard of in Constantinople), the marble had been shattered, and the library broken up. The face of Buda was radically changed by the Turks, who created a metropolis that would impress the seventeenth-century Turkish visitor Evliya Çelebi with its thirty-four mosques, four djamis, three dervish monasteries, six elementary schools, five high schools, hundred leather workshops, and four thermal baths.

The Royal Palace, at the centre of all this hectic building activity, was the main structure not to have been burnt down in 1541. A contemporary chronicler referred to Suleiman as having seized 'the immense wealth, household chattels, cannons and shells of the miserable king' (Louis II), while sparing the palace for use as his own residence. However the fate of the building was sealed when the Turks later decided to use Sigismund's 'New Palace' as a powder arsenal: when lightning struck the building in 1578, the ensuing explosion caused stones to be flung right over to the other side of the Danube. The various Christian attempts to recapture Buda consolidated the destruction of the palace, which was described early in the seventeenth century as looking 'like an empty skull with a candle burning inside'. When Lady Mary Wortley Montagu passed through a still devastated and largely unrestored Buda in 1717, she described the town as having been 'the royal seat of the

Hungarian kings, where their palace was reckoned one of the most beautiful buildings of the age, now wholly destroyed'.

But the concern of Christian Europe was centred mainly on the plight of Matthias's library, which had been disastrously neglected long before the arrival of the Turks. The copyists' workshop had ceased to function, and no more additions to the library had been made during the reigns of Wladislas I and Louis II; furthermore, according to contemporary sources, precious volumes had been ransacked, mislaid, or else abandoned to the dust, dirt, and vermin. The bulk of the library, it seems, none the less remained *in situ* at the time of Suleiman's entry into Buda; only afterwards did its fate become the subject of intense speculation and contradictory rumours.

Some said that Suleiman had burnt down the whole library; another claimed that he had torn up many of the books, and vandalized others by ripping off the silver ornaments. One Matthias Bremmer noted in 1541 that 'the library had been destroyed by Asian barbarism, for when I carefully examined it two years ago I could hardly find any trace of its former brilliance, except for a few Greek authors' (the latter volumes being thought, presumably, too plain to be worth bothering with). The possibility of the library's complete destruction was one that provoked anger and sadness throughout Europe, and prompted a Basle scholar of the 1530s, Salvianus Brassicanus, to quote a famous line from Virgil. '"On hearing this," he sighed, "who could retain his tears?"'

Yet other reports suggested that the damage to the library was not nearly as great as was feared. Many people went to Buda to try and see and even acquire what was left, though at least one of these potential visitors—a preacher in 1605—was refused admission. About two decades later a Hungarian scholar, Pál Enyedi, managed to gain entry and was afterwards able joyfully to report that 'the library of King Matthias is still in Buda, in its old place of before, and it has not suffered any loss, being watched by guards'. A different account of the place was given in 1666 by the Habsburg librarian, Peter Lambeete, who was hoping to purchase works for the imperial library in Vienna. He found the books lying about in heaps in a deplorable condition, and was only allowed to take away three plain volumes, none of which bore the Corvinus crest.

When Buda was recaptured in 1686, the Italian engineer Marsigli discovered the remnants of the library within the smouldering ruins of the palace. Three hundred works were rescued and taken to Vienna, and a handful of illuminated manuscripts or *corvinas* ended up in French and Italian collections. However, none of these survivals can match in brilliance the fabulous reputation that the library had enjoyed over the centuries—a reputation that had endowed it during the Turkish period with all the myth and mystery of King Solomon's Mines.

The fame of King Matthias has likewise proved more durable than the cultural artefacts that were meant to sustain it. He is an inescapable figure in the Hungary of today, and you will find his name attached to such diverse enterprises as Hungary's leading publishing house, Budapest's largest brewery, and one of the most popular of the city's long-established restaurants. But for a greater and more poignant awareness of the persistence of his legacy you should really visit his native Transylvania. During a long stay there in the early 1980s, I paid a visit to a remote Hungarian village in the county of Kolozsvár. I was intending to see one of the easternmost examples in Europe of the Italian Renaissance style.

The half-derelict village, renamed Mineu, lay at the end of a rutted track which, after a while, became impassable for the car I was in. Half an hour's uphill walk was required to complete my journey, at the end of which the local sacristan invited me into his home for copious quantities of *pálinka* (home-distilled fruit brandy) and lamentations about the sufferings of Transylvania's Hungarians. Finally, in a tipsy and emotional state, he led me to the church, where a sudden shaft of sunlight, emerging from behind a dark cloud, lit up the uncannily well-preserved object of my pilgrimage—an exquisitely carved red marble portal, executed possibly by a member of the same team of Italian craftsmen who had worked for Matthias at the Royal Palace of Buda.

2

Turkish Baths

SINKING into the murky, steaming waters of the octagonal pool, I slip into a gloomily mysterious world of naked figures floating around in an unmistakably Turkish setting of weathered marble columns and star-shaped openings in the dome. But I am neither dreaming nor in Turkey. I am in the Rudas baths of Buda, lying in a sixteenth-century Turkish bath encased within unprepossessing nineteenth-century walls. And, instead of the exotic female beauties that Ingres and other romantics might have imagined, I am surrounded by Hungarian men in varying stages of physical decrepitude, discussing business, reading newspapers, playing chess on floating boards—participating, in short, in a typical, everyday scene of Hungarian life.

The importance of Turkish baths in present-day Hungary, together with the local love of coffee, coffee-houses, and spicy, paprika-flavoured food, are the main features of a Turkish legacy that has left few actual monuments. After reconquering their country in 1686, the Hungarians demolished most of what had been constructed by their Eastern oppressors, leaving today in Budapest little more than a handful of Turkish structures. These include a couple of prayer-niches, a tiny group of modest wooden tombs, and the much venerated small shrine of the Dervish saint Gül Baba. More significantly, there remain four magnificent and still functioning baths where Hungarians can forget the more negative aspects of Ottoman domination and luxuriate in a world of proverbial oriental indolence.

Few other places were more suited than Buda and Pest to satisfy the Islamic passion for hot baths. At least 123 mineral springs lie below the modern city, which has been described as 'sitting on a heat accumulator of gigantic dimensions'. The presence of these springs was undoubtedly a principal factor underlying the foundation of the first settlement in the area: the name of Aquincum, appropriated by the Romans from the Celts, referred to the area's 'plentiful waters'. The heat of these would later prompt the Germans to rename Buda *Ofen* or Oven.

The Romans were the first to exploit the waters in any systematic way, and established here no fewer than eleven baths, the fame of which soon spread throughout the Roman empire (extensive remains of one of these, complete with under-floor heating, have been turned into a small museum in Óbuda). Bathing was regarded by the Romans not only as a hygienic necessity but also as fundamental to a person's mental well-being. As hedonistic places of entertainment, the baths inevitably came to attract moral censure, which was aroused especially by the practice of mixed bathing—common among the Romans up to the time of the emperor Hadrian. The widely held view of the baths as being almost synonymous with brothels was matched by the more sober image of them as places where the sick came in search of a cure. Roman soldiers suffering from rheumatism appear to have been sent to Aquincum from all over the empire, to judge from the deformed skeletons that were found on the site of a military hospital adjoining one of the baths. There is also circumstantial evidence suggesting that the waters here were already used for the alleviation of leprosy: the island of St Margaret (famous since ancient times for its springs) was known by the Romans as the *Insula Leporum* (Island of Hares), which might well have been a punning euphemism for *Insula Leprosorum*.

The dichotomy between the clinical and the steamily sensual has characterized thermal baths up to the present day. The Church, which would periodically condemn baths for their licentiousness, was also a major force behind the revival of thermal bathing in the Middle Ages, and did much to promote the healing properties of the waters. Religious orders were in fact responsible for turning Buda into a medieval thermal resort by as early as the mid-twelfth century, nearly 200 years before the foundation of the Belgian resort that gave such places their modern name, Spa.

Hospitals run by the nursing orders of St István and St John were established in the twelfth century alongside baths both in the northern half of Buda (on sites to be identified with those of the present-day Lukács and Császar baths) and at the foot of Buda's Gellért hill—an area which would form the nucleus of the modern spa town. A further hospital, next to another of the Gellért springs, came to be associated in the early thirteenth century with St Elizabeth, the future patroness of many of Hungary's hospitals and leper colonies. This much-loved saint was frequently portrayed in medieval art washing lepers in a crude wooden tub; but she might also have appreciated the more sybaritic aspects of bathing, for the dowry on her betrothal to the Markgraf Ludwig von Thüringen featured the then unheard-of luxury of a silver bath.

The renewed fashion for bathing continued to grow in Hungary during the reigns of Sigismund and Matthias Corvinus. A French traveller of 1432, Bertrandon de la Broquière, praised Buda's 'tres beaux baingz chaulx', but it was not until over a century later that the humanist bishop Miklós Oláh gave the first detailed description of them. Describing the baths that had flourished during the reign of Matthias, he mentioned how effective these were in healing rheumatism, fevers, and other diseases; he also indicated their wide-ranging appeal by writing one moment about the particular baths favoured by the king and the next about those where 'peasants and vine-dressers are usually bathing, in such a way that only their heads and shoulders can be seen'.

A common characteristic of the medieval public baths was the presence of a barber-surgeon, who, as well as being responsible at first for the rent and upkeep of these places, carried out blood-letting and other minor operations that tended to turn the waters a gruesome red. From the fourteenth century onwards some of his more appealing duties were taken over by the so-called 'bath-girl', a figure apparently comparable in reputation to the scantily clad female attendants of contemporary massage parlours. The ever-greater popularity of the baths was accompanied by their growing notoriety as places of loose behaviour where naked men and women shamelessly cavorted together. A manuscript belonging to Matthias Corvinus portrayed scenes from the life of a 'bath-girl' at the time of King Sigismund: the girl in question, naked save for a see-through apron, was shown engaged in such activities as washing her client, drying him with a towel, massaging and shaving him, and cutting his hair. She was also depicted holding the bunch of twigs that would be used to stimulate the circulation of those emerging from the Nordic-style saunas that seem to have caught on in Hungary during this period (one such structure has been found within the ruins of the royal palace of Visegrád).

Despite the enormous popularity that thermal bathing acquired in Hungary in the Middle Ages, it is unlikely that the taste for hot baths would have attained such a central position in Hungarian life had it not been for the arrival of the Turks in the early sixteenth century. By this date fewer and fewer Europeans were taking baths, thanks to a combination of the increasingly firm moral standpoint adopted by the Church and the growing preference for dousing the body with perfumes rather than with water: Isabella of Castile was even able to claim in old age that she had had only two baths in her whole life, once before her betrothal and the other time before her coronation.

For the Muslim inhabitants of North Africa and the Middle East, who appear to have inherited the bathing practices of the Greeks and Romans, bathing was undertaken not just as a pleasure or as a cure but as a necessary part of Islamic ritual. This explains how the Turks, on reaching Buda, devoted so much energy to preserving springs, embellishing old baths and building new ones. There were essentially two types of Turkish bath, the more traditional one being the *hamman* or steam room; the other type, the *ilidje*, comprised a cupola covering a central pool of round or octagonal shape. The earliest of these baths in Buda were the work of the first of the town's Turkish rulers, Mohammed Pasha, who fashioned one of the pools out of Christian marble plaques that had had their inscriptions removed; further baths were built by him directly below another of his creations—the shrine to Gül Baba. But the Turkish baths that attract today's visitor to Budapest (notably the Rudas and Király Baths) are the *ilidjes* that were erected in the late sixteenth century by the man known as 'the great bath-building Pasha of Buda', Mustapha Sokolli.

Robert Townson, a late eighteenth-century British traveller who found the hot baths 'the most remarkable things of Bude', wrote that 'the Turks, who so often have had possession of the city, could not fail of applying it to their favourite pastime; some of the baths, and the greatest, are Turkish remains.' These baths were no less objects of praise during the Turkish period, when they even drew lengthy and excited comment from Turkish travellers such as Evliya Çelebi and Mohammed Omar Ben Bejazid (the latter being a visitor of the late sixteenth century who marvelled at the waters' 'healing effects on malignant diseases', on their being hot enough to boil an egg in, and—in the case of those of the Rudas baths—'so abundant as to enable the driving of two water mills'). Numerous other lengthy descriptions of the baths have come down to us from this period, beginning with one featured in the *Hypomnemation de admirandis Hungariae aquis*—a pioneering work on Hungarian mineral waters written in 1551 by a German doctor, Georg Wernher, who approved of the loving care that the Turks bestowed on their springs. A German preacher on his way to Constantinople in 1573 was amazed by the lavishness of the baths' marble decorations, while a Belgian diplomat visiting Buda in 1584 commented on their cleanliness, and on the efficiency of the staff who worked there. And at least one Westerner— Josef Wilden, the mayor of Nuremberg—had personal experience of the beneficial qualities of the waters. Wilden, taken prisoner by the Turks in 1610, was allowed by his captors to visit the baths every day to try and cure a leg swollen from the cold. After two months of this treatment, Wilden had fully recovered the use of this leg and had gained from his time in the baths such a favourable impression of Buda that, had he been a free man, he would have liked nothing better than to have spent the rest of his life there.

Unlike those who frequented the baths before and after the Turkish period, the Turks insisted on a rigid separation between male and female bathers, the former being allowed into the baths only in the mornings and the latter only in the afternoons and evenings. Adam Wenner, a German seventeenth-century traveller, emphasized how the women, prevented from walking the streets unveiled and unchaperoned, could enjoy a freedom in the baths that was granted to them in few other areas of their lives: here, unaccompanied for once by their servants, they could gossip openly with their friends, and give themselves up to a wholly sybaritic existence.

The longest and most famous account of Turkish baths and bathing customs was that given in 1638 by the English doctor Edward Browne, who prefaced this by declaring:

The natural Baths of Buda are esteemed the noblest in Europe, not only in respect of the large and hot springs, but the Magnificence of their buildings. For the Turks bathe very much and though little curious in most of their private houses, yet are they very sumptuous in their public buildings, as their Chars or Caravansaii's [sic], Mosques, Bridges and Baths declare.

According to Browne there were eight public baths in Buda, the individual peculiarities of which he went on to list, dwelling on such features as the heat and smell of the waters, and their architectural setting: thus the Rudas baths, known then as the 'Bath of the green Pillars' ('though at present they be of red colour'), had water of tolerable heat that was let out at night after the women bathers had left. For Browne, the 'noblest' of the baths was that of Velibey (the present Császár baths), which had an exceptionally large antechamber and a capacious and high-arched bathroom adorned with five domes, one great one over the central pool and four lesser ones over each of the four corners. Unfortunately the water had a strong sulphurous smell, and was so hot that it needed the addition of cold water to be made bearable.

Browne left to the end a description of the actual rituals taking place within the baths. As in the baths today, visitors would be greeted in the antechamber by attendants who provided them with a towel and an 'apron'. After undressing and putting on the 'apron' (today's male visitors are provided instead with a loose-fitting loincloth), they would proceed to the bathroom, where, before sinking into the waters, they would be attended to by a barber, who would rub them all over with his bare, outstretched palms, then stretch out and lift their limbs. When the men had bathed the barber would shave their heads, and—in the case of the younger men—their beards, leaving only the hair on the upper lips. Then, while they were either sitting or lying face downwards on the ground, they would be vigorously rubbed all over with a hair cloth, soaped, and soaked in cold water. At the end of all this they would finally be left to linger lazily in the steam.

Edward Browne was a witness to the bath culture of Buda immediately prior to its entering a long period of decline. During the siege of Buda of 1686, three years after the publication of Browne's travels, some of the baths were destroyed completely and others, such as those of the Császár, were greatly damaged and reduced both in size and splendour. An Italian traveller, Domenico Sestini, came to Buda in 1717 after having read descriptions of what the town's baths had been like under the Turks. He was inevitably disappointed: they had lost for him all traces of their 'oriental luxury'.

The baths that survived the siege were variously sold off, rented out, donated as gifts, and granted to the municipality; for a period following an outbreak of plague in 1693 they were even closed down completely. Though some of the new private owners were able to make reasonable sums of money from the baths, bathing was no longer the fashion of the town's rich and came to be practised almost exclusively by what contemporary travellers dismissively referred to as the 'lower classes'. The medical and hygienic aspects of bathing became subsidiary once again to the purely pleasurable ones. Mixed bathing was reintroduced, and—as one Georg Johann Keyssler commented in 1723—the bathers, being of the 'lower classes', rarely bothered with the 'aprons' and shifts that were obligatory respectively for men and women. Decrees issued by the Buda City Council in 1713 and 1785 prove that the baths had become once again the scene of 'revelry and moral mis-deameanour'—behaviour that Robert Townson found incomprehensible in the context of the often unbearably hot and steamy conditions. 'In a common bath', wrote Townson in 1797,

I saw young men and maidens, old men and children, some in a state of nature, others with a fig leaf covering, flouncing about like fish in spawning-time. But the observer must be just. I saw none of the ladies without a petticoat, though most were without their shifts. Some of the gentlemen were with drawers, some without; according, no doubt, to their degree of delicacy, and as they thought themselves to be favoured by nature or not. But no very voluptuous ideas arise in these suffocating humid steams; and as a further sedative, the surgeon is seen hard at work, cupping and scarifying.

While thermal bathing declined in fashion in the eighteenth century, scientific interest in the waters grew, thus fostering the nineteenth-century craze for balneology. A number of scientific analyses of Hungary's mineral waters were carried out, including, in 1721, Laurence Stocker's *Thermographia Budensis*, the first study devoted exclusively to Buda's thermal springs. In this work, reprinted in 1729, Stocker criti-cized the inhabitants of Buda for not taking sufficient advantage of the healing springs that God had blessed them with. Sebastian John Dill-mann, the then mayor of Buda, obviously took this to heart, for in 1733 he tried to improve the town's shattered finances by having the town council bring out in German a compendious guide to the town's thermal resources. This piece of propaganda did not prove effective, and the town had to wait for nearly a century before bathing became widely fashion-able once again.

A report on Buda's baths undertaken in 1815 by a group of Viennese scientists concluded that the baths were still places of 'lower-class amuse-ment' rather than serious healing institutions. By 1822, however, a book on Buda written by Francis Schams indicated that all this had begun to change, and that the general standard of baths had improved immeasur-ably. The rapidly developing science of balneology, which had begun transforming spas such as Karlsbad and Baden-Baden into some of the most sophisticated resorts of Europe, was bringing the Buda baths back into fashion, and initiating the process that would make Budapest today the only place in the world that is both a spa town and a city. Decayed Turkish baths were restored and given a neo-classical casing incorporating not only all the paraphernalia of balneology such as steam chambers, massage rooms, tub-baths, and showers but also guest rooms, billiard rooms, and elegant restaurants. The Rudas baths, once shunned by the more refined elements in Budapest society, now led one visitor to opine that he had 'never had a more comfortable bath'; the Császár baths, meanwhile, remodelled by the great neo-classical architect József Hild, regained their reputation for splendour and, though tending at first to the impecunious sick, also flourished as a luxurious dancing venue and 'place of delight'.

New springs were discovered, and new baths opened, not only in Buda, but also on St Margaret Island, and in the previously unexploited Pest. The first bath of note in Pest was built at the beginning of the century by the town's medical officer, Sebastian Rumbach, who had come across a mineral spring while digging a well on a plot of sandy land that the town council had auctioned off near the Városliget or City Park. Other baths soon followed in Pest, including, in the 1820s, the sumptuous Diana bath, the architecture of which (by Hild) inspired the writer Kazinczy to comment that this was 'Beauty's dwelling-place'. Improved digging techniques from the 1850s onwards allowed the boring of holes ever deeper into the ground and encouraged the search for further spring waters. The principal Hungarian engineer specializing in this was Vilmos Zsigmondy, who, in 1866 and 1868 respectively, started making borings on St Margaret Island and in the City Park. Within three years he had discovered on the former site an abundant spring which would prompt the building of a magnificent spa complex by Miklós Ybl, the architect of the Pest opera house. However, it would take him nine years of digging, amidst mounting criticism, before uncovering the spring in the City Park that would later provide the waters for the present Széchenyi Baths.

The interest in steam and vapour baths that developed in Europe in the mid-nineteenth century merged with a romantic obsession with the orient to bring Turkish baths to the height of their popularity in the West. At a time when a pseudo-oriental style of architecture was being adopted throughout Europe in the construction of bath-houses, the presence in Buda of four genuine Turkish baths must have seemed a real boon. Their presence certainly helped to further the town's romantic image among foreigners, who often approached these baths with pre-conceptions based on the sensual reveries of orientalist painters and writers. One of these foreigners was the French traveller Victor Tissot, whose characteristically high-flown account of the Rudas baths ('one of the greatest curiosities of Buda') must in turn have fuelled feverish Western visions of what these baths were like.

'Imagine', he wrote in 1881, 'a vast rotunda supported by eight large pillars, the entrance to which is by a black vault-shaped door, orna-mented with a Turkish inscription; all around the walls are fixed stone seats, on which men, women, and children were dressing and undress-ing, showing bare arms and legs, bodies arched, backs foreshortened.' The 'sleepy haze' that fills every corner of the room gives an added sen-suality to a scene in which Tissot is soon picking out such sights as a bending woman taking off her stockings, the supple body of a young girl disappearing into a chemise, a bare-breasted girl fastening the ends of her hair, 'young girls playing with the limpid water with the grace of nymphs and naiads'. Eventually his eye rests on a naked gypsy girl who is leaning drying herself against a pillar: with her perfectly rounded throat that 'would have delighted a sculptor', her finely shaped head, harmoniously proportioned figure, and thick dark hair falling in waves over her shoulders, she appears to him as 'the strange divinity of some mysterious Indian temple'. However, despite the 'interest one might have taken in these pictures from an artist's point of view', the fully clothed Tissot soon finds himself unable to withstand the heat, and is forced to leave. As he does so the door-keeper strongly recommends him to return early on Sunday morning, when all the peasant women of the neigh-bourhood come to bathe: 'My faith,' the man sighs, 'there are some pretty ones!'

A rather more realistic idea of what to expect from a visit to one of Buda's public baths was given in 1869 by the Englishman William Byrne, who was taken to see the Turkish bath-chamber of the Császár baths. He found himself in a 'gloomy, cavernous-looking place' where, after adjusting his eyes to the dark, he could just about make out 'some dozen or more of living creatures, either sitting on the edge, or floating about in the water, men and women bathing promiscuously together, or rather lazily enjoying the tepid temperature of the air and water'. The sight, he concluded, 'was by no means an attractive one. They were for the most part haggard, wrinkled creatures, with dark hair hanging over their faces and shoulders, in forms resembling rats' tails; so we bade a rapid adieu to these elderly naiads and forbidding tritons, who seemed equally pleased to be rid of our presence.'

While the human sights to be observed in the baths might not have been as generally beautiful as Tissot had led visitors to believe, the architectural settings became ever more lavish and seductive, with the development of an official municipal spa policy after the unification of Buda and Pest in 1873: all the privately owned baths became gradually the property of the newly created city of Budapest, which promoted its uniqueness as a spa city to the extent that it was to host in 1937 the first International Congress of Balneology. The restrained neo-classicism of the earlier baths was succeeded by a wide range of grand and playful styles from the neo-Turkish to the neo-Renaissance to the spectacular neo-baroque of the Széchenyi baths (built between 1909 and 1913). But the city's crowning spa complex was the one developed between 1908 and 1933 on the site where St Elizabeth and the knights of the Order of St John had once tended to lepers—the foot of the Gellért hill. The Gellért Spa Hotel, described by one visitor of the 1930s as 'classical in its proportions but Hungarian in its details and ornaments', is from the outside an expressive, twisting mass of light grey stone crowned by domes of a fantastical and vaguely oriental appearance; hidden at the back is a curvaceously terraced area dominated by an enormous 'wave-pool' decorated at the bottom with flowing ceramic lines. The interior is even more impressive, with an echoing entrance hall where light filters through a series of stained-glass windows portraying scenes from an epic poem by János Arany; gilded brass and a profusion of blue and green majolica tiles from the Zsolnay workshop adorn the men's thermal bath, while columns that seem straight from some maharajah's palace support the two-tiered arcade that surrounds the enormous 'Bubble-Pool'. The whole forms the glowing centrepiece of the present-day spa resort of Budapest, and has been used on the covers of tourist brochures and guidebooks to evoke the spirit of Budapest itself.

Budapest today remains a city obsessed with both baths and swimming. The many Turkish and other indoor baths are complemented by a vast array of outdoor pools, ranging from the Olympic-sized Palatinus swimming-pool on St Margaret Island to the 'Roman baths' at Óbuda and the warm thermal pool of the Széchenyi baths, where one can laze in the middle of an open-air amphitheatre of statuary and colonnades. 'The Hungarian's relationship with water is entirely naïve, entirely elemental,' wrote the German writer Franz Fühmann in a passage evoking 'the pleasant hours of chitchat and gossip, sitting in the water, on proper stone seats and chairs, smoking in the water, nibbling candy in the water, playing chess in the water, drinking mineral water in the water, enthusing over bathing experiences in the water, totally at ease in the relaxation of their hot and sulphur-immersed bodies'. What he could also have mentioned was the prowess at swimming and water-sports which has led Hungary to produce an exceptional number of outstanding swimmers, such as the current Budapest heroine, Kristina Egerszegid, who, by the age of only 26, has won gold medals at three consecutive Olympics and even has her own restaurant, the Mousehole, the name of which plays on her nick-name 'Little Mouse'.

A visit to one of Budapest's bathhouses and thermal pools has become a prerequisite of any stay in this city, though it is an experience that might at first baffle the foreigner. Those with little command of Hungarian will probably be confused as soon as they reach the ticket office, where a long notice lists the prices for the various facilities on offer, from massage and family changing cabins down to such specialities as 'ultra-sound' and pedicure: the acquisition of a basic ticket will probably be enough for most people, and—despite what is written on the notice— enable you to remain in the Turkish baths for longer than the statutory one and a half hours.

Once inside a bathhouse, you are likely to find yourself in what Fühmann described as a 'labyrinth of passages, nooks, crannies, angles, cubbyholes, corners, alcoves, cubicles sprouting sties and stalls . . .'. The white-coated attendant who takes your ticket (a tip will prevent you from queueing during the more crowded times of the day) will direct you to the changing-rooms, where a further attendant will open a locker for you, and provide you either with a second key to this or else with a numbered tag. If you are visiting an outdoor thermal pool, a swimming pool, or a mixed Turkish bath, a bathing costume is needed, together (usually) with a plastic bathing-cap (a bare head can often earn you a recriminatory whistle). Almost all of the better-known Turkish baths have reverted to the Turkish practice of having separate bathing times for men and women: it is in these places that men are supplied (by the locker attendant) with their 'modesty cloth' and women with the rather more extensive 'apron'—items of clothing that are usually discarded by the latter but kept by all but the more exhibitionist of the former.

Proceeding now into the baths, you will generally be confronted by a central pool surrounded by smaller pools of differing degrees of heat—a sight that Fühmann compared to the 'maw of Hell: clouds of steam, aura of sweat, rising vapors, drifting mist, swaying lights, gliding figures, gasping and rumbling, pillars looking like wraiths, grottoes, caves, steps going down and up and pools with heads and fluttering hands . . .'. The sybaritic pleasures of the waters make you soon forget the infernal aspects of the scene, though the unsuspecting heterosexual male who visits the Király or Rácz baths (notorious gay meeting-places despite characteristically Hungarian denial) might soon be made tense again as a result of the sexually predatory atmosphere—an atmosphere that quashes once and for all Townson's theory that 'no very voluptuous ideas arise under these hot, humid conditions'.

Whether you move from hot to cold water or vice versa seems very much a matter of personal constitution, as is the ability to withstand the heat and claustrophobia, let alone the steamy behaviour, of the adjoining steam-rooms and saunas. But whatever bathing regime you adopt, or whether you go on to have massages, pedicures, or other treatments, you should always leave yourself time at the end of the visit to cool off in the 'relaxing room', where the apron or loincloth is exchanged for a towel that covers you as you lie stretched out on a deckchair trying to make sense of the whole strange experience.

The strangeness of a visit to the Turkish baths is a sensation that can be felt to an even greater degree in Budapest's outdoor thermal pools, especially in those such as the Széchenyi that remain open throughout the autumn and winter, when they lose their crowded, festive character. Iván Mándy, one of the greatest recent writers to concern himself with the minutiae of Budapest life, beautifully evoked this in a short story in which he described such details of the autumnal pools as the bursts of distant laughter from a changing-room, the brisk rush of girls making their shivering way into the warm pool, and the melancholy waltz of frog-like leaves being rocked by the water that they are slowly covering. But more suggestive still than the autumnal pool as portrayed by Mándy are the Széchenyi baths in winter, when the snow is falling, the statuary is disappearing under a white blanket, and clouds of steam are rising into the frozen pale blue sky, revealing old men playing chess, solitary smokers, isolated walrus moustaches, and other apparent figments from a dream.

I am now in the 'relaxing room' of the Rudas baths, wrapped up in a towel and stretched out on a deckchair in between other bodies. The baths leave you in a pleasantly sleepy state, with barely the energy to contemplate anything afterwards other than the relaxing prospect, say, of going out for a meal or a drink. Now that my body has been purged of its impurities, I can only think about contaminating it again in smoky rooms serving copious quantities of coffee, lard, paprika, pastries, alcohol, and cream.

3

The Ghost of Gyula Krúdy

AMONG the homely, pastel-coloured survivals of eighteenth-century Óbuda, stranded between tower-blocks and Roman fragments, is a traditional Biedermeier inn, single-storeyed, steeply roofed, and with a tree-shaded courtyard where guests can eat in the summer months. The Kéhli restaurant is no longer the simple inn that it once was, but it preserves the memory of the turn-of-the-century Hungarian writer whose name is immediately suggestive of the pleasures of good food and wine—Gyula Krúdy. A stone plaque in the corner of the dining-room marks the seat and table favoured by this great epicurean, whose writings are liberally quoted from in a menu steeped in nostalgia for a bygone era when Hungary was great and life leisurely.

The works of Krúdy are themselves descriptive of a world that exists largely in the past tense but which can instantly be recalled in dishes that have the same power of suggestion as Proust's lime tea and *madeleines*. The subject of food is one that brings out all the sentimentality of the Hungarians, especially among those with a strong sense of having been deprived in later life of the gastronomic delights that they knew in their youth.

'Not being nostalgic by nature,' wrote the Hungarian-born Kató Frank in her *Cooking the Hungarian Way* (London, 1963), 'it needed those special Hungarian dishes to remind me of those enchanting little restaurants in the old town of Buda, where we ate spring chicken with fresh cucumber salad, the taste of which I shall never forget.' The way in which food can momentarily bring back a world that has gone is emphasized in that most poignant of Hungarian novels, *Skylark*, by Krúdy's outstanding contemporary, Dezső Kosztolányi (translated by R. Aczel, 1996). The book deals with two elderly parents whose taste for life is rekindled when their abstemious stay-at-home routine is disrupted by the departure for a week of their sensible, spinsterish daughter; long-forgotten pleasures are rediscovered the moment they decide to have lunch at the local inn, where the spicy flavours of fattening food, enhanced by drink and good company, begin to seduce them almost against their will:

The smells of the restaurant still lingered about his nose, stubbornly, unavoidably, assertively. That stuffy fragrance, fragrant stuffiness, that cruel, aromatic combination of caraway, onions fried in fat, and the pleasantly bitter hop breath of beer.

The food that arouses such intense nostalgia and enthusiasm among Hungarians is often of the most basic kind—such as fresh peaches, goose fat spread on toast, pickled cucumber, garlic-flavoured sausage. Hungarian cuisine is known less for its subtlety than for its heartiness, the strength of its flavours, and its traditional reliance on onions, sour cream, paprika, and lard (a combination of ingredients that should be compared with what has been called the 'holy trinity' of French cooking—fresh butter, herbs, and truffles). But it is also a cuisine of remarkable adaptability which has managed over the centuries to maintain its essential strong character while responding to the many foreign influences to which Hungary has been subject.

The character of this cuisine seems already to have been established shortly after the arrival of the first Hungarian tribes from the East. Early sources, including an anonymous Codex of 1303, indicate that the first Hungarians did most of their cooking in a cast-iron cauldron known as a *bogrács*, which is used today for goulash and other typically Hungarian soups. These soups are often meals in themselves, just as they were in ninth- and tenth-century Hungary, and share other characteristics of present-day soups such as a sour or semi-sour taste achieved through the addition of sour cream, vinegar, sauerkraut, yoghurt, or horseradish, and being sometimes thickened with browned flour and fat, or with a mixture of flour, milk, and egg yolk. An accompaniment to these stew-like soups (the staple diet of early medieval Hungary) was a millet-sized pasta which, under the name of *tarhonya*, is still a feature of Hungarian beef stews. As for the meat that formed the basis of the soups, this had previously been dried so that it could be taken away on journeys, together with the ubiquitous *bogrács*: the drying process involved cooking the meat until all its liquid had gone, leaving it for three or four days in the sun, and then either pulverizing it into a fine powder or else keeping it in pouches made from sheep's stomachs. Sheep (whose milk was used for the curd known as *zsendice*, one of the oldest Hungarian foods) and grey cattle (whose descendants live on in the part of the Hungarian puszta around Hortobágy) were brought over from the East by the original Hungarian settlers; soon afterwards lamb and beef were supplemented by pork, which has remained to this day one of the primary elements in Hungarian cooking.

When the Mongols invaded Hungary in 1246, the Hungarians were able to display for the first time their remarkable ability to benefit gastronomically from political adversity: their country may have been left in ruins, but they had apparently gained from their invaders a knowledge of how to stew mutton in its own juice, the basis of today's *berbéc-stokány* stew. Furthermore, in the wake of the disaster Hungary acquired what would become the most internationally renowned of its wines, Tokay: vineyards had been flourishing in Hungary at the time of the Magyars' arrival, but it was the Walloon settlers whom Béla IV had brought in after the Mongol invasion who planted here the famous sweet Tokay grape.

With the reign of Sigismund came the first known Hungarian chef of distinction, Ferenc Eresztvényi, who was awarded a patent of nobility in 1414, together with a coat of arms featuring a chef's hat, a boar's head, and a sturgeon leaping over flames. But the most important advances in the early history of Hungarian food were made during the reign of Matthias Corvinus, the culinary life of whose court was recorded in meticulous detail by the humanists Galeotto Marzio and Antonio Bonfini. The enormous culinary sophistication reached during this period is revealed in the various accounts of banquets, the most spectacular of which was that celebrating the marriage of Matthias to Princess Beatrice—a marriage which brought the flavours and style of Italy to the Hungarian table. The great chefs of the Aldobrandini family were sent to Hungary, together with *pasta asciutta*, dill, capers, figs, pastries, and other delicacies, as well as the Italian habit of serving food on the finest majolica; turkeys, requested by Matthias from Ludovico Sforza, duke of Milan, came afterwards, and bred so well here that Hungarian turkeys are today considered among the best in Europe. Other later Italian imports included onions and garlic, which, despite their humble nature, apparently sent the king into raptures: Princess Beatrice, on acknowledging a gift of these vegetables from Ferrara, wrote that Matthias 'could not have been more pleased if they had been pearls'. Numerous documents such as these testify to Matthias's enormous love of food, which appears to have increased as he grew older and to have inspired many stories about his visits to the royal kitchens to check up on and even assist with what was being prepared for that day. Among the more popular foods served up at the royal tables were sturgeon, plover eggs (still a Hungarian delicacy), beef, ewe, pork, venison, hare, duck, quail, starlings, capon, and pheasant, all of the meats being stewed, as they are today, in their own juices rather than being enriched with a separate sauce.

Though deriving so much from Italy, Hungarian cuisine had already the reputation by Matthias's day as a cuisine which in itself was worth emulating, for dishes such as 'Hungarian soup' had already begun featuring in contemporary Italian menus. The ingredient still needed to give this cuisine the character we think of today as unmistakably Hungarian would come shortly with the Turks—paprika.

The way in which the branchy paprika plant came to Turkey has been much debated, one theory being that it was an Indian plant which was later introduced to Persia and then to the Middle East; more probably the plant originated in Central America, and reached Turkey by way of Spain and Italy. What is certain is that paprika was unknown in Europe before Columbus, and that it soon became, in the Turkish empire, a popular alternative both as a flavouring and a colouring additive to the increasingly expensive black pepper.

The Turks who cultivated the plant in Hungary felt so proprietorial towards it that they did not allow it to be grown by the Hungarian peasantry. However, this rule proved impossible to enforce, and by at least the early seventeenth century, the Hungarians had become the first nation to use paprika in its pure, powdered form. With the addition of this spice to chicken, fish, and meat stews, some of the most famous Hungarian dishes of today were created: when the Turkish traveller and gastronome Evliya Çelebi visited Hungary in the early seventeenth century, he was able to find eight inns in Buda alone serving both carp and chicken in the paprika-based stew known as *pörkölt* which, together with *paprikás* (a similar stew but with sour cream added at the last minute), *tokány* (in which the meats are braised in their own juices), and the paprika-free *gulyás* soup, constitute what has been referred to as the 'four pillars of Hungarian cooking'.

Paprika was by no means the only contribution made by the Turks to Hungarian cuisine. The Turks introduced strudel pastry, rice pilaffs served with spit-roasted meat, stuffed foods such as aubergine, pepper, and vine-leaves, the pizza-like fritters known as *lángos* (one of Hungary's many culinary terms of Turkish origin), and plants ranging from tomatoes to sweet and sour cherries, the latter being the basis of *Meggyleves*, a popular Hungarian soup. Not least they brought coffee to Hungary, in the process profoundly influencing the future social and cultural life of the country. Coffee had reached Constantinople in 1517, with the first coffee-house being opened there in 1554. The instant popularity that these establishments enjoyed (as was reflected in their ever more sumptuous interiors) was accompanied by the inevitable moral censure, with some Islamic commentators condemning coffee with the same fervour as they did alcohol; however, none of the steps taken to ban the drinking of coffee proved long-lasting, and coffee-houses continued to flourish throughout the Ottoman empire, from where they spread to the rest of Europe by the end of the seventeenth century. The coffee-houses that were founded in Buda and Pest after the departure of the Turks took on several of the characteristics of their Turkish predecessors, including the adjoining presence of a barber's shop, and the role of disseminating news and gossip. And though coffee itself might now have lost its controversial aspect, the institutions where it was drunk began acquiring reputations as centres of dissent, with one of them—the Pilvax in Pest—playing a central role in the Hungarian struggle against the Austrians.

Austrian rule in Hungary, and the accompanying Germanization of the country, affected every aspect of daily life, down to the people's gastronomic habits. While the Hungarian aristocracy began aping the French-inspired manners of the Austrian upper classes, the middle classes adapted their cuisine to accommodate such Austrian specialities as schnitzel, sausages, potatoes, and the cooking of vegetables in a roux made of lard and flour. Austrian influence can be felt too in the various kinds of eating and drinking establishments that were developed in Hungary from the seventeenth century onwards and which are still popular today, albeit in an increasingly luxurious form. Among these was the *csárda* or inn, which was often situated next to one of the stopping-places of the mail coach. Fisherman-*csárdas* grew up in the former wine-growing district of Óbuda, where, additionally, a number of cottage gardens were laid out with gaily covered tables where visitors could indulge in food and wine while listening to the sounds of *schrammel* (Austrian popular music) or gypsy music (one such garden is attached to Krúdy's beloved Kéhli inn). Simple food was always served at taverns or *kocsmas*, which can be compared in their unpretentiousness to the more urban *kisvendéglő*, a basic small restaurant where the seating was sometimes communal and the wine poured from an earthenware pitcher. Austrian-style pastries, tempered with a strong hint of Turkish influence, were the speciality of the *konditorei* or *cukrászda*, of which a magnificent example surviving from the 1820s is Ruszwurm's on Buda's Castle Hill.

Foreign visitors to Hungary of the eighteenth and early nineteenth centuries rarely showed much enthusiasm for the local cuisine, which they found occasionally exotic but more usually unsophisticated to a near-unpalatable degree. Attitudes began changing from the mid nineteenth century onwards, at a time when Hungarian food had started once again to influence foreign cuisines. After winning over the palates of the Austrians—who appropriated such Hungarian specialities as pancakes and chocolate roulade—Hungarian food went on to conquer even so distinguished a master of French cuisine as Escoffier, who in 1879 introduced to Monte Carlo *gulyas hongrois* and *poulet au paprika*. By the beginning of the present century the country's cuisine was held in a regard which has never been equalled since, its combination of the exotic and the creamily rich being ideally suited to the sensation-seeking tastes of Edwardian high society. And for the more health-conscious of those who visited the now fashionable Hungarian spas, there was always the freshwater fish known as the *fogas*, which, in its breaded form, achieved a reputation comparable to caviar and *foie gras*.

The transformation of humble Hungarian cooking into a sophisticated cuisine owes much to the Francophile tastes of the Hungarian aristocracy, after whom so many of the culinary creations of the nineteenth century were named, from 'Pálffy noodles' to the host of dishes rendering homage to Prince Pál Esterházy, including 'roast beef Esterházy', 'pudding Esterházy', 'beefsteak Esterházy', 'gulyás Esterházy', 'Esterházy sauce', and 'Esterházy cake'. The cooks responsible for these and other creations, and for generally lightening Hungarian food through the subtle artistry of French *haute cuisine*, constituted a remarkable foursome beginning with the French-born Josef Marchal, a passionate admirer of Escoffier.

Marchal, who had embarked on his rapid rise to fame through a spell as chef to Napoleon III, was brought over to Hungary by the gastronomically obsessed Prince Pál Esterházy, a man whose love and knowledge of food had been immeasurably enhanced by his travels as an ambassador. It was on a mission to St Petersburg in the mid-1850s, when Marchal was working as a chef to Tsar Alexander II, that Esterházy had first encountered the latter's cooking; but it was not until 1863 that he was able to carry out his long-cherished plan of luring this much sought-after chef to Hungary. Marchal turned down various other prestigious offers from elsewhere in Europe to accept the post of director-chef of what had been Buda and Pest's most important social club from the beginning of the century, the Casino. The timing was perfect, for within four years the pact with Austria known as the Compromise came into being, thus giving Buda and Pest a greater social prestige than ever and enormously increasing the Casino's clientele; and Marchal's own prodigious reputation was further boosted by his being asked to prepare the banquet for the coronation of Franz Joseph as king of Hungary. Marchal remained in Budapest for the rest of his life, becoming later the restaurant director of one of Budapest's most exclusive hotels, the Angol Királynő, a hotel fragrant with flower decorations and replete with mahogany walls and white and gold columns. While being seduced—as his mentor Escoffier was—by such characteristics of Hungarian cuisine as the use of paprika, Marchal also did much to modify this cuisine through perpetuating Escoffier's intelligent and poetic approach to cooking: he substituted butter for lard, and made use of such French subtleties as herbs and truffles.

An almost exact contemporary of Marchal's was József Dobos, who proudly claimed descent from the chef to Prince György Rákóczi, leader of the 1703 uprising against the Austrians. Dobos made an enormous impact on Hungarian gastronomy through his culinary classic, the *Hungarian-French Cookbook*, and through the fabulously stocked delicatessen that he owned in later life in Budapest—a shop that allowed him to indulge a love of showmanship which led on one occasion to the pouring out of a magnum of the finest Burgundy into a hollowed-out lump of cheese weighing fifty kilos. But the name of Dobos is perennially associated with the chocolate-layered cake that he invented in 1887, the Dobos torte. Hungary's first world-famous dessert, the Dobos torte was only matched as an international confectionery achievement by the near-contemporary cognac cherry—one of the many bonbons created by the Swiss-born Emil Gerbeaud, whose confectioners in Vörösmarty Square has been the most famous in Budapest since its foundation in 1870.

The culinary history of Hungary as it enters the twentieth century is to a great extent the story of János Gundel and his son Károly. This story, of almost fairy tale beginnings, goes back to the small Bavarian town of Ansbach, where János (then called Johann) was born in 1857. Brought

43

up by the proverbial tyrannical stepfather, and thwarted in his early desire to become a priest by the latter's unwillingness to continue paying for his education, Gundel left home at the age of 13 to work for several years as a wandering journeyman, undertaking odd jobs in return for lodging and food. During his travels he got to know a Viennese boy of his own age called Edward Sacher, who was then an apprentice in the specialty food shop of his father, the inventor of the Sachertorte. János himself worked for a while in this shop in Vienna before moving to Pest and getting a job as a waiter in a fashionable hotel restaurant frequented by the likes of Krúdy. As with Marchal, who settled in Pest at about the same time, János's career was aided enormously by the great urban changes that Buda and Pest were undergoing. The soon-to-be-united city of Budapest had become a land of opportunity in which the handsome, charming, and dynamic János was able by the age of 18 to rise to the position of head waiter and gain the nickname of 'Napoleon'. By the time he was 25 he had become the owner of the Blumenstockli restaurant (Virágbokor in Hungarian), which, with its excellent kitchen, wide selection of Czech, Austrian, and Bavarian beers, and (not least) its frescoes by the eminent Károly Lotz (the painter of the Opera House dome), soon become the most popular restaurant in town. The cuisine, heavily Austrian-influenced at first (this was the first place in Pest to serve Wienerschnitzel), became ever more imaginative and adventurous, while also catering to the whims of its many distinguished clients such as Liszt, whose favourite meal was beefsteak, and the painter Munkácsy, in whose honour János created 'eggs in aspic Munkácsy style'.

Married but childless, János surprised his clients by retiring at the age of 35 and selling his business to one of his brothers-in-law. He would surprise them even more by going on afterwards to have five children in quick succession, before coming out of retirement to take up the lease on the restaurant of the city's most elegant hotel, the István Főherceg Szálloda (the Archduke Stephen). Immediately regaining his old clients, he went now to such great lengths to satisfy them that a contemporary article on the restaurant observed:

All of the rare delicacies of the country end up here; if a mouflon is shot in the forests of Nyitra, it will be sent here; if a Danube salmon is hauled from the river Tisza near Máramaros, it will immediately be packed in ice and brought here; if a jar of especially fine cottage cheese is made of sheep's milk in Liptó, it will also find its way here; sausages are delivered from the Hungarian plains, trout from Transylvania, the best wines from Tokaj.

For the writer Kálmán Mikszáth, a regular client since the Virágbokor days, János devised a famous lamb and potato soup named after the mischievous Palóc people whose doings Mikszáth had frequently recorded; for Alexandre Dumas *père*, he provided a series of recipes that would later find their way into the latter's *Dictionary of Cuisine*, itself a work which had been motivated by the enthusiasm of a Hungarian, Count Teleki.

János Gundel continued running his new restaurant until 1904, when the establishment closed down following his failure to renew its lease. Mikszáth mourned its departure in an article predicting that the restaurant would one day be remembered as 'the last place where the cooks in the kitchen could still cook'. He would soon be proved wrong, for the name of Gundel would soon rise to greater heights than ever thanks to János's son Károly, who managed to outstrip the father not only as a progenitor (he ended up with 13 children) but also as a restaurateur.

Whereas János's mentor had been Sacher, Károly's was the Swiss-born shepherd boy turned hotelier César Ritz, whom he met in Switzerland. The example of Ritz persuaded Károly to apply the highest level in elegance, luxury, and professionalism to an already celebrated restaurant that he acquired in Budapest's City Park in 1910. This restaurant, which had previously been owned by Ferenc Wampetics, had thrived through its position, adjoining both the zoo and the part of town where the millennial celebrations of 1896 had been held. Under Károly and his Ritz-inspired regime, 'Gundel's', as this restaurant became known, prospered more than ever, so much so that by 1913 Károly had to expand into a neighbouring Transylvanian-rural-style building (this has recently reopened with its original name of Bagolyvár or 'Owl Castle'). The Bagolyvár's speciality in traditional Hungarian home-cooked food was deliberately meant to contrast with the ever more extravagant *haute cuisine* characteristic of Gundel's itself. Though constantly experimenting and responding to such wild gastronomic challenges as preparing 500 goose soufflés for a single luncheon, Károly remained always conscious of the importance of such basics of the culinary art as simple home cooking and freshness of produce: he grew vegetables and raised pigs in his own farms on the outskirts of Budapest, and personally scoured the markets at dawn in search of the finest ingredients. Károly's recipes and ideas on food were published in best-selling books that have recently been reissued; and both his fame as a restaurateur and Budapest's newly gained reputation as a gastronomic capital would reach their zenith in 1927, when Károly took over the five restaurants attached to the Gellért Spa Hotel.

This flourishing of *haute cuisine* in Budapest coincided with the liveliest years in the history of a café society more vital than almost any other in Europe. Thanks to the Turkish occupation, café life had been established in Budapest a good hundred years earlier than it had been in what are now better-known café centres such as Vienna or Paris; furthermore, none of these other centres could boast a place like the Pilvax, where an actual revolution had broken out. From the mid-nineteenth century onwards the café life of Budapest developed a spiralling intensity which was invariably commented on by foreign visitors to the city such as D. T. Ansted, who wrote in 1862: 'there are many coffee-houses in Pesth—many indeed, in every street, for the Hungarians seem to delight in such resorts more than the Parisians or the Vienese.'

By 1900 the vast pool of cheap labour that had become available in Budapest was sufficient to man over 600 cafés. The decor of these places was not of primary concern to most of their clients, who relished above all a sense of familiarity in their adopted café and who, on at least one occasion, were known to have protested at the prospect of their café-owner renovating his establishment's flaking, smoke-suffused walls. None the less, the turn-of-the-century spirit of renewal and civic pride could not fail to affect such an important aspect of the city's life as its cafés, many of which were rebuilt at this time and given interiors of neo-baroque indulgence. Few cafés in the world could surely have once compared with the still standing if insensitively restored Café New York, a gilded, balconied, and chandeliered extravaganza dating from 1894. And it is undoubtedly symptomatic of the exalted position that cafés had come to hold in Budapest life that this particular one should have been built by Alajos Hauszmann, architect of the Hungarian Royal Palace.

'If you ask a Hungarian exiled from his country what he misses most, nine out of ten will tell you: the cafés!', wrote one such exile, Paul Tábori, who used the title 'The City of Cafés' for one of the Budapest chapters of his book *The Real Hungary* (1939). Many of the cafés, such as the New York, were open twenty-four hours of the day, and many for 365 days of the year, making them enclaves of light and activity at times when the rest of the city was almost deserted. The very earliest coffee-houses served only tobacco and coffee, the latter meaning *café au lait* and Turkish coffee (espresso would only become widely available after the 1940s). However, in the course of the nineteenth century, with the emergence of cafés that favoured small round or square tables rather than the long communal ones of the earlier period, the range of fare on offer became increasingly extensive: by the late nineteenth century many people would visit a café for an after-theatre supper or for an early morning 'hangover soup'.

The café came to be associated with the most remarkably diverse activities apart from drinking and dining, including gambling, reading newspapers, negotiating business, writing, debating, and listening to gypsy bands and other musicians: 'A Budapest café', summarized Tábori, 'is a home from home, a meeting-place, and a stock exchange, a refuge and an intoxicant.' As was once the case with café society in general, the Budapest café world was divided into its various coteries, with particular professions favouring particular cafés—businessmen, for instance meeting up at the Café Orczy, actors at the Café Pannónia, pig-dealers at the Café King Mátyás, cartoonists at the Café Lánchíd, stockbrokers at the Lloyd. In terms of the city's cultural life the two most important cafés were the Japán and the New York, the former attracting artists and architects such as Ödön Lechner, Rippl-Rónai, and Csontváry, the latter being a renowned haunt of writers dominated by the playwright, novelist, and wit Ferenc Molnár, who, on the café's opening night, is said to have thrown its key into the Danube so that the place would never be closed.

The wealth of material relating to Budapest's cafés is such that one of the most exhaustive studies ever to have been devoted to the subject of cafés has been written about them—a massive, two-volumed work by someone boasting ancestry in the city's Coffee-brewers' Guild, Béla Bevilaqua-Borsody. This man's teetotal-sounding name did not prevent him from writing about such intoxicating themes as 'Drunken Waiters in the Pest Cafés'—one of the many social types featured in the book's absorbingly detailed index. Most writers on the city's cafés have similarly delighted in recording these characteristic types, another of whom was the 'telephone boy', whose task was to answer the telephone and call anyone who was wanted: Tábori defined this type as a 'wizened, old little man' and recalled one in particular who had a Schweik-like capacity to make stupidity seem like genius. The personality at the centre of the Budapest café world was the head waiter, who collected all payments and tips and was described by Tábori as 'father confessor, banker, adviser, and creditor to the motley crowd in the domain': in some of the more Bohemian cafés, where literary and stage folk and their friends had a 15 per cent discount, he would even grant credit to those low in funds. One such waiter was lovingly portrayed by the writer Ferenc Karinthy, who, after scribbling down his observations on the man, suddenly became conscious that his subject knew he was writing about him:

He almost certainly knows, he knows everything, only he does not talk un-necessarily. He has seen you, citizen of Pest, born and live in the Coffee-house and if one day you drop dead in your chair, you could not wish for a more brotherly hand than his to close your eyes.

For Tábori, the 'immense variety of types' to be found in the cafés made these places 'up-to-date caravanserai' in which a great many of Hungary's literary masterpieces were born. A writer whose debt to the cafés of Budapest was only equalled by his love to its restaurants was Gyula Krúdy, who captured more successfully than any of his liter-ary contemporaries the spirit of the city's culinary and coffee-house heyday.

A gourmet and a womanizer in equal measures, and someone after whom over 100 Hungarian dishes have been named, Krúdy was a larger-than-life figure with Gargantuan passions that belied his wistful, trimly elegant appearance. From his beloved taverns and late-night cafés came the many near-legendary and at times scarcely believable tales about a life apparently filled with prostitutes, mistresses, all-night drink-ing sessions, romantic duels, gambling, and horse-racing. These tales contributed to the popularity of his image while considerably detracting from his seriousness as a writer; but it is none the less difficult to sepa-rate the life from a heavily autobiographical œuvre in which reality and fantasy are completely interwoven.

Food and women recur throughout Krúdy's works, frequently at the same time, so that, for instance, a menu becomes a love letter, and a goulash soup triggers off a memory of an amorous proposition. He also applied these two favourite themes to his description of places such as Pest, which on one occasion is compared to a '*raffinée* courtesan', and on another described as smelling of 'imperial beer, fresh draught beer and Wiener sausages' and having squares resembling confectionery boxes.

Sensual and gastronomic experiences constantly colour Krúdy's short stories, and are sometimes pivotal to the plot, as in his two stories that deal with the two main protagonists of the same duel, *Death and the Journalist* and *The Last Cigar at the Grey Arab*. In the first of these, a down-at-heel journalist who has offended a military club with one of his articles spends what he thinks are his last hours on earth indulging in *haute cuisine* and other previously unimaginable luxuries. In the second, the colonel who has been chosen to fight him tries to imagine what his opponent's life must be like by going to a modest tavern and eating the sort of simple food and drink he has not had in years but has secretly craved for—pork crackling, stale beer, the scraped-up remains of a midday stew. Only at the end, fifteen minutes before the duel is meant to take place, does the colonel decide to allow himself a final luxury and to take out what is probably the first havana ever to have been smoked on the premises. The final image is of the colonel savouring the exquisite flavour of what turns out to be the last cigar of his life.

The stories for which Krúdy is best known (*The Adventures of Sinbad*, translated by George Szirtes, 1997) feature an ageless traveller named Sindbad, who is constantly returning to half-remembered places where he has enjoyed amorous adventures or experienced food that has never tasted better than in those particular locations. Sindbad is of course the *alter ego* of Krúdy himself, a person afflicted with nostalgia for a vanishing past, as well as someone capable of making a large detour in the middle of the night after suddenly recalling a remote country restaurant where he had once eaten an incomparable chicken Újházy. All Krúdy's writings, but especially his later ones, are tinged with a sense of a world that has gone forever: 'How charming it used to be', he recalled of Pest,

to see the old shop sign-boards on Rákóczi Street, to drive by the familiar restaurants and coffee-houses and know for certain who was sitting in them and where, to see in one's imagination the tables reserved for regular guests at the Metropole, the neat dining-rooms of the Pannonia, the acquaintances drinking black coffee in the Balaton, the regulars of the Hungaria and all the other people of Pest, whose habits, way of sitting, luncheons, and amusements we knew as precisely as the calendar. Do not try to find them at the old chairs, at the old tables. Strangers are sitting there, people you have never seen.

It was perhaps fortunate that Krúdy died in 1933, before the Second World War and its aftermath destroyed the last traces of the social and gastronomic life that he had so cherished.

The culinary fate of Hungary after 1939 was mirrored in the sad later history of the Gundel family. Károly Gundel stayed on in Budapest throughout the war, struggling with stringent rationing, constant air raids, and failing eyesight but managing against all the odds to maintain the Gundel and Gellért restaurants as sanctuaries of scaled-down elegance: when the severe winter of 1944–5 finally forced Gundel's to turn to the neighbouring zoo in search of fresh meat, Károly was even able to respond by devising such dishes as lion cutlet and giraffe ragout. However, Károly was to die a poor man, all the money he had earnt having been continually reinvested in improvements to a business that would eventually be seized by the communists. Deprived of everything he owned, interned, and deported to the country, Károly and his large family would finally be allowed to emigrate to Austria.

With the years of communist rule, political oppression no longer had the positive impact on Hungarian cooking that it had had in the past: indeed, gastronomy seems rarely to have benefited from any communist regime. Nationalization and shortages in fresh produce resulted in a bland uniformity, and put the majority of restaurants beyond the pockets of most Hungarians. The tentative introduction of a mixed economy in the early 1980s brought marked culinary improvements to the country, though I remember no memorable gastronomic experience from that period, despite having had once the enjoyable task of trying out the best of Budapest's restaurants for the still-to-be-published American Express Gold Card Guide to Europe. Within days I had begun judging restaurants on their friendliness and atmosphere rather than on their food, which I found depressingly similar from one establishment to the next, all of it being overcooked and smothered in excessive quantities of cream and lard. The most popular of the tourist restaurants were characterized by their impersonal, unfriendly waiters (who earnt at this time far more than doctors, teachers, or lecturers), and their ubiquitous gypsy bands (by now the ultimate Hungarian cliché); sometimes these places were only bearable on account of their decoration—as was, for instance, the case with the Kárpátia, which is still worth a visit solely for its fantastical, neo-Gothic interior. I enjoyed the surviving old restaurants that had gone slightly to seed while retaining such endearing traditional features as a murky fish-tank. But I ended up with a preference for the modest and wholly unpretentious *kisvendéglő*, and strongly urged the Gold Card carrier to make the trek to an outlying, barn-like establishment revealingly named the Sport, which promoted itself with a photograph showing Coca Cola bottles on all the tables. I also acquired a taste for the most basic wine and beer cellars (respectively *borozók* and *sörözők*), where you daily risked food poisoning in what seemed like the nadir of squalid soup kitchens: one of the places I fondly remember, a short distance from the Art Academy, was straight out of Gorky's *Lower Depths*, complete with drunken tramps, lugubrious lighting, and a floor where you slipped on the dark grease.

The collapse of communism, and the consequent increase in tourism and Americanization, have radically altered the culinary map of Hungary, and have threatened the existence of the simple and often run-down places that I had grown so much to like. Stricter sanitary requirements, the burgeoning of fast-food chains, and the urge towards ever greater luxury have led to the closing down of many of the older establishments, or else deprived them of much of their original character; in compensation, the variety and overall standard of food on offer have greatly improved. Some of the best traditional food is now served at the so-called 'shirt-sleeve' restaurants, which are comfortable but unshowy, and where seasonal produce and freshness of food are emphasized at the expense of gypsy music and other tourist fripperies. But the place which most famously expresses the new, rejuvenated spirit of Hungarian cooking is Gundel's, which is run today by a worthy successor to the Gundel dynasty, George Lang.

Born and educated in Hungary, Lang made his name in America, where he heads a large culinary empire that includes today one of New York's finest restaurants, the Café des Artistes. 'The planet will know that Lang was here,' concluded the *Los Angeles Times* food and restaurant critic in an article on this dynamic individual who had first eaten at Gundel's during the 1960s, while researching his lively and encyclopaedic book, *The Cuisine of Hungary* (1st edn., 1971). The historian John Lukacs, comparing the communist-run Gundel's with the restaurant of before, commented:

That harmony of Gallic refinement with Hungarian solidity is no longer extant. There are, instead, strenuous efforts to decorate the rich Hungarian dishes with all kinds of accoutrements. But the result is at best a culinary cohabitation instead of a good marriage.

Lang was even more critical of the Gundel's that he had first known, finding that 'the restaurant's socialist-cooperative-designed interior was difficult to swallow, not to mention the food which would have had to be improved before one would call it pedestrian'.

No sooner had the Kádár regime fallen than Lang began a series of intensive negotiations to try and buy Gundel's, and to compensate the founder's family for what they had lost. Achieving these ambitious aims within less than a year, he set about restoring the building and reconstructing its interior in a style suggestive of its *belle époque* glory. By the winter of 1994, when I went to interview him in his Budapest office, I found him organizing a banquet for Elizabeth II and on the point of reopening the neighbouring Bagolyvár Restaurant.

Short and bald-headed, with a dark suit, a handkerchief in his lapel, and a smile suggestive of charm, mischievousness, and complicity towards his listener, Lang struck me at first as being like some munificent gangster. The room seemed too small to contain a boundless energy that, in between transatlantic calls and rushed snatches of conversation, had him springing continually from his chair in search of the hundreds of articles either written by or about him. Eventually, after showing me in confidence the menu and wine list he had devised for Queen Elizabeth, he proposed that I should join him on a tasting tour of inspection of the Bagolyvár's kitchens—an outing he was convinced I would find 'quite amusing'.

We descended into the bowels of his empire, together with a group of his flunkeys, all of whom behaved as they would in the presence of an emperor. His staff were like an extended family, he told me as chefs and their assistants continued to curtsy in front of him or humbly lower their eyes. In each of the kitchens we would be offered different, delicious dishes, which he would savour with a child-like enthusiasm, pausing every now and then to reflect on the clear, fresh flavours of traditional Hungarian cooking, or else to issue sharp instructions as to how a particular dish could be improved. 'He has an unfailing palate, he can remedy anything,' whispered his elegant press officer, as Lang continued to charm and to flirt and to reveal the occasional sign of a man of exacting standards with whom it is better not to cross swords. At the end of the tour I was taken over to Gundel's itself, to see a collection of turn-of-the-century Hungarian paintings in chocolate-box frames, and to enjoy the 'cocktail of the house' in a lavish bar presided over by a jazz pianist. I could have been in New York.

Lang has successfully brought back to life one of the famed institutions of turn-of-the-century Budapest; but the atmosphere of the new place is wholly international, as is the clientele. Tourists and the city's growing numbers of foreign residents continue to predominate in the restaurants, as they do both in the handful of surviving old cafés and in the plethora of fashionable new drinking-haunts bearing such international names as 'Incognito', 'Piaf', 'Picasso Point', and 'Paris, Texas'.

Even someone with the energy of Lang cannot bring back what Budapest has apparently lost for ever—a flourishing café life with a distinctively Hungarian character. Such a magnificent old café as the cavernous Lukács on the Andrássy út has recently closed down to be replaced elsewhere in the city by such a monstrous pastiche as the Café Mozart, with its plastic, post-modernist rococo, costumed waitresses, and historically insensitive Austrian details. But it is the combination of loud music, television, and escalating prices that have deprived café life of its principal driving force—the belief in the café as a place where like-minded individuals can come together to discuss issues of common interest. The politician and author of the best recent guidebook to Budapest, András Török, tried in the early 1990s to reinstate an intellectual café life in an institution which had by now been almost entirely given over to tourism, the New York. However, this and other attempts to revital-ize Budapest's café society not only have been short-lived but seem also to have been motivated less by intellectual necessity than by nostalgia.

The ghost of Gyula Krúdy continues to haunt the streets of Budapest, intensifying the nostalgia for what is in many ways this city's most seduc-tive feature—its turn-of-the-century past.

4

Sinful City

LOFTY patriotism tempered by foreboding and disillusionment accompanied the spectacular transformation of Buda and Pest from quiet provincialdom into the vast industrial metropolis that the dictator Miklós Horthy alluringly described in 1920 as 'sinful city'.

The tensions and the energy underlying the creation of modern Budapest were fuelled by the Hungarians' growing desire to assert their identity in the face of oppressive Austrian influence. Following the departure of the Turks, the Habsburgs had done their best to turn the devastated and depleted townships of Buda and Pest into provincial versions of baroque Vienna. Major buildings were commissioned from leading Viennese architects such as Anton Erhard Martinelli, who created a majestically sized hospital for disabled soldiers (now, more appropriately, the City Hall) in the very heart of Pest—a town that had begun growing at a greater speed than Buda after the latter had been almost entirely destroyed by fire in 1723. In Buda, the efforts of the Austrians were concentrated largely on the Royal Palace, which, under Maria Theresa, was reconstructed on a scale that corresponded neither to the amount of time that the empress was in residence there nor to the reduced political status of a town that had still to recover from its Turkish occupation, when its role as Hungarian capital had been assumed by Pozsony (present-day Bratislava).

As well as imposing their culture and language, the Austrians repopulated Hungary with settlers from throughout the Habsburg realms. The greatly diminished Hungarian element in both Buda and Pest was augmented by the arrival of large numbers of Jews from Moravia and Galicia. When Robert Townson entered Buda in 1793, bringing with him the typical anti-semitic prejudices of the time, his first impression was of the Jewishness of the place: 'as the Jews have occupied the first part of the town, it is not necessary to say that the first thing that strikes you is poverty and filthiness.' The Jews were no less in evidence in Pest, where they too were obliged to settle at first in what were then the outskirts of the town—beyond the demolished city walls.

Against this background of increasing foreign and specifically German-speaking dominance, there developed an ever more vociferous Hungarian nationalist movement. Towards the end of the eighteenth century many of Hungary's radical intellectuals, inspired by the Jacobins of the French Revolution, came together to form a secret society led by the unfrocked monk, philosopher, and freemason Ignác Martinovics. The severity with which this conspiracy was dealt with by the Austrians in 1795 was a foretaste of repressive measures to come: Martinovics and his closest companions were executed, while many other intellectuals perished in prison, often for having just the slightest association with the 'Hungarian Jacobins'. Among those implicated was Ferenc Kazinczy, who was sentenced to death merely for having copied one of Martinovics's pamphlets; in the end his sentence was commuted to a period of imprisonment that would last 2,387 days. Pardoned at the age of 42, he later became a figurehead for those devoting themselves to the reform of the Hungarian language—a language that had been maintained up till then largely by the peasantry.

The revival of Hungarian as a literary language went hand in hand with intensive research into the language's obscure origins: one scholar, Sándor Csoma de Kőrös, walked all the way from Transylvania to Tibet in search of these, while another, István Horváth, even claimed in the 1820s that ancient Greek was Magyar in origin. The mood of growing national pride began to influence artists and architects, who developed an obsession not only with Hungary's past but also with the idea of a national Hungarian style; right up to the middle of the nineteenth century, however, their patriotic interests could find relatively little outlet in their works. The three main artistic figures from this period to have been linked with national preoccupations were the painter Károly Markó the Elder, the sculptor István Ferenczy, and the architect Mihály Polláck. The first of these was a landscapist who fell in love with Italy, where he spent the last years of his life: his credentials as a 'national painter' stem largely from his pioneering early portrayals of the Hungarian landscape (most notably the fresh and glowing *Visegrád* in the Hungarian National Gallery). Greater patriotic claims can be made for Ferenczy, a neo-classical sculptor who, at a time when Hungarian artists were forced to train abroad, actively campaigned for the cause of artistic tuition in

Hungary. Much encouraged by the enthusiasm shown in his work by his compatriots, he became one of the earliest Hungarian artists to make a reasonable living in his native country. However, he failed in his two most cherished ambitions: to set up a publicly funded sculpture academy in Pest, and to persuade the government to commission a monumental bronze equestrian statue of Matthias Corvinus.

Hungarian architects, headed by the Viennese-born Mihály Pollack, were initially more successful than painters or sculptors in establishing a future for themselves in Hungary itself. They received considerable support from Archduke Joseph, who served as palatine of Hungary from 1796 to 1847, and was the most enlightened of the Habsburgs to have lived in this country. It was under Joseph that Buda and, above all, Pest started to acquire something of the character of the future metropolis. Before his rule the military commanders and municipal authorities of the two towns had allowed buildings to be put up without any regard to town planning. Joseph changed all this in 1805 by ordering a local master builder to design the layout of Pest on more modern lines (the project that was eventually chosen, involving a series of concentric ringed boulevards, was not executed until after 1838, following severe flooding). More significant still for the development of Hungarian architecture was Joseph's creation in 1808 of the so-called Royal Committee for Embellishment, which had the job of supervising all construction work in Hungary. Though Joseph reserved for himself the right of supreme control and decision, the committee greatly increased the building opportunities for local architects by making them no longer subordinate to the Court Office of Architecture in Vienna.

Mihály Pollack, who soon assumed the leadership of the committee, promoted a monumental and virtually unornamented neo-classicism, which, while having nothing that was specifically Hungarian about it, became widespread throughout the country, and offered an alternative to the more elaborate and baroque tastes of the Viennese. After establishing a reputation with the suitably austere Lutheran Church off Pest's Deák Square, Pollack went on to create numerous private residences in Pest, including the adventurously simple Festetics house, at the junction of Nádor and Zrínyi Streets. But the Pest building on which his fame as a patriotic architect largely rests is the National Museum, which features a marbled circular hall of mausoleum-like solemnity, and an exterior dominated by a projecting, pedimented portico. Begun in 1836, the building was completed in 1847, less than a year before its steps became the scene of one of the most stirring moments in modern Hungarian history.

The foundation of a national museum, together with that of a national theatre where plays and operas in the Hungarian language could be performed, were among the more emotive cultural moments leading up to the Hungarian Revolution of 1848–9. The driving spirit behind both these institutions was Count Ferenc Széchenyi, whose fame was none the less overshadowed by that of his son, Count István Széchenyi, a man of extraordinary energy and complexity whose career reflected the rising and then suddenly deflated hopes of his generation of romantic nationalists. He was in many ways a Byronic figure, impulsive, dandyish, strikingly good-looking, and notorious in his amorous affairs. But he was also a pragmatist who differed from many of his patriotic contemporaries in preferring to face the realities of the present rather than dwelling too much on the glories of the past: 'Many think that Hungary has been,' he once wrote; 'I like to believe that she will be.' His attempts to improve his country led him one moment to advocate such a radical programme of social reform as the full emancipation of the serfs, and the next to draw up a proposal for the introduction of steam-shipping on the Danube. A man of practical ideas, he is perhaps best remembered today for having promoted the first permanent bridge between Buda and Pest—the Lánchíd or 'Chain Bridge'. This revolutionary ironwork structure, begun in 1842 by the Scottish engineer Adam Clark, must have seemed in the early days of its construction an eloquent symbol of a country projecting itself boldly into the future. Sadly, however, it was not completed until 1849, when the country's political circumstances had changed in a way that Széchenyi, in his darker moments, had always feared.

For all the Byronic and radical tendencies in his character, Széchenyi was wary of the idea of outright revolution, and believed instead in material progress as the first stage in attaining independent nationhood. These views brought him into conflict with the rising Hungarian political star of the 1840s, Lajos Kossuth, a landless aristocrat who had come to prominence after founding the leading Hungarian language newspaper, *Pesti Hírlap*. Széchenyi's influence waned in proportion to the growing popularity of Kossuth, who caught the confident and emotional mood of the decade with his provocative articles and stirringly delivered speeches arguing for immediate separation from Austria. Kossuth had also the advantage over Széchenyi in having his uncompromising stance towards

Austria echoed in the writings of Hungary's best-known and most popular poet, Sándor Petőfi.

Impecunious rebel and restless wanderer, Petőfi was born in 1823 in a village in the middle of the Great Hungarian Plain—a place whose vast, flat expanses, so suggestive of freedom, came to be perceived by him as the most beautiful landscape in the world. Much of his short life would be spent walking around it, as is suggested by one of the more touching exhibits in Budapest's Literary Museum: the poet's battered travelling-case. Though compelled through his work and political interests to come to Pest, Petőfi was obviously much happier in the countryside, where he drew much inspiration for his characteristically direct and uncomplicated poems, which—from the time of his first anthology, entitled simply *Versek* ('Poems', 1844)—were heavily influenced by the themes and rhythms of folk-songs. With Petőfi, Hungary began to emerge as one of Europe's greatest if also most undervalued poetic nations. Petőfi's own verse has been far more widely translated than that of any of his compatriots, but its full power is difficult to convey to those not used to the idea of the poet as the spokesman of his people. For this is effectively what Petőfi became from the mid-1840s onwards, when his poetic outpourings helped to incite a nation to war.

The revolution of 1848-9 was sparked off by a meeting attended by Petőfi in the greatest literary and political café of its day—the Café Pilvax in Pest. The building where it was housed was demolished in 1911, but a café bearing the same name was later put up on the rebuilt site; this is now a restaurant in pseudo-Biedermeier taste, surrounded by wooden cabinets displaying plates, cups, coffee-pots, prints and other mementoes from the days when the café (opened in 1838) was the most up-to-date in Pest, with a spacious, multi-arched interior and the earliest gas lamps of any Pest coffee-house. A visit to the nearby Literary Museum, where some surviving chairs and a table are kept, helps further to recreate the setting where, on 15 March 1848, Kossuth inspired prominent members of Hungary's liberal intelligentsia to take part in a demonstration that would turn Petőfi overnight into a national hero.

The demonstration, two days after rioting had broken out in Vienna and twelve days after Kossuth had given a parliamentary speech calling for the total abolition of the feudal system, involved Kossuth and his group leaving the Café Pilvax and distributing radical leaflets through the streets before ending up at the recently completed National Museum. Here, standing on the steps before a huge crowd, Petőfi recited his

National Song, a work which would be as important to the Hungarian revolution as the *Marseillaise* had been in France. The first printed document in Hungary to reach the public without going through the censor, the *National Song* employed a masterly use of refrain to convey a stark choice between freedom and slavery. In reading out this poem in front of the National Museum, Petőfi succeeded in making this institution a vital part of the Hungarian history that it was commemorating: a plaque to him was later placed on the steps, which became the scene of an annual patriotic rally.

The massive show of support for Kossuth revealed on 15 March frightened the authorities in Vienna, who responded positively to the proposal for a liberalized constitution in which freedom of religion, assembly, and the press would be granted, Hungarian established as the language of the state, serfdom abolished, and the nobility's privileges heavily curtailed. By 7 April the Habsburg emperor had sanctioned the formation of a Hungarian ministry headed by Count Lajos Batthyány, and including Ferenc Deák, Kossuth, and Széchenyi (who was given the lesser post of minister of transport). However, this was still not enough to satisfy an extremist such as Kossuth, who, in his new capacity as finance minister, insisted on both a financial and military system separate from the Austrians. War became inevitable after Kossuth persuaded the government to continue opposing the Habsburgs and to form a 200,000-strong Hungarian army.

The first retaliatory action against the Hungarians was led by a Croatian, who, like others from the non-Hungarian ethnic minorities within the country, preferred domination by Austria to that by Hungary. Buda and Pest fell early to the Austrian army, forcing the Hungarian government to move to Debrecen. But by the spring of 1849 the Hungarian army had fought back with such determination that they had retaken Buda, and would probably have gone on to win the war had not the newly enthroned Austrian emperor, Franz Joseph, made a desperate appeal for help to the tsar of Russia. The Russians' subsequent intervention resulted in a swift defeat for the Hungarians, who would lose in the process the great poet who had done so much to maintain their patriotic fervour. Petőfi, an aide-de-camp during the war's last stages, had enrolled as a soldier partly to counteract accusations in the press of being brave only in word and not in deed. He fought his last battle on 31 July outside the Transylvanian town of Segesvár (in Romanian, Sighişoara). With his typical disregard for the minor details of army life, he apparently faced the Cossack enemy dressed in an open-necked white shirt: witnesses claimed to have seen him holding up his sword in the air before being run through with a lance.

The Hungarian surrender thirteen days later at the lowland village of Világos is often thought of in the same momentous terms as the defeat at Mohács. The reprisals were certainly brutal, with the captured Hungarian generals being put almost immediately before the firing-squad, and Batthyány being executed in October at Buda (the victorious Austrians reputedly toasted the death sentences with beer, which is why the clinking of beer mugs is still regarded by Hungarians as an offensive act). Kossuth spent the rest of his life in exile, first in Turkey and later in France and England, from where he continued to canvass support for his country. Széchenyi, suffering a nervous breakdown, entered voluntary seclusion in a mental hospital near Vienna, where, in the last years of his life, he was continuously harassed by the secret police, who suspected him of having been the author of a pro-Hungarian publication brought out by exiles in London. The strain proved too great for him, and on Easter Sunday in 1860 he finally killed himself—a gesture which was as telling a sign of Hungary's post-revolutionary depression as the Chain Bridge had been of its hopes.

But the feelings of despair and frustration that followed the revolution, together with the memories of Hungary's brief moments of independence, eventually provided rich material for writers and artists, who consoled themselves for political defeat by renewing their efforts to create a national mythology. Literary life, hindered at first by the intensified atmosphere of persecution and censorship, slowly revived, not so much through the emergence of young, new talents but through the rediscovered voices of older writers such as the novelist Mór Jókai and the poet János Arany. Jókai, an immensely precocious and prolific writer who had published his first poem at the age of 10, represented Hungarian literature and nationalism at their most escapist. After an early novel in the spirit of Victor Hugo, and effusive political writings that one critic had described as 'love-letters to liberty', he went on to publish anonymously a collection of short stories based on his experiences of the revolution (*Battle Sketches*, 1850). However, it was when he turned to the fictional re-creation of a glowing Hungarian past that he won for himself a huge readership both in his own country and abroad. Though setting some of these novels in as recent a past as the so-called 'Age of Reform' (the early nineteenth century), it was with his discovery of seventeenth-century Transylvania that he found a place and an era ideally suited to his talents as a vivid teller of adventurous, fast-moving tales with an exotic background and a patriotic appeal. Transylvania, with its dramatic scenery of mountains and forests, its associations with Matthias Corvinus, and its semi-autonomous status during the sixteenth and seventeenth centuries, seemed to epitomize the greatness of an independent Hungary; but it was also a land that interested those of romantic, orientalist leanings, thanks to its traditional reputation as the gateway between the West and the East. Jókai, from the time of his novel *'Midst the Wild Carpathians* (1851), used Transylvania as the starting-point for a series of Turkish tales that mirrored Hungarians' changing attitude towards their former oppressors—an attitude in which hatred was being replaced by a vague, mysterious sense of affinity with all Eastern peoples.

Jókai was a born optimist who treated Hungarian themes in a way that made them picturesque for the foreign reader; Arany, in contrast, was a profound pessimist, whose genius cannot fully be appreciated by anyone who does not share his obsession with the destiny of the Hungarian people. Merging elements from Virgil, Homer, the *Nibelungenlied* and Scottish and Transylvanian folk-ballads, Arany forged a Hungarian tradition of nationalist epics. Perhaps the greatest of these was his *Toldi* trilogy, which was based on the life of the semi-legendary medieval hero Miklós Toldi—a man of minor nobility, but treated as a peasant by his brother, who becomes, through his bravery, a knight at the court of Louis the Great only to end as an embittered old man living in a decaying house surrounded by an overgrown garden. The concluding part of the trilogy, *Toldi's Eve*, was written in 1847–8 but not published until 1854, by which time the disillusionment of the hero reflected that of Arany.

In 1861, when Arany was the undisputed arbiter of Hungarian literary taste, a hitherto obscure writer called Imre Madách showed him a manuscript that conveyed, more than anything that Arany himself had written, the mood of Hungary in the years between the revolution and the Dual Compromise. This work, a dramatic poem entitled *The Tragedy of Man*, did not immediately impress Arany, who dismissed it as a flawed imitation of Goethe's *Faust*. Arany put the manuscript aside, but took another look at it a short time later, after its author had given a speech on Hungary's constitutional position that had been enthusiastically received. This time he saw its merits, which was fortunate, as Madách said afterwards that he would have thrown the work away had Arany's opinion been wholly unfavourable.

The Tragedy of Man, perhaps the single most important work in Hungarian literature, echoes Goethe, Byron, and Milton in its portrayal of mankind's hopelessness and fall from grace. Its hero, Adam, expelled from Paradise and anxious to know the future of his race, is led by Lucifer on a tour embracing such disparate periods of human history as the Egypt of the Pharaohs, ancient Rome during its decadence, Constantinople at the time of the Crusades, Kepler's Prague, Danton's France, a Dickensian London where the rich oppress the poor and even the poor quarrel, and on into the future. Adam's values are those of a romantic liberal, but in the course of his journey every human system and creed is represented as a failure, from democracy to nihilism, from revolutionary socialism to free-market capitalism. In the end Adam wishes to spare his race's future sufferings by committing suicide, a fate from which he is spared by Eve's announcement that she is going to have a baby. Madách had written plays, poems, and essays since the 1840s, but nothing in his earlier work had prepared his contemporaries for such an ambitious undertaking as *The Tragedy of Man*, which was also an unprecedented achievement in Hungarian literature. Personal grief, as well as national tragedy, had contributed to the gestation of this work: imprisoned shortly after the Revolution for having harboured a prominent Hungarian activist, Madách returned home two years later to find that his wife had been unfaithful to him; he separated from her and from society generally to spend the remaining few years of his life in an isolated rural retreat that he called 'The Lion's Den'. But *The Tragedy of Man* is a drama that aims for universal significance, and, in so doing, tries to transcend the context in which it was written: unusually for a Hungarian work of this period, it makes no reference to specifically Hungarian issues.

In contrast, scenes from Hungarian life and history—including numerous moments in the life of Petőfi—became the staple inspiration of Madách's artist contemporaries, few of whom attained more than a provincial importance. The facilities for studying art in Hungary had improved after 1846, when an Italian artist called Giacomo Marastoni founded an academy of painting in Pest, which continued to function after the revolution. However, the opportunities for working as an artist in Hungary remained limited, unless one was able to make a living from society portraits, as was the case with the Transylvanian-born Miklós

Barabás, who settled in Pest in 1836 and stayed there until his death in 1898. Barabás, a painter also of landscapes, genre paintings, and even signboards (a selection of which are in Budapest's Historical Museum), enjoyed a pre-eminence in the Pest art world of the middle years of the century rivalled only by Markó's conservative pupil Gusztáv Keleti. Though limited in his pictorial output, Keleti held enormous power both as an art bureaucrat (he eventually became the first director of what is now the Budapest Academy of Fine Arts) and as a critic, in which capacity he did his best to humble any potential competitors. His vicious criticisms succeeded in destroying the confidence of many a Hungarian painter, and were even a final determining factor in persuading some of these artists to spend the whole of their lives abroad. Among those who suffered from his attacks were Viktor Madarász and Miklós Zichy, who were the first important Hungarian painters to portray scenes from their country's past. Madarász, a friend of French Romantic writers such as Hugo and Gautier, lived for most of his working life in Paris, where he made his name in 1859 with his gloomily atmospherical *The Bewailing of László Hunyadi* (Budapest National Gallery). Zichy, one of the first students in Marastoni's academy, finished his studies in Vienna, where he executed his ambitious, allegorical piece *The Life-Boat* (Budapest National Gallery), a homage to Géricault's *Raft of the Medusa*. He was invited afterwards to Russia, which would become his near-permanent home after he failed in his attempts to settle both in Pest (where he was driven away by Keleti) and in Paris, where his works were admired for the brilliance of their draughtsmanship and inventiveness, but criticized for their greyly monotonous colouring, hard handling of paint, and darkly symbolical content, the full significance of which was often difficult for the non-Hungarian to understand.

The art produced in Hungary itself during these years rarely attained the verve or originality that was now being exhibited in Hungarian architecture, which began seriously to respond to the challenge of developing an unmistakably Hungarian style. The neo-classicism propagated by Pollàck and his circle became so ubiquitous in Hungary that eclecticism came to be favoured instead, with the two main architects of this period (Miklós Ybl and Frigyes Feszl) incorporating elements that alluded to their country's new-found affinity with the East. Ybl, who is known today principally for his lavish neo-Renaissance monuments dating from the 1860s, worked up to then in a romantic vein that mingled romanesque with occasional oriental features, as in his Unger House in

Pest (Múzeum Körút 7), which has a façade featuring romanesque arcading crowned by a Moorish cornice. The concern of architects to stress the Turkish rather than the Germanic aspects of their country's heritage was expressed with particular boldness in the works of Frigyes Feszl, who had first made use of oriental motifs in his competition-winning design of 1845 for a Hungarian Parliament building. Though this project was thwarted by the War of Independence, Feszl received other important commissions in Pest in the 1850s and 1860s, culminating in his idiosyncratic rebuilding of Pollack's Municipal Concert Hall (now the Vigadó Concert Hall), which had been devastated by shelling in 1849. Obliged by the town authorities to keep Pollack's neo-classical basement, Frigyes used this as the starting-point for an eclectic *tour de force* whose arcaded, richly encrusted façade is held together by giant fluted columns crowned by minaret-like turrets. Begun in 1860, this powerful, imaginative, and radiantly self-confident work heralded a new phase in Hungarian history: by the time the building was completed, in 1864, the prospect of a pact with Austria that would fulfil the dream of a politically revived and economically powerful Hungary seemed closer than ever.

The need for the Austrians to reach some form of reconciliation with Hungary had become increasingly apparent after they had suffered serious defeat in Italy in 1859. Six years later, in Pest, Ferenc Deák gathered together the remnants of the Hungarian Liberal party to work out the terms for such an agreement. A further Austrian defeat, against the Prussians in July 1866, led finally to the discussion of an accord between the two countries, despite the warnings of the exiled Kossuth, who predicted that with the inevitable and doubtless imminent collapse of the Habsburgs, the oppressed subjects of their empire would treat the Hungarians with the same contempt reserved for the Austrians themselves. The short-term interests of industrialists and the more blindly patriotic proved more persuasive than these forebodings, and in 1867 Hungary and Austria were established as a Dual Monarchy with two separate governments, parliaments, and armies, though with common foreign, defence, and finance ministries. The Viennese writer Musil described this hybrid new land as a place whose 'mysteries were as difficult to penetrate as those of the Holy Trinity'.

Luckily, under the Dual Monarchy Hungary was transformed at such a dizzying speed as to give its inhabitants little time to ponder either the labyrinthine workings or the long-term viability of their new constitution. These changes were particularly apparent in Pest, which was radically expanded and altered within only two years of the Compromise: an English traveller, Arthur Patterson, in a book on Hungary published in 1869, wrote: 'my Hungarian friends tell me that since I left the country in 1867 the town is so much altered as to be scarcely recognizable.' With the creation of Budapest in 1873, Pest became the focus, as well as the colloquial abbreviation, for what would emerge as Europe's fastest-growing metropolis.

The combined population of Buda and Pest grew from 280,000 in 1867 to 733,000 in 1900, when construction fever reached its peak; by then the city had spread over more than eighty square miles of land, making it the largest municipality on the continent. The most important port on the Danube, and the hub of an impressive national railway network (with two of the biggest and most up-to-date terminals in the world), Budapest acted as a gigantic spider that drew into its web thousands of new settlers from all over Hungary. Though Budapest's population in relation to the rest of the country was comparable to that of other major capitals such as Paris and London, the city was unusual in being nearly ten times larger than the Hungarian town closest to it in size, Szeged. Thus the exodus from country to town that was a feature of Europe generally during this period became in Hungary essentially an exodus from country to Budapest, which attracted to its burgeoning suburbs peasants whose families had been working the land for nearly 1,000 years. A large proportion of the city's new inhabitants supplied meat, fruit, and vegetables to the metropolis; and a remarkable one in five of the population worked as servants. But the chief draw was the city's extensive industries, which had flourished after 1867 as a result of extensive foreign investment and the reduction of trade tariffs.

One of the legacies of Hungary's communist regime is the large number of predominantly unvisited museums chronicling Hungary's technological advances and industrial development. From these places it can be surprising to learn how many of the great scientific inventions of the nineteenth century originated in Budapest, from Tivadar Puskás's telephonic switchboard of 1881 (on display in the Telephone Museum at Úri utca 49) to the steel rollers used in mills to produce the extra-fine flour needed for pastry (in the Milling Industry Museum at Soroksári út 24, in the heart of the working-class Ninth district). The fascination of the objects and the accompanying information panels (translated, if at all, into the quaintest of English) is eclipsed by the atmospheric nature of some of the settings, which are often authentic relics from the city's industrial past: the Foundry Museum (at Bem József utca 20) is in the original mid-nineteenth-century building of the Ganz Foundry, while the unpromisingly titled Capital Sewerage Works Museum (at Zsigmond tér 1–4) is in an actual sewerage works, complete with a faint odour of rotting eggs and a pre-First World War control room that seems like the set of some early science fiction film. Museums such as these transport one back to the days of the city's technological prowess, as does (at times) the public transport system itself: the present extensive tramway system is a reminder of Budapest's pioneering electric streetcars of the late 1880s, while the underground line running just below the Andrássy út dates back to as early as 1896, when it was the oldest such line in continental Europe.

The progressive aspects of turn-of-the-century Budapest, combined with the city's extraordinary growth rate, had once prompted comparisons with America. The Old World's 'Yankee City' was how the place was described in 1896 by New York's most famous newspaper reporter, Richard Harding Davis; 'Chicago' was the name popularly given to the Pest district of Ferencváros, while 'New York' was the one chosen for the palatial office block housing the city's most fashionable café. Yet in most respects turn-of-the-century Budapest had little in common with an American city, not least in terms of its appearance, which was characterized by a relatively low skyline—the result of exceptionally stringent building regulations, which stipulated that none of the imposing new blocks should be any higher than five storeys.

A more fundamental difference between Budapest and somewhere like New York was the enormous cosmopolitanism of the latter in comparison with the growing chauvinism of the former. At the beginning of the nineteenth century Buda and Pest were places where a variety of ethnic communities (Germans, Magyars, Slovaks, Serbians, Greeks, Armenians, Romanians, and others) were very much in evidence, all speaking their own languages; but by the end of the century this sense of diversity had been lessened by the mood of Magyar fervour that had swept through the metropolis.

The Hungarian language, with its non-Indo-European roots and limited international viability, superseded German with extraordinary rapidity. German, which had been the principal language of over half the total number of inhabitants of Buda and Pest in 1848 (the bulk of the German community remained based in Buda), was spoken by only 34.4 per cent of the population in 1880, as opposed to the 65.6 per cent who spoke primarily Hungarian; by 1910 the proportion of German speakers had decreased to 10 per cent, while that of Hungarian speakers had risen to 85.5 per cent. The declining fortunes of the German language and culture were reflected in the fate of Pest's German Theatre, which was fast surpassed in popularity by the Hungarian Theatre that had been founded in Pest in 1837 by Count Ferenc Széchenyi. Already, in 1840, the English traveller Julia Pardoe was describing the latter as 'by far the most interesting theatre in Pesth', and praising the female singers for their unrivalled beauty; she also noted the enormous difference between the audiences of two theatres, that of the Hungarian displaying all 'the joyousness, the restlessness, the enthusiasm of the national character'. When the German Theatre burnt down in 1848, anti-German feelings ran so high that no immediate attempt was made to rebuild the place. In the meantime the Hungarian Theatre reopened after only a brief period of closure, and continued to win the praise of foreign visitors, one of whom, Charles Pridham, was so taken by the 'sweetness and flexibility' of the Hungarian singers that he could not help feeling that he was witnessing an Italian opera. A new German Theatre was eventually opened in 1853, but the quality of its productions began seriously to decline after it had been taken over at the end of the decade by a succession of mediocre directors; kept going purely through inviting guest artists from abroad, then given over to operettas at the end of the 1860s, the theatre was destroyed a second time by fire in 1889, and was never again replaced.

'It will be seen from this that our Teuton friends are not great favourites with the Magyars,' wrote the traveller Louis Felberman in 1892, when almost all the German names in Budapest had been Magyarized, and the main cultural organ of the city's German-speaking community was the ever more conservative and pro-Hungarian journal *Pester Lloyd*, the equivalent of America's *Wall Street Gazette*. The assimilation of Hungarian culture by non-Hungarians was a remarkable feature of Budapest's late nineteenth-century development, and particularly evident in the case of Hungary's ever-increasing Jewish community. The Jews, whose enthusiastic support of Kossuth during the revolution had finally led to their emancipation in 1867, became so completely Magyarized in so short a time that, by the end of the century, some had been raised to the nobility and others had taken a seat in the Chamber of Deputies.

Settling mainly in the traditionally more Magyar Pest, they provided much of the dynamic impetus that helped turn the city into a great financial and industrial metropolis. The Jewish community came to include not only a high proportion of Budapest's most prominent bankers and industrialists (notably the creators of the city's all-important textile and milling industries) but also, by 1910, two-fifths of the city's lawyers, three-fifths of its doctors, and two-fifths of its journalists: by then, Jews accounted for a quarter of the city's population and had earnt the place the nickname of 'Judapest'. This large Jewish element undoubtedly added a necessary cosmopolitan element to a city which had become progressively more xenophobic. However, the irony was that this community, though featuring some of the city's more progressive and internationally minded intellectuals, also included some of Hungary's most fervent and conservative nationalists, including the long-time editor of the *Pester Lloyd*, Miksa Falk.

The nationalism that helped to create an ever more unified if also less liberal Hungary found its focus in the celebrations that took place in Budapest in 1896, which marked the 1,000 years since the arrival in Hungary of Árpád and his hordes. A celebratory mood had already been established in Budapest in 1892, when, in commemoration of the quarter-centenary since the foundation of Austria-Hungary, Franz Joseph had declared Budapest a capital and royal seat equal in rank to Vienna. Two years later the city's inhabitants had been brought together, under less official and cheerful circumstances, to pay homage to Lajos Kossuth, whose body had been transported here from Turin: Franz Joseph refused to nominate the funeral a state occasion, and insisted that the bells of the city's Catholic churches remain silent; but the municipality went ahead with its three days of mourning, during which time the Protestant bells rang and the city was draped in black.

While all this was happening, preparations for the millennium celebrations gathered pace. Over in Buda, neo-Romanesque fortifications were erected to provide a more dramatic setting for the newly remodelled medieval church of Our Lady, known as the Matthias Church, which was chosen as the starting-point for the imperial procession planned for New Year's Day 1896. The projected nucleus of the celebrations was in Pest, at the northern end of the recently built Andrássy út, which was the city's closest equivalent to Vienna's Ringstrasse, but without the latter's overwhelming symbolical associations in support of state and empire. Ybl's Opera House, at the southern end of this street,

was the most prominent public building in a thoroughfare lined principally with fashionable private residences: symbolism became blatant only
in the monumental Heroes' Square, which was created as the solemn
heart of the millennial celebrations. A column testifying to Hungarian
greatness, flanked by the pedimented Fine Arts Museum and Exhibition
Hall, served as the portentous prelude to the grounds of a world fair in
which a spectacular architectural complex uniting elements from many
of the great Hungarian buildings of the past (from the fantastical Renaissance castle at Vajdahunyad to the baroque Esterházy palace at Fertőd)
was incorporated within a setting that would be animated by music, electrical illuminations, balloons, panoramas, the first Hungarian movie
newsreel, and other such attractions.

The celebrations, originally planned for 1895, were delayed a year
allegedly by the untimely death of the exhibition's designer, which entailed an official declaration that Árpád's invasion had taken place in 896
rather than in 895, as had originally been stated. Other, more controversial historical adjustments were needed to point out the glorious contribution to Hungarian history made by the Habsburgs, whose image was
being promoted almost as much as that of Hungary herself: the original
millennial monument on Heroes' Square featured not only Hungarian
heroes but also five Habsburg rulers (they were removed after the First
World War), including Franz Joseph, who, like Matthias Corvinus before
him, was thought of by his apologists as a latter-day Attila.

Details such as these emphasized the underlying hollowness of the
celebrations and, by extension, of the whole period of Hungarian alliance
with Austria. Similarly, the more glamorous aspects of Budapest's fre-
netic turn-of-the-century expansion served as a front to cover the city's
growing social and political problems: the famous Hungarian disciple
and confidant of Freud, Sándor Ferenczi, used the term 'magical thinking' to describe his countrymen's tendency to turn away from reality and
chase what he called a *délibáb* or mirage. The reality, in the case of
Budapest, was a city becoming dangerously overcrowded and filled with
destitute people. The sumptuous homes of the haute bourgeoisie often
occupied the front section of buildings otherwise taken up by one-room
proletarian flats, in which, by 1910, there lived four out of every nine of
the city's inhabitants, with an average of four to five people crowded
within each of these single-room dwellings; by this date no less than
one third of the city's population consisted of sub-lessees, many of whom
could afford only to rent a bed or mattress on a nightly basis. It is no

wonder that many Hungarians of this period, like the writer Gyula Krúdy, looked back nostalgically to the days of István Széchenyi, whose vision of urban greatness must now have seemed as quaint and old-fashioned as his aristocratic liberalism.

But the heady combination of dramatic change, commercial wealth, millennial jingoism, and *fin-de-siècle* angst, was one that inspired in Hungary a flowering in the arts no less intense than that of turn-of-the-century Vienna. Sadly, unlike Vienna, the products of this renaissance are, for the most part, little known outside Hungary, partly for want of translated texts and partly because of the nationalist element that dominates this period: whereas in Vienna political concerns were subservient to aesthetic and psychological ones, in Budapest the opposite was true. This obsessive nationalism accounts also for another major feature of the arts of Hungary's so-called 'Golden Age'—a love of folklore to the exclusion of any interest in the life of the city. Although most of Hungary's artists, writers, and musicians were concentrated in Budapest, and indeed were enthusiastic participants of its café life, they differed from their counterparts in places such as New York and Paris by hardly ever depicting the city in their works. Even architects began turning their back on the city through their increasing appropriation of motifs derived from traditional rural architecture. In 1911 the young French architect Charles Édouard Jeanneret (the future Le Corbusier) planned an 'oriental journey' in which he sorted the places he wished to visit into the categories 'industry', 'culture', and 'folklore'. Budapest, as an architectural centre, was envisaged by him as being essentially of folkloric interest.

The Budapest that Le Corbusier actually visited was rather different from the one he had imagined, despite the existence of quiet, quasi-rural enclaves such as the Buda district of the Tabán, and the attempts of some of the architects to 'reintegrate folklore into the life of a large city'. Though Budapest did not have for him the same degree of sumptuous vulgarity as he found in Vienna, he none the less described the place as an industrial metropolis whose factories encased a centre made up of 'monstrous modern apartment blocks' displaying 'diverse and discordant styles'.

Yet some of the city's most memorable buildings date from this period of intense architectural eclecticism that would persist up to as late as 1936, when a neo-baroque church was built with inner vaults of plaster suspended from a reinforced concrete shell. One of the protagonists in the revival of historical styles was Miklós Ybl, who shook off his earlier medieval and oriental leanings to embrace the architecture of Renaissance Italy: he brought this style to perfection in his elegantly Palladian customs house building (now the University of Economic Sciences), and in his exuberantly decorated Opera House. Under Ybl's influence the neo-Renaissance became for a while the dominant architectural style of the city, until eventually weariness set in, and architects began experimenting again with a wide variety of historical periods, often in the same building.

Eclecticism, in the hands of lesser architects, easily degenerated into pure pastiche—as in the various replicas of Florentine *quattrocento* palaces that grew up in the city—or else resulted in buildings that freely borrowed elements from the past without any concern for the structural and spatial features of the architecture that was being imitated. The pompous absurdity of so many Budapest dwellings of this period was ridiculed in 1907 by the critic Géza Lengyel, who commented on the way in which façades imitative of such grand structures as medieval castles or pagan temples generally shielded the smallest and most ordinary of apartments.

But eclecticism also produced works of stunning boldness and originality, such as Imre Steindl's (1885–1904) parliament building, which impressed the young Patrick Leigh Fermor as being an example of 'architectural dash' which 'could scarcely go further'. Steindl, who had begun his career in a neo-Renaissance style before switching to the neo-Gothic (as in the parish church of the Erzsébetváros district), here welded the two styles together in a structure of baroque dynamism. The influence of Britain's own Houses of Parliament is evident in the predominant Gothic detailing and mass of crotcheted pinnacles; but the symmetrical arrangement of a circular central hall flanked by two long arms is wholly baroque, while the ribbed dome, minus its pinnacles, could easily be imagined as that of Brunelleschi's Duomo in Florence.

Whereas the Parliament's baroque ground-plan was devised as a way of giving symbolical unity to the two chambers corresponding to Britain's Houses of Lords and Commons, the building's Gothic and early Renaissance elements were intended to have a patriotic purpose. Though there was nothing specifically Hungarian in either of the latter styles, they evoked a period of Hungarian independence that had reached its climax with the reign of Matthias Corvinus; furthermore, they were meant as a provocative riposte to the late baroque grandeur of the Royal

Palace on the opposite side of the Danube—a building and a style now permanently associated with Austrian oppression.

Other architects of Steindl's day, in their continuing search for a Hungarian national style, turned again towards the Orient, but did so in a more ambitious way than Feszl and the young Ybl had done. No longer limiting themselves to the appropriation of Turkish motifs, they now expressed their affinity with the Orient in their use of neo-Moorish and neo-Byzantine elements (notably in the two main synagogues of Pest), and even ended up evolving a neo-Indian manner. But it was with their adoption of Hungarian folklore traditions, often in conjunction with this imagined Orient, that a truly Hungarian style was formed.

This concern with national identity was a major component of the Hungarian art nouveau—a term which in Hungary has not been restricted to describing the ornamental style of undulating forms that spread rapidly around Europe and America after 1890. The term was so broadly interpreted in turn-of-the-century Budapest that the poet Mihály Babits could describe even Monet as an art nouveau artist; more ridiculous still was his colleague Endre Ady's definition of the term as 'the struggle for unfettered individualism'. Even today the concept of the art nouveau has a different significance for the Hungarian than it has, say, for the Englishman: its connotations are as emotive and nationalistic as are those of its Catalan equivalent, *modernisme*.

The Hungarian architect who occupies a position in the history of the Hungarian art nouveau comparable to that of Gaudí in Catalonia is Ödön Lechner. Born to a wealthy and cultured Pest family in 1845, Lechner trained in Pest, Berlin, and Italy and began his career working in a conventional eclectic manner, executing, for instance, a sgraffito, neo-Florentine apartment house at Bajcsy-Zsilinszky utca 43 in Pest. In a short autobiographical note written in his late 60s, he admitted he was 'rather successful' at a very early age, but that he was also unhappy for not having devoted himself as yet to realizing his 'distant ideal of creating a national Hungarian style'. Architectural peers of his such as Pollack and Ybl had harboured the same ideal, but, according to him, had all 'come to the conclusion that it was impossible to have a building in the Hungarian style because there had never been such a thing'. For Lechner the one architect who had managed to invest a building with a 'truly Hungarian spirit' was Feszl, who had done so by using 'his creative imagination to break through the barriers of tradition'.

Depression at the death of his young wife when he was only 27, together with his continuing, 'tormenting' quest for a national style, took Lechner in 1874 to Paris, where he worked for three years with an elderly architect who restored many of the French châteaux. French culture was seen by Lechner as a shield to protect him against the prevailing German influence of his background. But he also developed a strong interest in the early history of French architecture, which helped him with an important problem that neither Pollack nor Ybl had apparently considered: how did national styles come into being in the first place? Focusing on the early French Renaissance, with its mixture of Gothic and classical detailing, he studied the way in which this style had evolved through the exposure of the nobility to a variety of different influences in the course of their travels. He wondered if 'some similar cross-fertilization' could be used to forge a new style in Hungary.

Shortly after his return to Budapest, Lechner borrowed heavily from French sources to build what is now the Hungarian Dance Academy (formerly the Hungarian State Railway Pension House); but he also reached the conclusion that the refinement of French culture could not be aligned with the 'primitive roughness of popular Hungarian art' which would come increasingly to absorb him in the 1880s.

During this same decade he made two very influential visits to England, on the first of which he was struck by how 'the atmosphere of the real countryside still lingers in country houses and cottages'; on his second visit his attention was largely engaged by the 'Colonial style of the English', in particular the way in which 'the English in India had accommodated to native taste.' Lechner's consequent fascination with the 'Hindu style', sustained by visits to Britain's oriental collections, was later allied with his growing interest in Hungarian folklore after he was directed to the theories of a Transylvanian drawing teacher called József Huszka.

Huszka, who was urging Hungarian architects to seek inspiration in their native peasant traditions, had begun in 1881 to collect and copy Hungarian peasant drawings and decorative motifs. His special mania was for the richly embroidered woollen garment known as the *cifraszűr*, which had already featured prominently in a proposed monument by Feszl to the victims of the 1848 revolution. The garment was the purest expression of the Hungarian soul, according to Huszka, who compared its decorative motifs with those on the metallic buckles of ninth-century Hungarian tribes. Uncovering further links with ornamental objects from the East, he went on to propose an elaborate theory about the oriental, and specifically Indian and Persian, origins of Hungary's folk art.

The building that most famously expresses the architectural ideals of Lechner's maturity is the Applied Arts Museum in Pest (1891–7), which was received by the inhabitants of Budapest with the same mixture of astonishment and outrage that greeted the opening of the Pompidou Centre in Paris in the 1970s. Some of the critics contemptuously dismissed it as 'the palace of the gypsies'; and even Lechner himself, reviewing the building in later life, found the exuberant main entrance 'a little too Hindu for me'. This extraordinary blend of the folkloric and the oriental was made doubly sensational by the gaudiness of the colouring, which has been lessened in recent times by the decision to repaint the neo-Mogul interior a uniform white. The colour on the exterior was provided by what would become the hallmark of the Lechner style—the use of Zsolnay ceramics. Lechner had acquired a fascination with this medium as a teenager, when he had spent many hours in a brickworks that his father had inherited. This factory turned out not only bricks but also glazed majolica and terracotta, including the tiles designed by the Viennese architect Förster for the main synagogue of Budapest. Ceramic surfaces, being non-porous and washable, offered a practical solution to the problem of maintaining the colour on exteriors exposed to the dusty, smoky air of Budapest. They also enhanced the building's Hungarian aspect, having traditionally been a substitute for stone in rural Hungary, where stone had nearly always to be brought in from far away.

Native influences dominated Lechner's subsequent work, such as the Institute of Geology, whose ornamentation and Zsolnay-tiled pyramidal skyline echo the traditional architecture of Upper Hungary. However, he returned once more to an imaginary Orient in his Post Office Savings Building, which belies its prosaic name by having an exuberantly inventive roof-top in which yellow tiling, pagoda-like turrets, and art nouveau scrolls bring a chinoiserie flourish to the 'national style'.

The folk arts and crafts of Hungary became the main obsession of Lechner's followers, some of whom, such as Aladár Árkay and the much-travelled Béla Lajta, combined this with a new interest in the traditional brick architecture of Scandinavia, above all that of Finland, whose people shared with the Hungarians the same obscure Eastern origins. Scandinavian architecture, with its Protestant puritanism and large expanses of unadorned brick, helped to temper the more frivolous, art nouveau elements present in Lechner's work. A stylized use of Hungarian folk motifs within a restrained and partly Scandinavian-inspired setting characterizes such jewels of early twentieth-century Pest as Lajta's Jewish Institute for the Blind and Árkay's Calvinist Church on Városligeti fasor.

Perhaps the most striking development in Hungarian architecture during the years leading up to the First World War was the impact of Transylvania—a region where Hungarian folk traditions had been preserved in their purest form. One of the architects who travelled widely here was István Medgyaszay, whose small home in Buda (today an eccentric 'memorial museum' hidden off a bosky, suburban alley) is full of sepia photographs tracing his fascination with the stylistic links between the architecture of Greater Hungary and that of India and the Far East. But the man who did most to promote Transylvania was Károly Kós, who was only 17 when he first encountered the region that would be the guiding inspiration for the rest of his life. A key figure in the Arts and Crafts movement in Hungary, Kós was influential not only as an architect but also as a scholar, designer, and illustrator. Among the hallmarks of his style are his steeply pitched roofs, timber detailing, and witch-hat spires that spread out at the base to form a broad overhang— the latter feature, so characteristic of Transylvanian churches, was used by Kós even in such a secular and unlikely context as the Buffalo House of the Budapest Zoo.

Hungary's folkloric traditions remained the dominant preoccupation of Hungarian architecture up to the First World War, and impeded the development here of modernism, which in Vienna and other major art centres had evolved rapidly out of the art nouveau or Secessionist movement. Lechner and most of his followers had incorporated modern materials such as steel and reinforced concrete into their works; but none of them had gone the way of their great Viennese contemporary Otto Wagner (the teacher of Medgyaszay), who had espoused a functional, international style of growing uniformity. Wagner was indeed highly critical of the Hungarian belief in cloaking a basic structure with what Lechner described as a 'national costume': in 1915 Wagner declared that a specific national style was an impossibility because 'modern urban life was virtually the same in all large cities'. The Hungarians retaliated by saying that Wagner's views were merely a reflection of a place such as Austria, which they thought of as a 'conglomerate of small German counties without a national identity'.

Yet folklore and the search for a national style were not always incompatible with modernism, as is proved by the one aspect of turn-of-the-century Hungarian cultural life to have achieved widespread international recognition—its music. The two great protagonists of Hungary's musical scene were Béla Bartók and Zoltán Kodály, both of whom embarked in 1905 on what would be the first serious field study ever undertaken of Hungarian folk music. Carrying with them a phonograph and a stock of waxed cylinders, they travelled through villages all over Greater Hungary, amassing over 16,000 recordings of both the music and the performances of peasant musicians—an archive that would greatly affect the composition of their own works. Kodály, a much more conservative and romantic figure than Bartók, emulated folk melodies in music that has been described as constituting 'a real profession of faith in the Hungarian soul'. His Budapest 'house-museum', overlooking the Andrássy út, is a warmly atmospherical place, filled with folk mementoes, and very different in character from the now ascetically modernized Buda home where Bartók lived in his later years. Bartók's 'house-museum', like his music, belongs more obviously to the twentieth century than does Kodály's. Unlike Kodály, Bartók made use of folk music in a way that was profoundly original: never composing in a 'folk' idiom, and rarely borrowing textually from this music, Bartók was inspired by it to break away from the confines of tonality. He experimented with the strange sounds of traditional Hungarian instruments, among which percussion figures prominently; and he interested himself in a form of melody derived from ancient pentatonic Magyar airs, with their firm but complex rhythms.

The imaginative interpretation of folkloric motifs helped Bartók to create a 'national style' no less distinctive than that attained by architect contemporaries of his such as Lechner, Lajta, Medgyaszay, and Kós. In contrast, few of the Hungarian sculptors and painters of this period expressed their national identity other than in their choice of subject-matter. Sculptors concentrated their energies largely on the creation of public busts and statues of famous Hungarians, which began to proliferate in Budapest after 1897, when the German Kaiser, Wilhelm II, complained about the lack of such statuary in the city and persuaded Franz Joseph to give 400,000 crowns from his privy purse to remedy this situation: whereas only twenty-six statues had been erected in the city during the forty-six years prior to 1897, thirty-seven appeared between 1897 and 1910. However, despite this increased demand for sculpture, and the lifting of earlier political restrictions, there was no corresponding rise in the artistic quality of the city's public monuments, which remained largely conservative in character, and without any of the dazzling virtuosity to be found, say, in Saloun's Hus monument in Prague's Old Town Square. A baroque solemnity typifies the public work of the two most successful sculptors of these years, János Fadrusz (the creator of the Matthias Corvinus statue at Koloszvár) and Alajos Stróbl, who executed the sculptural decorations for the Kossuth mausoleum in Budapest's Kerepesi Cemetery.

The many Hungarian painters active during these years were generally much livelier than their sculptor contemporaries, even if they were similarly unsuccessful in forming a cohesive and immediately recognizable national school. Though the Hungary of the Compromise offered painters far greater opportunities than before for working in their home country, the atmosphere remained at first too stiflingly conservative to encourage the more talented of them to do so. Mihály Munkácsy, the one Hungarian painter of this generation to win a truly international reputation, emulated his predecessor Madarász by spending most of his working life in Paris, where he enjoyed a close friendship with his compatriot and fellow-painter László Paál.

Munkácsy and Paál worked together in the 1870s in the pioneering French artist colony at Barbizon, a refuge from the constraints of the studio and the academy for Paris-based artists from all over the world. The surrounding forest was a particular source of inspiration to Paál, who was reminded here of his native Transylvania: the short-lived Paál, who lost his mind after hitting his head against a gas-pipe in 1877, evoked the forest in a number of large and boldly painted landscapes (in the Hungarian National Gallery) that combine the mystery of a Corot with the broad, sombre brush-strokes of a Courbet. Munkácsy too depicted the landscapes around Barbizon in a dazzlingly free and suggestive manner; but his temperament inclined him towards figure scenes, which he painted mainly in his Paris studio, where he nostalgically recorded the plight of the Hungarian peasantry or else moments in the Hungarian War of Independence. The epic sweep of so many of his works led to major decorative commissions in places as far apart as the Kunsthistorisches Museum in Vienna and the Public Library in Boston, Massachusetts: his sense of drama, sureness of brush-stroke, and vivid use of thick impasto gave these works a vitality lacking in the conventionally neo-baroque decorations of his prolific counterpart in Hungary

itself, Károly Lotz, the painter of the Budapest Opera House. His down-
fall proved to be his love of dark tonalities and bitumen-black surfaces,
which came to seem increasingly anachronistic in a Paris exposed to the
colouristic experiments of the Impressionists. Changing artistic fashions
triggered off in Munkácsy the familiar Hungarian tendency to insanity:
he was eventually confined to a mental hospital, shortly after an
American painter, William Hickock Low, had found him endlessly
repeating that the only way to maintain his success in the salons was to
paint lighter and lighter. His popularity in the Hungary that he had
abandoned as a young man grew none the less to such enormous
proportions that, on his death in 1900, his body was brought back
to Budapest to a funeral even grander than that of Kossuth six years
earlier. The body was placed on top of a 45-ft. catafalque in Heroes'
Square, and the city was once again draped in black. But the overall
mood of the city on that cool May day was more triumphant than
mournful: the gypsy bands who played Munkácsy's favourite Hungarian
songs outside the coffee-houses emphasized the celebratory, holiday-like
character of an occasion that glorified the most famous painter that
Hungary had ever produced.

Munkácsy's funeral came at a turning-point in Hungarian art, when
Hungarian artists had begun taking more seriously the prospect of a lifetime based in their own country rather than in an international art centre
such as Paris or Munich. Munkácsy himself would never have achieved
his degree of fame had he stayed in Hungary, nor would his pupil József
Rippl-Rónai, who became Hungary's most widely known turn-of-the-
century painter after establishing contact in Paris with such Post-
Impressionists as Maillol, Bonnard, Vuillard, Cézanne, Toulouse-Lautrec,
and Puvis de Chavannes. However, for most Hungarian painters of
Rippl-Rónai's generation, nostalgic yearnings for the homeland began
to prove stronger than any reservations about the artistic conservatism
of their native environment. The philosophy of this new generation was
summarized in a letter written in 1896 by a group of Munich-based Hungarian painters anxious to return to Hungary to establish an artist colony
at what is now the Romanian town of Baia Mare (formerly Nagybánya):
'Only if nurtured by the soil of our native land, only beneath a Hungarian sky and by renewed contact with the Hungarian people, can Hungarian art acquire strength, achieve greatness, and become genuinely
Hungarian.'

For Hungarian historians, the story of modern art in Hungary begins essentially with the so-called Nagybánya School, which was headed by a painter of enormous promise and charisma called Simon Hollósy. Hollósy, an inspirational teacher, made his first journey to Nagybánya in the spring of 1896, together with a group of his pupils and his main Hungarian rival in Munich, Károly Ferenczy. On their way from Munich they passed through Budapest, where they enjoyed the excitement and patriotic fervour of a city at the height of its millennial festivities; but they were also shocked by the turgid, academic nature of most of the art on display there, and by the level of ignorance about the latest developments in French art. The one exhibition which impressed them was of an idiosyncratic painter from a wealthy, aristocratic background called Szinyei Merse, who had executed colourful, *plein air* works in Munich in the 1870s before becoming disheartened through lack of a positive critical response towards his work; he had taken up painting again in Vienna in 1882, but had then decided to give up altogether following one of Gusztáv Keleti's characteristically scathing attacks. Merse's exhibition of 1896 was largely of works painted over twenty years before, including the startling *Picnic in May* (1873), which the Hungarians now proudly claim as an example of Impressionism before its time. As a figure scene executed out of doors in bright, sunny conditions (and prefiguring by one year Manet's *Déjeuner sur l'herbe*), *Picnic in May* was certainly a work more in keeping with the ideals of Hollósy and his circle than with those of Merse's own generation.

The artists who began visiting Nagybánya from 1896 onwards have come in recent times to be known as the 'Hungarian Impressionists'—a term indicative of the popularity they have enjoyed in Hungary since the time of their first and highly successful group exhibition in Budapest in the autumn of 1897. Their numerous *plein air* landscapes and figure studies on show in the Hungarian National Gallery come as a colourful relief after the many dark and bombastic historical scenes that precede them; but few of the works will strike today's viewer as being other than a pleasing reflection of the main international trends of the day. Hollósy himself, a lazy man enamoured of socializing and drinking (he married one of the barmaids at Nagybánya), did not live up to his early promise, and spent much of his time in Transylvania engaged on an ambitious and expressive figure scene—*The Rákóczi March*—that was never completed. The one truly exceptional member of the group, worthy of inclusion in any general history of European painting, was Károly Ferenczy, who made Nagybánya and its surroundings come alive in vivid, lush green canvases bathed in a magical sunlight.

Ferenczy, though dying in relative obscurity in Budapest in 1917, enhanced Nagybánya's reputation as the most important artist colony in eastern Europe; in turn, the example of Nagybánya encouraged Hungarian artists in their desire to search for inspiration in the countryside rather than in the city. In the wake of Nagybánya, artist colonies grew up along the Danube valley, and in the middle of the Great Hungarian Plain; meanwhile, at Gödöllő, on the outskirts of Budapest, there was founded an Arts and Crafts community led by the William Morris-like figure of Aladár Körösfői-Kriesch. Nagybánya itself later attracted other progressive Hungarian artists of the pre-First World War years, such as the Eight and the Activists, who viewed rural Hungary with eyes influenced by the stylized, Arcadian vision of a Cézanne.

During this same period, when the fashion for artist colonies was at its height, there lived in Budapest an eccentric and now much-venerated painter who called himself Csontváry. By far the most original Hungarian artist of the turn of the century, if also one of the least accomplished technically, Csontváry worked for much of his life as a pharmacist in a village now in Slovakia. In his late 20s he claimed to have heard a voice telling him that he would be 'the greatest . . . painter the world has ever seen—greater even than Raphael'. In 1881 he went off to Rome so that he might 'catch up with the great, or outdistance them'; by 1894 he had leased his shop and enrolled in Hollósy's Academy in Munich. On settling a few years later in Budapest, he tried unsuccessfully to present one of his canvases to the newly completed Parliament building, and, with his long beard, strange, gaunt appearance, and biblical pronouncements, found himself being continually teased by the many artist habitués of the Café Japán, where Lechner held court. He escaped to exotic destinations all around the Mediterranean, and drew on his memories of these to paint vast, luridly coloured canvases that recall in their ambitiousness (but not their artistry) the works of visionaries such as John Martin, Edward Lear, and the Douanier Rousseau. Most foreign visitors to Budapest still fail to appreciate Csontváry's works, as did virtually all his contemporaries, who either shunned or ridiculed his two large exhibitions that were held in Budapest in 1908 and 1910, in halls intended for industrial displays: whether persuading passers-by in the street to visit the shows, or else explaining to those inside the meaning of his unframed and unsigned masterpieces (genius required no signature), he frequently reduced people to titters, and certainly convinced them of his lunacy. Lack of recognition exacerbated his megalomania until eventually he moved his studio from Pest to Buda, and did not allow anyone to enter it or to buy his works other than as a complete entity (for which he fixed a price of five million Hungarian crowns). As a painter, he differed from his Hungarian contemporaries in virtually every respect save one: he never painted the city that had become his adopted home.

'Where are the painters of Budapest?' asked a Hungarian art historian as late as 1947. The same question could also be asked of Hungary's turn-of-the-century writers, so many of whom distanced themselves from the city by going to live in the leafy suburbs and hills of Buda. One of the writers from an older generation who settled in these near-rural surroundings was the then grand old man of Hungarian letters, Mór Jókai, from the grounds of whose Buda home the city appeared as a picturesque, distant blur, framed by trees (these grounds still survive, as does his reconstructed study, now an unvisited memorial museum to him). 'The secret of my fertility is communion with nature,' said Jókai, who died in 1904, shortly after completing his 202nd novel.

None of the many brilliant writers to emerge from turn-of-the-century Hungary achieved the international fame of Jókai, with the exception of Ferenc Molnár, a truly cosmopolitan figure who divided his life between Budapest and Vienna, and ended his days as an exile in Hollywood. Molnár made his name not only with his witty plays of amorous intrigue (usually involving flirtatious young wives and jealous husbands) but also with his much-translated short novel for children, *The Paul Street Boys* (1907). The latter work, though dealing with school gang rivalry in a typically congested district of modern Pest, extols the values of a now threatened Hungary: an old-fashioned code of honour governs the boys in their struggle to keep possession of a vacant plot of land which, for children who have been brought up like them in a 'mournful, many-storeyed apartment house', has all the beauty of wide, open fields.

Molnár, a conservative writer whose talent lay essentially in light comedy, did not play any part in the intellectual debates that divided Budapest's intelligentsia into conflicting factions, each of which claimed to represent modernity. Sociologists and political scientists were associated with the journal *Huszadik Század* ('Twentieth Century'), which was founded in 1900 as a forum for new, radical ideas about social reform in Hungary. The best known of Hungary's marxist thinkers, however, were the intellectuals who belonged to the so-called 'Sunday Circle', which, to begin with, was interested primarily in metaphysics. Gathering irregularly and informally in private apartments, this circle was presided over by one of this century's most influential Marxist philosophers, György Lukács, and included the librettist of Bartók's *Bluebeard's Castle*, Béla Balázs, and the art historian Arnold Hauser, who matched Lukács's creation of a sociology of literature through writing a pioneering social history of art.

Lukács's cultural formation and way of thinking were essentially German, and he exposed in his writings the limitations of Hungarian as a vehicle for philosophical thought: language other than as a means to an end ultimately held little interest for Lukács, who failed to appreciate the linguistic brilliance of a writer such as Krúdy. Lukács's disregard for language and national tradition earned him the rebuke of the poet Mihály Babits who, together with the novelists Krúdy and Zsigmond Móricz and the poets Dezső Kosztolányi and Endre Ady, formed the mainstay of the outstanding literary group linked with the journal *Nyugat* ('West').

Nyugat, which first appeared in January 1908, was recognized immediately as the ultimate in literary modernity in Hungary. As its name suggests, the journal aimed to promote greater cultural links between Hungary and the West, and in so doing free the country both from provincialism and the prevailing influence of Germany. Both in its stance and in the avant-garde nature of its writings, *Nyugat* incurred the wrath of many a conservative nationalist, including a journalist Dénes Gorcsoni, who, less than a month after the first issue had appeared, wrote:

it is treason and slander what they do in *Nyugat* under the pretext of civilizing the barbarian Magyars. They want to ruin our morals, they want to disillusion us of our faith, and they want to crush to pieces our national pride. (Mary Gluck, *Lukacs and his Circle* (1985), p. 113).

And yet the writers of *Nyugat*, for all their attacks on the 'oriental backwardness' of the Hungarians, were remarkably contradictory in their attitudes towards conservatism and nationalism. Raised in provincial Hungary, some of them even descended from minor landed gentry, they had an underlying nostalgia for their country's past, and were certainly not as comfortable in its industrial present as was their unabashed modernist contemporary, the socialist poet and artist Lajos Kassák, who took great pride in living in the Budapest working-class district of Angyalföld. Rural Hungary was the main inspiration of Móricz's highly realistic fiction, as it was of the more lyrical writings of Kosztolányi, who in 1913 concluded that the Hungarian countryside was 'a land of miracles' and that those 'who are born there will have a wider horizon than anybody brought up in the industrialized capital'. As for Krúdy, who evoked so wonderfully the sights and smells of Budapest, he did so through the haze of memory and alcohol, and an ethereal prose style; and he main-tained all his life sentimental feelings for the *Nyírség*, one of Hungary's most backward agricultural regions.

The contradictions and greatness of this period in Hungarian culture were summarized above all in the tortured figure of Endre Ady, the most popular Hungarian poet after Sándor Petőfi. Born in the Transylvanian village of Érmindszent, Ady worked initially as a journalist in the nearby town of Nagyvárad (now Oradea in Romania), where, around 1900, he fell obsessively in love with the older married woman whom he called 'Léda'. Léda lured him to Paris, opened up for him the pleasures of bohemianism and cosmopolitanism, and unleashed some of the most passionate love poetry in the Hungarian language. Returning to Buda-pest, Ady caused a sensation with the publication in 1906 of his *Új Versek* ('New Poems'), the impact of which was not just on literary circles but on a whole new generation conscious of an impending historical crisis, doubtful of the patriotic certainties of the past, and, in the words of Móricz, desirous of poetry that would direct their burning passions as if it were a 'searchlight' or a 'flame-thrower'. 'Shall I break through below Dévény / With new songs for new times?', announced Ady at the beginning of this book, referring to the westernmost village where the Danube enters Hungary. With these famous two lines, Ady embarked on a heavily symbolical journey embracing a heady mixture of patriotic despair, messianic prophecies, radical politics, love of money, morbid pre-occupation, and erotic passion, which was treated here as the highest experience of life.

Ady encapsulated in his person the decadent fascination of his verse. Darkly handsome with large, Picasso-like eyes, he drank heavily (usually at the Pest tavern of The Three Ravens) and suffered from a slowly advancing syphilis. Both in his life and work, he had much in common with his beloved Baudelaire; but, though he must have seemed to his critics as the epitome of all the vices of the modern urban world, he was not intoxicated with this world to the same degree as the French poet was. In one of his short stories, he described the life of daytime Budapest as 'one huge, protracted groan'; and he returned frequently to his native Transylvanian village in search of spiritual renewal—the theme of his poem, *I Shall Return to My Village*. It is perhaps symptomatic of his deep-seated rural yearnings that at the height of both the First World War and of his illness he should have married a young woman who, like him, came from the Transylvanian gentry.

The city that Admiral Horthy would shortly reproach for its sins had by now come to be seen by both the Left and the Right as a symbol of a darkening Hungary. The viewpoint of the conservatives was eloquently expressed in the popular and widely translated novel *The Old House*, written on the eve of the war by Cecile Tormay, one of the few Hungarian writers of these years actually native to Budapest. Tormay, a contributor to *East* (a direct retort to *Nyugat*), was influenced by Thomas Mann's *Buddenbrooks* in her account of the declining fortunes of the Ulwing family, whose beautiful and isolated family home on the Pest side of the Danube is soon hemmed in by all the new buildings that spring up once the Chain Bridge is completed. Anna, the youngest member of the family, finds that she can no longer see from her window 'the lovely wide river, the Castle hill, the spires . . . Morning came later to the rooms than formerly. The houses opposite sent their shadows into the windows. The sun shone into them no more and night fell earlier than of old.' In the end Anna is forced to the conclusion that 'the only families that survive are those which have their roots in the soil. The seed drops in vain on the city's pavement; no tree will grow out of it.'

The First World War and its aftermath confirmed all the fears that had developed in the course of Hungary's rapid industrial development since 1867. In the immediate aftermath of the war, when the country became briefly a liberal republic under the leadership of Count Mihály Károlyi, many Hungarians would have found consolation for defeat in the idea of a country building a new future for itself on a basis other than short-term capitalist goals. This was a world in which official recognition could at last be given to Ady, who, on the day the republic was declared, received a governmental delegation welcoming him as 'the poet of the Revolution'. Unfortunately, the poet was unable to reply to this other than with an unintelligible stammer, for his health had declined markedly since his marriage in 1915. Dividing his last days between the pretentious Transylvanian country estate of his parents-in-law, a small apartment in Pest (now a pathetically neglected museum), and a sanitorium in a Buda suburb, Ady died on 23 January 1919, only a few weeks before the demise of Károlyi's regime. This was an inauspicious start to a year which saw in May the death of Csontváry, who by now had lost all that was left both of his mind and of his faith in 'unbelieving humanity'.

Károlyi, driven to resignation on hearing of Allied plans to divide up Hungary, handed over his government in March to a group of mainly Jewish and Budapest-born communists led by Béla Kun. The writer Arthur Koestler, even as a staunch anti-communist, recalled the Hungary of 1919 (when he was still in his teens) with such sentimentality and indulgence that he could describe as 'idyllic' one of the worst years in modern Hungarian history. Kun's government, far from fulfilling the dreams of those envisaging a socialist dawn for Hungary, managed merely to destroy the economy through nationalizing the banks, and to anger neighbouring countries through trying to forge links with Lenin and the Bolsheviks, on whom were focused unrealistic hopes for military aid. And it proved unsympathetic to such genuine socialist writers and artists as Lajos Kassák and László Moholy-Nagy, whose avant-garde work, like that of Mayakovsky in Russia, fell foul of the communists, in this case through expressing a view of art as being above class and party loyalties.

Kun and his 'Republic of Councils' lasted only 123 days, eventually collapsing as Romanian troops advanced on Budapest. Kun fled to Vienna, together with his ministers, among whom was the future Hollywood actor of Dracula, Béla Lugosi, who had been appointed under-minister of culture. Other prominent socialists also escaped into exile, including Lukács, Kassák, and Moholy-Nagy, the latter establishing himself in Berlin as one of Hungary's most important artists this century. Those who stayed behind in Budapest had to suffer at first the many provocations of the Romanians, who did little to improve the traditional enmity between them and the Hungarians by bivouacking in the smart Oktogon intersection of Pest, and then plundering the city of all that they could find. But worse was to come with the arrival in November of a former admiral in the Austro-Hungarian navy, Miklós Horthy, who rode into Budapest at the head of a 25,000-strong Hungarian national army. Horthy, soon to be appointed regent of Hungary in place of a claimant to the throne, instigated a 'White Terror' that set about beating up and hanging anyone who had been associated with the communists.

Taking his revenge on a regime that had been largely Jewish and from Budapest, Horthy made his famous comments on the 'sinful' state Hungary's capital, and, in so doing, greatly exacerbated the mood of anti-semitism that had been gaining ground in Hungary since 1900.

To the sufferings of communists and Jews was added the national tragedy of the Treaty of Trianon, which was signed on 4 June 1920. Black flags were hung, shops were closed, trams were stopped, and the street life of Budapest came to a standstill as all of Hungary mourned a treaty that deprived her of two-thirds of her kingdom and one-third of her Magyar population. Budapest, with its one million inhabitants, now contained one-seventh of the total population of Hungary; and it would occupy an ever greater proportion of the country over the coming years, when thousands of refugees from former Hungarian lands began crowding into the city.

The devastating reduction of the Hungarian countryside, and the now uniquely disproportionate size of the capital in relation to the rest of the country, had the inevitable effect of increasing those literary and artistic yearnings for Hungary's rural life and traditions. 'Transylvanianism', aided by the influx of refugees from this region, became more popular than ever, with Budapest even gaining a garden suburb (the St Imre Colony) designed as a Transylvanian village complete with Transylvanian names. A related phenomenon was 'Populism', Hungary's answer to the German Völkisch movement, with its back-to-nature ideals and exploration of the proverbially harsh lives of the peasantry. One of the main exponents of this movement was the poet and prose writer Gyula Illyés, whose realistic tales of the Hungarian peasantry were most famously related in his semi-autobiographical classic *People of the Puszta* (1936), which astonished middle-class Hungary with its account of the primitive rural conditions that existed almost on the threshold of Budapest.

The surviving original contributors to *Nyugat* also reacted to the postwar upheavals by distancing themselves yet further from the contemporary urban world. Móricz became involved with Populism, while the scholarly and ever more spiritual Babits (the last editor of *Nyugat*, which died with him in 1941) retreated in his last years to an isolated house on the Danube bend, where, terminally ill with cancer of the larynx, he wrote poetry chronicling the helplessness of man. An increased profundity distinguishes also the later work of Dezső Kosztolányi (another victim of throat cancer), who, after beginning his career as a self-confessed aesthete and supremely elegant symbolist poet, wrote after 1921 a handful of deeply perceptive novels. Two of these (the best-known is the wonderful *Skylark*) were set in the author's native town of Szabadka (now Subotica), which was handed over to Yugoslavia in 1920. Though Kosztolányi spent most of his later life in Budapest, his home here was in the village-like district of the Tabán, where he set his novel *Anna Édes* (1926), which portrays this district as being almost totally cut off from the rest of the city. The novel, covering the period between Kun's flight to Vienna and the Treaty of Trianon, deals with a simple, hard-working maid from the countryside who ends up killing her employers. Kosztolányi himself makes an appearance in a self-mocking epilogue written with an otherworldly detachment from the politics and affairs of the world. Three friends are taking a walk in the Tabán where they catch sight behind a fence of a tall, untidy man smoking and drinking coffee in an idyllic garden. After one of them identifies him as Kosztolányi 'the journalist', they exchange conflicting rumours about his religion and political views, the general conclusion being that he is neither a Christian, nor a Jew, nor a Communist, nor a supporter of the White Terror, but that instead he's a clever opportunist who's 'for everybody and nobody':

The three friends concurred in this. They stopped again at the end of the fence. It was obvious they still didn't fully understand. One could see that they were indeed used to thinking one thing at a time; one could see that two thoughts were beyond them.

Kosztolányi, as this passage reveals, was able to confront the complexities of this period with irony and a quiet humour. Hungarians generally showed a remarkable resilience in the wake of national tragedy, and succeeded soon after Trianon in giving Budapest a reputation as a major European centre of elegance and pleasure. The Hungarian-born humorist George Mikes, the author of the best-selling *How to Be an Alien* and other similarly titled books, remembered the interwar Budapest of his youth as 'one of the pleasantest, most amusing and most intriguing cities in a turbulent Europe which was hoping against hope, but which knew at the bottom of its heart that the carnival would not last'. But it needed a more subtle and less perpetually cheerful humourist than Mikes to capture the tragicomic ambiguity of mood that characterized this era known sometimes as 'the Silver Age'. Such a person was Frigyes Karinthy, an associate of *Nyugat* who made a living as a prolific journalist, writing witty sketches that punctured pretensions, exposed the absurd, and gave bizarre twists to ordinary situations. 'When it comes to humour, I'm in dead earnest,' said Karinthy in a phrase that acquired an added resonance in the late 1930s, when he was found to have a tumour of the brain. He went on to write the extraordinary *Journey Around my Skull* (1938), which records with an amused, anti-heroic objectivity every detail of his illness, down to the moment when he endures brain surgery under local anaesthetic. The words that he used to describe his literary development—'from humourist to tumourist'—was also wittily evocative of an interwar Hungary poised between emotional extremes.

Whereas with Karinthy a humanitarian optimism triumphs over physical frailty, it is the darker forces of life that eventually gain the upper hand in the case of Attila József, the most outstanding poetic talent to emerge during these years. Brought up in the industrial Pest district of the Ferencváros (where the dark and cramped apartment where he was born has been preserved as a memorial museum to him), József was one of the first Hungarian writers to find beauty and inspiration in the grimmer aspects of city life. His lyric poems—such as the famous *A Night in the Slums* (1932)—use powerful images of poverty and industrialization as the starting-point for existential meditation. A committed socialist, with a lifelong concern for the plight of the working-classes, József became a member of the underground Communist party, but was sacked from this for trying to merge Marxism with the teachings of Freud. Ultimately a loner, always unhappy in love, József finally succumbed to insanity. In 1937, in a gesture which unwittingly ensured that his name would later be given to Budapest's principal psychiatric hospital, the 32-year-old writer threw himself under what could easily have been an image from his poetry, or indeed a symbol of Budapest's sudden rise as a metropolis—a moving freight train.

5

The Moving World

IN 1937, the year of Attila József's suicide, a young Scottish woman visited Hungary on the invitation of a Lutheran pastor with whom she had recently fallen in love. The outbreak of the war precipitated the marriage and prevented her from making her first return visit to Scotland until the summer of 1956, three years after the collapse of Stalinism. Arriving in Britain one day too late to see her father alive, she stayed only a few weeks there before returning to her husband and two sons in a Budapest that she found reduced to a chaos of sandbags, snipers, burnt-out cars, and overturned trams.

When I got to know her, during the last decade of Hungarian communism, she was a widow living in an old flat in Óbuda. I was introduced to her by her artist son, Árpád Szabados, who told me how pleased she would be to meet someone from Britain, where she had no family left and only one remaining friend. Her Hungarian, which had never been perfect, was already deteriorating; and she spoke in an English full of prewar archaisms such as 'forenoon' and 'bloody circus'—idiosyncrasies inherited by her son, whose name she anglicized to 'Paddy'. Strong, determined, and unsentimental, she never gave any hint of what she must have suffered in abandoning her homeland for a Hungary under the successive grip of fascism and the Soviet Union. But whenever I saw her, I could not help thinking about how her life highlighted the sense of loss and isolation of the Hungarian generation to which she had half-belonged—a generation whose memories have been distilled to their bleakest essence in the semi-autobiographical fiction of György Konrád, who prefaces his novel *A Feast in the Garden* (1989) with an opening line unwelcoming even by Central European standards: 'The house is on the side of the hill, the cemetery to the right, the mental hospital to the left.'

At a time when my Scottish friend was settling into Budapest, many of Hungary's anti-fascist intellectuals such as the poet György Faludy and the journalist György Pálóczi-Horváth (the future authors of two of the finest Hungarian memoirs of this period) were leaving, unable to support a regime that in 1939 allied itself with Germany by becoming a signatory of the Anti-Comintern pact. Those who stayed behind in Hungary often found themselves in the unenviable position of being communist sympathizers forcibly conscripted into an army that participated in the German attacks against Yugoslavia and Russia. However, Hungary itself survived the war relatively unscathed until as late as 1944: Budapest was only hit by a single bomb, food shortages were few, and the presence of impoverished widows and maimed war veterans on the city's streets was not nearly so great as it had been during the First World War. Furthermore, the ailing Horthy and his government did not prove wholly subservient to their German allies: in 1940 they welcomed into Hungary 100,000 refugees from occupied Poland; and in 1943, following the loss of the entire 2nd Hungarian Army near the River Don, they refused to send any more troops to the front, and even entered into secret negotiations with the Allies. Furthermore the country's large Jewish population was treated by the Hungarians far more mildly than the Nazis would have wished: though the Jews were restricted in their freedom by legislation passed before the war, they were neither herded into ghettos nor deported; indeed, thanks to Horthy's government, they were safer in Hungary than they were in any other country under German influence.

The unreliability of the Hungarians as allies, combined with the rapid advance of the Russians towards Budapest, finally forced German troops to move into Hungary on 18 March 1944. The prolific novelist and diarist Sándor Márai, on the point of going to bed after a candle-lit dinner party, was rung up at midnight to be told by a civil servant friend that German tanks were advancing on the Castle Hill. Márai sat up for a few more hours in his study, wondering about what would happen to the 6,000 volumes that lined its walls; later he remembered the whole night in the most momentous terms—as the prelude to 'what was nothing less than the total destruction and extinction of an entire way of life'.

The next day, over on the Margaret Island, 270 German officers were billeted at the Hotel Palatinus, where the poet Ernő Szép had been living for over thirty-three years. Hurriedly forced to pack a lifetime of belongings before moving to a flat on Pest's Pozsony út, Szép was offered reassuring words by the hotel's elderly desk clerk: 'This was not a real military occupation', the man said; 'it was only a *transitory passage to secure supply lines.*' But Szép had every reason to take a more pessimistic view of the situation, for he was one of the city's 230,000 remaining Jews, who would soon begin to feel, more acutely than the rest of the population, the realities of war. Within weeks of the occupation, Anglo-American aircraft had embarked on a bombing campaign of Hungary, and the Germans had begun rounding up from all over the country nearly half a million Jews for eventual transportation to Auschwitz. Governor Horthy, with his waning powers, attempted to slow down the process of deportation; but a more realistic hope for the Jews lay in the efforts made by representatives of neutral states—above all Sweden—to issue protective passes and offer shelter in 'protected houses'. Thousands of the city's Jews were saved by the wealthy Raoul Wallenberg, a Swedish Schindler who would be rewarded for all his good work by being 'disappeared' after the war into the oblivion of some Soviet camp.

On 15 October 1944 news came that had the residents of Ernő Szép's apartment block prematurely taking out bottles of carefully hoarded champagne: Horthy, realizing that there was no point in continuing the war, had made a speech calling for an armistice. Unfortunately, this only had the effect of bringing to an end a right-wing government which by now had come to seem almost benign. Horthy was immediately kidnapped by the SS, and power in Hungary was seized by the Nazi puppet Ferenc Szálasi and his Fascist Arrow Cross party. The champagne was put back again, and with it the last hopes of avoiding the fate that finally befell Szép later that day, when he was sent, together with many others from his block, to a forced-labour camp on the outskirts of Budapest.

Szép stayed in the camp until 9 November when, during the chaos accompanying the arrival of the Russians at the perimeter of Budapest, he was allowed to return to the city, and endure the bloody siege that would last until February of the following year. Two of his brothers were killed, a sister 'disappeared', and many of the inmates of his camp perished while accompanying the retreating Hungarian units; but Szép miraculously survived to write *The Smell of Humans*, a memoir of the holocaust in Hungary as human and unsensational in tone as the more famous works of his younger Italian contemporary, Primo Levi. This memoir, so full of irony and quiet humour, displays a tolerance towards his fellow human beings that extends even to those 'anti-semitic Jews' who tried to save their lives by betraying both their faith and their neighbours.

And it renders the horrors of war more believable by dwelling on such absurd details of everyday life as the constant sewing on and taking off of the yellow stars of David, and the baffling inconsistencies of the bureaucratic mind. 'Boring, isn't it?', he wryly comments at one particularly complex stage of his narrative.

Márai, in his own powerful account of this period, *Memoir of Hungary*, lacked the light touch of Szép, but made up for this with a daunting erudition, and an analytical and reflective brilliance, capable of conveying the full emotional and psychological complexities of this critical moment in Hungarian history. Whereas Szép had braved it out in Budapest after the arrival of the Germans on 18 March, Márai had managed to escape to a nearby village under Russian control, where he had passed his time studying the Russian character and forming conclusions about this that did not bode well for a Soviet-dominated Hungary. But his primary concern, once the Russians had taken control of Budapest, was to see what had become of his home and of his beloved city. His eloquent account of the ruins that awaited him reveal how much the city had suffered in less than a year of fighting.

Three bomb hits and more than thirty grenades had left his Tabán home (where his friend and neighbour Kosztolányi had set his novel *Anna Édes*) as 'a mushy pile of ruins', over which lay scattered some photographs, a French porcelain candlestick, and his top hat. Looking for keepsakes to take with him, he eventually made his way into what had been his study, to find that the blasts had ground his rare editions of Eckermann, Marcus Aurelius, and other authors into a pulp: out of his 6,000 books, the only one to have survived with its title-page intact was a volume entitled *On the Care of a Middle-Class Dog*; he had a sufficient sense of humour and pathos to put this straight into his pocket. Afterwards he went on to visit the nearby house where Kosztolányi had lived until his death in 1941, and found that this too, with its equally fabulous collection of books, had been turned into 'a pile of mouldy debris': 'this was the most a Hungarian author could acquire in years past through respectable literary work', he bitterly reflected. Continuing his morbid tour, he walked up into the Castle district, of whose former 6,000 residents only 600 were still living there. His stroll along its narrow streets reminded him of 'that of Ulysses when he looked down into the pit of Hades'. The Royal Palace had lost all trace of its splendour, while inside the battered Matthias Church he was shocked by the sight of two dead horses lying abandoned 'in front of the tombs of princes'. Looking down to the banks of the Danube, he would have seen only the stumps of bridges, and a long line of rubble marking the grand apartments that had once formed the riverside in Pest.

Slowly Márai tried to rebuild a life for himself in the changed city, but became increasingly preoccupied by the country's new political situation. As someone who disliked all forms of political extremism, he found his fervent anti-fascist stand of before the war being transformed now into a comparable hatred for the Communists, who had come to power in 1945 as part of a four-party coalition including the Small-holders' Party, the National Peasants' Party, and the Social Democrats. Though it was not until after 1948 that a Stalinist, one-party state would be consolidated in Hungary, Márai noted how already a red terror—the ringing of doorbells late at night, the disappearance of individuals, the ubiquitous presence of the 'uniformed man'—had begun to pervade the air of Budapest like some 'fetid, life-threatening gas'. One spring afternoon, walking down Andrássy út, he had a chilling glimpse into the future while passing at No. 60 the austerely ornamented block where the Fascist Arrow Cross Party had once been quartered: looking up at one of the balconies, he recognized as former members of this party a group of laughing, cocky young men now dressed in the uniforms of the AVO—the secret police force who would make this building one of the most feared addresses of the Stalinist period. Had Márai stayed on longer in Hungary, his belief in the essential sameness of all extreme political groups would have received further confirmation in the huge monument that was built on top of the Citadel Hill in honour of the 'Soviet Liberation': a version of this work had originally been planned as a memorial to Horthy's son.

In this Hungary that was becoming ever greyer and more oppressive, Márai noticed how people were escaping from 'everyday dreariness . . . loneliness and hopelessness' by turning to the other Hungary that had been evoked in the nostalgia-steeped works of Krúdy. Even those who had never read or heard of Krúdy came to be addicted to what Márai called the opiate of 'Krúdyism', which suddenly took hold of the inhab-itants of Budapest and made even those who had barely touched wine or been before to a Turkish bath spend their days and nights in the penumbral glow of taverns and steam-rooms. But for Márai himself the only real escape from the realities of postwar Hungary was to leave the country for good: the prospect of not being able to write freely did not bother him so much as not 'being allowed to be silent freely'. He spent his last year in Budapest reading the works of Hungary's 'forgotten, unsuccessful' writers, the example of whom gave him 'rich provisions for the journey in solitude, for the heretical life in a cave'. Settling eventually in America—where he took up citizenhood after the failure of the 1956 uprising—he adamantly refused to set foot again in Hungary until democracy returned. Twenty-five years into his exile, he confessed that barely a day had passed without some image of Budapest coming to mind; he would have to endure almost a quarter of a century more before dying alone and obscure in San Diego, California, only a few months before the collapse of communism in Hungary.

Márai at least never had any illusions about communism, which saved him from the acute disappointments and physical sufferings experienced by those who had returned to postwar Hungary with a sense of optimism about the future. György Pálóczi-Horváth, a man of aristocratic birth, was one of many Hungarian intellectuals who had come back to Budapest as a dedicated communist, only to be dragged off a few years later into the cellars of the AVO building at 60 Andrássy út; an account of his 1,832 days of torture and imprisonment (many of them in solitary confinement) form the basis of his shocking but clear-headed memoir, *The Undefeated* (1959), which was written during his exile in Britain.

No less vivid as a personal memoir of Stalinist oppression was György Faludy's *My Happy Days in Hell* (1962), the title of which gives a good idea of the difference in personality between him and Pálóczi-Horváth. Faludy appears from this book as representative of a less earnest side to the Hungarian character: charming and witty, he seems happy to let politics and intellectual matters rest for a while in the pursuit of what was for him ultimately far more important—friendship, wine, and, above all, women. At the outset of his memoir he writes how he fled Budapest in 1939 not simply to avoid having to fight as an ally of the Germans but to get out of a disastrous lightning marriage. Later in the book he reveals his priorities in life in an anecdote relating to a leading Hungarian communist whose fall from grace in 1948 coincided with the start of the Stalinist terror—László Rajk. Faludy describes how he had met Rajk in a Paris café shortly after the latter had returned from the Spanish Civil War, 'where he was said to have fought heroically'. He was interested in hearing about Rajk's experiences in the war, but found himself subjected instead to a long diatribe about there being only two roads open to mankind—'that of the *bourgeoisie* and that of the proletariat'. Faludy, becoming increasingly bored and irritated with Rajk, then went on to brand himself forever as a flippant bourgeois by getting up from the table to 'follow the road' of two 'very beautiful Annamite girls'.

Though finding Rajk a 'ridiculous' man in Paris and a 'fanatical, cruel, incorruptible, reckless and boring' minister of the interior in a Hungary under the Stalinist rule of Mátyás Rákosi, Faludy could not help feeling sympathy for him on hearing in 1949 the alarming and absurd accusation that the man had been a spy for the Horthy police, and a fascist agent for the Spanish nationalists. The subsequent trial and execution of Rajk and his fellow 'conspirators' left Faludy with few illusions as to the true nature of the Rákosi régime, and even sent a chill into the hearts of devoted communists such as Pálóczi-Horváth: from now onwards Hungary was gripped by a mood of paranoia and suspicion in which no one could feel safe any more, even with close friends. Faludy, a voluntary member of the American army during the war, could hardly have felt surprised when, in the aftermath of the Rajk trial, he himself was taken off to the AVO headquarters, and thence to a prison camp, where he needed all his amatory fantasies and sense of humour to survive the years of forced labour that followed. Many of his companions had died from hunger and torture by the time he was finally released, in September 1953, shortly after the death of Stalin.

Stalin's death gave Hungary a brief respite from Rákosi, whose ugly, swollen face (the result of a glandular disorder) had been reproduced to such an extent on posters and monuments that even Stalin had been embarrassed. The far more moderate communist Imre Nagy took his place, but lasted only two years in power before being ousted by the Moscow-backed Rákosi, who accused him of 'deviationism'. However, by now a mood of open dissent was growing among the Hungarians, who took heart from Khrushchev's denunciation of Stalin at a supposedly secret meeting held early in 1956 at the 20th Congress of the Soviet Communist Party. By June of this year, Hungarian writers and intellectuals used the forum of the Petőfi Writers' Circle to voice freely their criticisms of Rákosi, who was subsequently removed by Khrushchev, only to be replaced by the no less odious Stalinist Ernő Gerő. On 6 October, in the middle of an abnormally hot and sunny autumn, the Hungarians stepped up their provocative stance by reburying the now pardoned Rajk in a ceremony that brought 200,000 people onto the streets of Budapest.

Seventeen days later, as the Indian summer continued, a large crowd of students expressed solidarity with reform policies in Poland by planning an afternoon march to Buda's Bem József tér in honour of the eponymous Polish general who had fought with Hungary during the War of Independence of 1848–9. Sándor Kopácsi, the then head of Budapest's police, remembered having woken up that morning to 'yet another radiant day'. His wife had already gone off to her job in the ministry of the interior, and their daughter Judith was preparing to walk to her school, accompanied by 'Tango the dog and Fifi the cat'. He told Judith that he would be home that evening at the 'usual' time, not knowing that the events of the day would bring about the most dramatic decision of his life, and ultimately separate him for many years from the woman and child he adored.

Kopácsi, who had just returned from his holidays, entered his office later that morning in a relaxed frame of mind, only to find out that leading members of the Politburo were urgently searching for him, anxious to know how he was going to handle the 'grave situation' caused by the afternoon's planned march. Believing the participating students to be all good communists, he himself found it difficult to share the panic of the authorities, who at this stage were refusing to allow the march to take place. An emergency meeting was held in which Kopácsi narrowly succeeded in having this ban retracted after he had pointed out that his police force was not sufficiently well equipped to stop the students had they gone ahead with the march regardless of the consequences. Afterwards, when he went to follow the procession in his car, he experienced his first real moments of anxiety as he waited for the marchers to cross the Erzsébet bridge. Held up in the traffic behind him was a black limousine carrying the future Soviet premier Andropov, who asked Kopácsi through an interpreter if he thought things were not 'going a bit far'. It was only later that Kopácsi noticed a large Hungarian flag with the communist emblem cut out from its centre.

The demonstration, swelled by thousands of workers, turned rapidly into an uprising as it moved from the Bem József tér to the Parliament building, and from there to the Hungarian Radio headquarters on Bródy Sándor utca, behind the National Museum. The students protracted the journey by pausing at the museum to recite the patriotic poem 'Arise Hungarians!'

Kopácsi returned quickly to his office, to be met this time by messages sent from twenty-one police precincts around the city, desperately awaiting his orders. The most pressing of these messages came from a small police post at the edge of the Városliget park, telling him that an irate crowd was pulling down the large statue of Stalin which had stood near Heroes' Square. Kopácsi was not so much concerned by the fate of the statue, which was already earmarked for removal to a less conspicuous place, but by the estimated 100,000 to 200,000 people who surrounded it.

An even larger crowd, amounting perhaps to half a million, had by now gathered outside the Parliament, where they hoped optimistically for an appearance by Imre Nagy, whom Kopácsi described as a man who 'couldn't imagine taking any step without a direct order from the party leadership'. Eventually, a group of Nagy's close friends managed to persuade him to leave his Buda house to come and address the crowd, whom he promptly disappointed by urging them all to go quietly home. By this time Kopácsi's attention was diverted by reports that the AVO ('arseholes and animals' in the opinion of one of his colleagues) had stationed themselves with heavy machine-guns on key roofs in the city centre. Kopácsi, foreseeing a catastrophe in the event of 'one hasty order' or 'a single misunderstanding', picked up the emergency telephone line to Gerő, only to be told by the man's secretary that he could not be disturbed as he was busily preparing a speech for the radio.

Everything now depended on this speech, which had the power to silence the volatile city if only Gerő could admit to past errors, announce reforms, and give in to the general demand for Nagy Imre to be returned to power. Everyone in Kopácsi's office listened in a tense silence as the radio began broadcasting a speech that opened promisingly with Gerő stating his 'firm and unshakeable intention to develop, enlarge, and deepen democracy in our country'. By the end of the speech, however, one of Kopácsi's senior officers was taking out his pistol and threatening to go to Gerő's office and shoot him. 'Because of that bastard Gerő', the man said while being forcibly restrained, 'we're all going to die.'

Around eight-thirty that evening, the revolution broke out when AVO marksmen guarding the Radio headquarters fired shots from the top of a neighbouring building. No one was injured, but hopes that this would be an isolated incident faded as reports came in of irate civilians surrounding a motorized army detachment and successfully pleading for arms to defend themselves against the 'murderers in the AVO'. A gun battle ensued, which escalated when two further motorized units, sent to try and put a halt to the carnage, ended up by distributing more arms to the crowd. Later that night news came that Soviet tanks were entering the city from the south-west corner of Buda. Soon they were firing indiscriminately at lighted windows, endangering even the lives of Kopácsi's men and other supposed friends.

Kopácsi, as horrified by this Soviet invasion as he was by the brutalities of the AVO, found himself increasingly unsure about his loyalties, and was naïvely surprised to discover that many of the rebelling citizens whom he was struggling to control were card-carrying members of the Communist party. Left by his besieged superiors to fend for himself, and with a minimum of ammunition, he also faced the very real possibility of being soon unable to defend his own headquarters. The next day, when his building was under attack from young snipers positioned in the block opposite, his wife paid him a visit to persuade him to hang out the Hungarian flag of the insurgents. An hour or so later Imre Nagy was reinstated as prime minister.

Intense fighting continued throughout the city over the next few days, during which time Kopácsi helped bring about negotiations between the Hungarian army and the insurgents, three of whose leaders had been turned overnight into working-class heroes—the brothers Pongrátz (who established their headquarters in the Ferencváros of Attila József fame) and István Angyal, who had as his stronghold one of Budapest's oldest cinemas, the Corvin. They defended themselves with anti-tank weapons and other arms obtained from a factory in Angyal's home district of Csepel, which had the reputation of being the most staunchly communist part of the city. 'Red Csepel', as it was still known, now played a major role in forcing the Soviet army to beat a hasty retreat from Budapest as early as 29 October. A dazed and jubilant Hungary, foolishly confident about receiving the support of the West, enjoyed a few days of relative calm in which the AVO was disbanded and a National Guard formed in its place.

The major and most horrifying disturbance took place on 30 October outside the Budapest Party Committee headquarters at Köztársaság tér 26–7 (this is now the Hungarian Socialist Party offices), where ex-AVO and other army officers had assembled, together with a huge arsenal of weapons. Soon they were opening fire on anyone who approached the building, until they were finally forced to surrender after the insurgents used tanks to break down the walls. Though carrying a white flag as they walked out into the street, many of the building's occupiers were executed on the spot, including the former partisan and Spanish Civil

War veteran Imre Mező—a friend of both Kopácsi and the member of Nagy's government who would soon become Hungary's Soviet-appointed premier, János Kádár. The killing of Mező, a relatively moderate politician, was reputedly influential in making Kádár opportunistically switch his allegiance from Nagy back to the Soviets.

The hot autumn of 1956 came symbolically to an end with the arrival of November, which brought a heavy frost to the streets of Budapest; by 4 November the Soviet tanks were back. Armed workers fought to prevent them from entering the city at the Széna tér; students along the Móricz Zsigmond körtér stalled the vehicles by throwing oil on the cobblestones; and heated battles broke out at the Kilian army barracks (at the junction of Üllői út and József körút) and at the Corvin cinema. But there was a limit to the amount of resistance that the Hungarians were able to put up, given the relatively small number of their civilian fighters (an estimated 5,000) and the reluctance of Nagy to lose thousands more men in an outright war against the Soviet Union in which Hungary, unaided by the West, stood little chance of winning.

Nagy took refuge in the Yugoslav embassy, which overlooked the bronze boots which were all that remained of the city's destroyed statue of Stalin. Captured shortly afterwards on his acceptance of an armistice agreement, he was taken to Romania and kept prisoner for almost two years, together with members of his revolutionary council. They were secretly returned to Budapest and executed in the Kozma utca prison; their bodies were buried in unmarked graves in the most remote corner of Pest's Új Köztemető cemetery. Kopácsi, arrested for his refusal to aid the returning Soviet forces, expected a similar fate, but instead languished in prison until 1963, when an amnesty was reached between Khrushchev and Kennedy; his father, whom he had not seen since 1956, died just a few hours before his release. He spent a further twelve years subject to constant harassment and surveillance before being allowed to emigrate to Canada, where he worked as a janitor while writing his sarcastically titled memoir *In the Name of the Working Class* (1979).

The uprising, though lasting only two weeks, was enormous in its impact: apart from making 200,000 Hungarians flee the country, it irreparably damaged the international communist movement (in Britain alone one-third of the entire party membership resigned in protest), facilitated the eventual emergence of more liberal approaches towards radical politics, and provided a model for Prague in 1968 and for the East European revolutions of 1989–90. It also helped significantly to change the way in which Hungarians thought about their capital city. From having been once regarded as a centre of cosmopolitan modernity antagonistic to the true Hungarian spirit, Budapest became a place associated with one of the bravest patriotic rebellions of the twentieth century: the 'sinful city' had finally atoned for its sins, and could claim to be as profoundly Hungarian as the most traditional parts of the countryside.

Despite the executions and multitude of imprisonments, the aftermath of the uprising could not nearly compare in its grimness with the Stalinist period. Kádár, who had himself spent time in prison under Rákosi, was by no means the hardliner whom one might have expected the Soviets to have chosen as Nagy's successor. Attempting to normalize a country devastated by revolution, Kádár adopted a conciliatory policy that was expressed in his slogan 'Who isn't against us is with us'— an inversion of the famous Stalinist threat 'Who isn't with us is against us'. The recovery of the country's economy by 1963 was accompanied by a political thaw, which in turn developed into a process of economic reform that encouraged decision-making at a local level and gave greater emphasis to market forces; after 1979, when Hungary entered its period of so-called 'goulash socialism', a limited amount of private enterprise was allowed, and Hungary came to be known among cynical capitalists as the country where Marxism 'almost works'. Kádár, who had overseen all these changes, was Hungary's ruler for nearly thirty-three years, at the end of which he had come to inspire—as the elderly Franz Joseph had done—a certain degree of fondness among the Hungarian people.

One of the more enlightened pronouncements from the early days of Kádár's rule was a statement made by his then minister of culture, György Aczél, calling for the publication even 'of works that are not socialist in their conception but that possess artistic merit'. This statement, almost heretical in the context of the eastern Europe of this time, heralded a resurgence in Hungary's cultural life, which had been so greatly constrained in the postwar years by Stalinist demands of realism and political relevance.

To the outside world this resurgence was manifested at first above all in films, which had been characterized during the Stalinist period by the application of an Italian neo-realism to the rural themes of Hungarian populism. The change towards a more adventurous cinema was initiated in 1958 by the foundation in Budapest of the Béla Balázs Studio (named after Bartók's librettist)—an experimental workshop which gave graduates of the Film Academy the unique opportunity of making their first films, independent of official production. Of the many new Hungarian directors to come to the fore in the subsequent decade, the most promoted abroad was initially Miklós Jancsó, whose typical themes and distinctive style were first fully displayed in *The Round-Up* (1965): set in Hungary in the wake of the revolution of 1848–9, it features ritualized, balletic movements, long tracking shots of the Great Hungarian Plain, faceless, interchangeable oppressors, and metaphors of innocence in the shape of naked young women.

Other directors of this generation, such as Márta Mészáros, Károly Makk, István Gaál, Péter Bacsó, and István Szabó (best known abroad for his *Mephisto* of 1981), were united in their refusal to work from meticulously prepared, ideologically approved scripts, and in their obsession with their country's recent past, which was often treated obliquely (in particular the uprising), both so as to avoid political censorship and to escape from the heavy-handed naturalism that had weighed down so many of the films of their predecessors. The past was often viewed either with surreal humour, as in Bacsó's hilarious satire of Rákosi's Hungary, *The Witness* (1969), or else through the veil of memories, as in Szabó's poetic chronicle about an old Budapest block *25 Fireman's Street* (1973).

These cinematic developments were echoed in the finest fiction of this period, which, escaping from the worthy realism and populism of the 1950s, rose to new heights of irreverence and daydreaming. Two writers of an earlier generation who came into their own during the 1960s were Iván Mándy and István Örkény, both of whom represented a type of author conspicuously absent in earlier Hungarian literature—an unashamedly urban type, unimaginable outside the context of Budapest, and unaffected by sentimental, rural longings.

'I was born in Budapest in 1918,' wrote Mándy; 'I cannot think of a better phrase to sum up my life. I owe everything to that city: she has profoundly influenced my life and my career . . . I've rarely left it, and always for very short periods, but whenever I've done so, if only to visit a suburb, I'm seized by a violent nostalgia.' After spending much of his childhood and adolescence in extreme poverty and living out of a suitcase, Mándy had looked forward to a better life in the socialist Hungary of the postwar years; but instead he was denounced as a bourgeois writer, and made to eke out a living through a variety of literary hack jobs, including transcribing the radio plays of others. Able to return to the

writing of his own novels after 1963, he wrote in a fragmentary and surrealistic style largely about the poorer inhabitants of the Józsefváros or
Eighth District. His protagonists are usually barely disguised *alter egos*
who look back with dark humour to their absurd ways of subsistence
during the 1950s, and who share his overwhelming passions for football
and the cinema, which provide them with the main outlet for their
dreams.

The history of Hungary since the First World War, with its bewilder-
ing succession of political systems, was reflected at its most absurd level
in the writings of Örkény, who was born in 1912 but had to wait until
the mid-1960s to find the perfect literary form in which to express his
elliptical and grotesquely funny talent. His 'one-minute stories', which
the author intended to be read in less than the time it takes to boil an
egg or dial a phone number, were seen by him as the inevitable outcome
of having had to write largely in secret and in the 'precious few hours'
that he was able to 'wrench from the inexorable march of history'. His
One-Minute Biography gives a characteristically witty account of a life
which he describes as having been 'one of continual decline' from the
time when he was a beautiful baby: 'Not only did I lose much of my
extreme good looks, but some of my hair and a few of my teeth as well.
What's more, I haven't been able to live up to what the world has
expected of me.' He went on to evoke a life in which his early ambition
to become a writer was constantly being thwarted—by his father's insistence that he study first pharmacy and then chemical engineering, by
the outbreak of war immediately after he had completed these courses,
by the wasting of a further four and a half years as a prisoner of war in
Russia, by the trials and tribulations of the Stalinist years . . .

Not even the *samizdat feuilletons* of the Czech writer Ludvík Vaculík
achieved the ironic concision that Örkény did in such commentaries on
totalitarian terror as this four-line story about the Rajk show trial:
'Foreign Minister László Rajk, the respected Party man, was sentenced
to death today. His execution, carried out at his own request, will take
place before a select audience of invited dignitaries.' This is humour
wholly in the spirit of Budapest, born amidst the gossip, cafés, petty
bureaucracy, and at times hypocritical gentility of a city that Örkény lovingly mocks in a story featuring 'The Great Hungarian Lexicon':
'BUDAPEST,' the entry reads, 'pop. 1,800,000. Founded by the weaver
Antal Valero in 1776 as a silk works and built in accordance with blue-
prints by architect Hildin Valero. The rest did not turn out so well.'

Something of Örkény's humour and concision might perhaps have benefited the writings of György Konrád, who was the first of Hungary's postwar novelists to be widely translated. He achieved international renown with his first and most powerful novel, *The Case Worker* (1969), a 'one-day story' drawing on his own experiences of working for a Budapest child-welfare organization. Virtually plotless, it holds the reader's attention with its stream-of-consciousness reflections of life spent in a Budapest whose grey, decaying apartment blocks and suicide-obsessed lives have rarely been so well conveyed in prose. In later works such as *The Loser* (which was published in Paris in 1980, three years before being allowed to appear in Hungary), his style becomes more rambling still as it expands to embrace memories that stretch over forty years of misery.

The historical soul-searching that is such a feature of post-Stalinist Hungarian culture was developed even further in the early novels of Konrád's younger contemporary Péter Nádas, whose *A Book of Memoirs* (1986) is thought by many to be a masterpiece on the themes of memory, personal identity, and historical continuity. But with the work of Péter Esterházy, the current international star of Hungarian fiction, profound questions about national destiny were replaced by a post-modern playfulness that challenges the Hungarian writer's perceived role over the centuries as social reformer and national spokesman. 'It might be more reassuring', he reflects at one point in his literary compendium *An Introduction to Literature* (1986), 'if the writer thought less in terms of the people and the nation, and more in terms of subject and predicate.' Esterházy's love of linguistic virtuosity over subject-matter can prove trying and tiresome, despite the rich vein of humour shown in such a work as *A Little Hungarian Pornography* (1984), which contrasts the elemental terrors experienced by Hungarians under Stalinism with the hypocrisy and fear underlying most people's attitudes towards sex. Only perhaps in his *Helping Verbs of the Heart* (1985)—which is centred around the author's visits to his dying mother—is the cleverness of the style matched by a text that is also emotionally engaging. This moving short novel, the product of a Hungary under a dying communism, has a foreword significantly dated 16 June, which is not only Joyce's 'Bloomsday' but also the day when Imre Nagy was executed—and the day on which Nagy would be publicly reburied in 1989 in a ceremony marking the beginning of a new era in Hungarian history.

My own contact with Hungary had begun in the early days of

'goulash socialism', when I had come to know, through my artist friend
Árpád Szabados, a group of dissident intellectuals associated with a
provocative cultural journal called *Mozgó Világ*, 'The Moving World'.
Shortly before my first visit to the country, the journal's entire staff had
resigned in protest against the sacking of the main editor, who had commissioned articles on such controversial subjects as homosexuality in
Hungary, and the acute housing shortage in Budapest. Faced now with
a great amount of free time, and anxious to maintain a sense of solidarity, those who had been connected with the journal sought the slightest pretext to organize alcohol-fuelled group activities, to which I was
sometimes invited. On one occasion I found myself picking cherries in
a Chekhovian private garden in Buda; on another I was confronting Péter
Esterházy across a football pitch.

Wholly unfit, and barely aware of the rules of football, I had agreed
to take part in this match under the mistaken illusion that a game involving teams made up respectively of writers and artists would be an effete
and unchallenging affair even by my own low standards. All that daunted
me was having to play against Esterházy, whom I did not know then as
a writer, but as a virtual embodiment of Hungarian history—as someone
whose descendants included a seventeenth-century palatine of Hungary,
the patrons of Haydn, a minister in Hungary's revolutionary government
of 1848, the dedicatee of one of my favourite cakes, and Hungary's prime
minister during the First World War. Fortunately I was unaware until the
match had begun that he—like the rest of the group—was a player of
almost professional standard, and that he had a brother who indeed
formed part of the national football team.

The fanaticism and aggression that the *Mozgó Világ* group revealed on
the football field were matched by the intensity of their passion for
culture. Though unable still to travel or publish freely, or enjoy many
material comforts, they seemed at least to find spiritual consolation in
the arts, which were then supported by the state to an extent that would
be unheard of in most Western countries of today. My artist friends might
have lived simply, but they did so in state-provided studios that their
Western counterparts would have envied. And on my many visits to the
city's bookshops I was unfailingly impressed by the range of world literature available in cheap Hungarian editions, including many works by
foreign authors who had yet to be translated into English. All this was
to change over the coming years, in keeping with the rapid process of

liberalization that the dissidents of *Mozgó Világ* had so strongly campaigned for.

Every time I returned to Budapest in the 1980s, I observed the growing signs of a society becoming more materialistic and less willing to devote money to culture. The famous Adidas store that was opened on the Váci utca in 1985 drew the sort of crowds that might once have formed on the day of publication of a new Hungarian novel or book of poems. Publishing houses meanwhile were concentrating ever more on subjects such as cooking and dieting; and cultural journals such as *Mozgó Világ* were being crowded off the shelves by fashion and lifestyle magazines. The prospect of imminent political change became increasingly the main focus of interest of Hungary's intellectuals.

Early in 1988 Árpád took me into one of Pest's typically dark and decaying apartment blocks to attend a political meeting: the occasion had a subversive feel to it, but in fact the meeting had been organized by one of Hungary's first democratic movements officially tolerated by the Communist party—the future Association of Free Democrats. On 15 March of that year, the day of Petőfi's revolutionary address to the Hungarian people, the traditional large-scale celebrations on the steps of the National Museum were allowed for the first time in nearly forty years. Many Hungarians, remembering 1956, feared that the celebrations of that day would spiral out of control; but when communism eventually collapsed in Hungary, it was to do so in an orderly and entirely peaceful way.

The beginnings of the end were signalled during the party conference held in May, when Kádár and other members of the old guard were removed from the Politburo and replaced by a younger and more liberal leadership headed by Károly Grósz. Kádár died in July the following year, and was buried in grand style in the same cemetery—the Kerepesi—where such great heroes of Hungarian history as Deák, Batthyány, and Kossuth had also been laid to rest. Grósz was disagreeably surprised by the enormous amount of respect that the dead Kádár seemed to inspire; but the crowds who lined up to see the grave were there to commemorate the passing not only of a person but also of an era. A few weeks earlier, in the more distant Új Köztemető, another event of great symbolic resonance had taken place—the reburial of Imre Nagy, whose skeleton, with its bound feet and hands, had been identified among the unmarked graves where the victims of 1956 had been placed.

An undertaking was made to create for the site a large memorial to be built by a leading avant-garde artist.

During this same eventful summer of 1989, thousands of East Germans were allowed to enter the West through Hungarian territory; the barbed-wire fence on Hungary's border with Austria was ceremonially cut; and a declaration was made allowing political parties to form with a view to their taking part in democratic elections in the near future. Later that year the government announced that these elections would be held in March 1990.

The communists, split now into the Hungarian Socialist Party and the hardcore Workers' Party, were heavily defeated in these elections by the Hungarian Democratic Forum, which won only a small victory over the Association of Free Democrats. The Democratic Forum, led by József Antall, was an alarmingly conservative and nationalistic party that espoused many of the views on Hungarian racial purity associated with Populism: significantly, it had taken shape at a meeting organized not in Budapest but in the outlying village of Lakitelek.

My first encounter with the new democratic Hungary did not take place until late in 1993, a few weeks before the death of Antall from cancer. Árpád, collecting me from the airport, tried to bring me up to date with all the changes that had occurred since my last visit. From a personal point of view, the most significant was that the close-knit circle of friendships that had once existed in the orbit of *Mozgó Világ* had been irreparably damaged. No one had time to see anyone any more, particularly as so many of them had exchanged a full-time dedication to the study or practice of the arts for prominent positions in the new cultural and political hierarchy: thus, a specialist in medieval architecture had become minister in charge of the Hungarian minorities, while a former university lecturer in English was now running a leading conservative newspaper. Politics had in turn set friends and colleagues against each other, with everyone accusing everybody else of being either former communist collaborators or else extreme nationalists with racist tendencies. Charges of virulent anti-semitism were even being levelled against the visionary architect Imre Makovecz, who was now attracting worldwide fame (and the attentions of Britain's Prince Charles) for his traditionally crafted wooden structures; I found it difficult to reconcile this image of a nationalist fanatic with the kind and courteous man I remembered from the cherry-picking days.

I spent the next weeks adjusting to a Budapest from which all obvious traces of its communist past had been removed: streets had reverted to their nineteenth-century names ('why get rid of poor Mayakovsky?', Árpád had complained); and statues of Lenin and other Soviet heroes had been taken away to a specially created park beyond the city limits, where they could now be enjoyed as amusing kitsch by tourists and young Hungarians alike. Rampant Westernization had somehow accentuated the evocative shabbiness of so much of the city: crumbling, shrapnel-marked masonry stood out the more for being next to the glistening steel and glass headquarters of Western banks, or to giant billboards promoting a suggestive use of Magnum Bars. The past was being papered over by the symbols of American-style consumerism: the four corners of the elegant Oktogon, which the Romanians had once desecrated, were now all occupied by American fast-food chains, one of which had even taken over the magnificently appointed turn-of-the-century restaurant attached to the Western Railway Station. A job in McDonald's, I was told, was one of the most sought after in the city.

Young foreign settlers had become very much in evidence, and included numerous young Americans of bohemian aspirations who thought of the city as a new Paris. They enjoyed the cheap prices, the atmosphere of sexual promiscuity, and the burgeoning 'alternative' night life of a kind disappearing elsewhere in Europe. One of the more popular of the new nocturnal venues was the music bar called Tilos Az Á (on the Mikszáth Kálmán tér), which absurdly took its name from the new cult book of the city's teenagers—Milne's Winnie the Pooh. The bar's chaotic, perpetually noisy interior was populated by a mixture of foreigners and privileged young Hungarians, notably members of the FIDESZ, a liberal political party that reputedly attracted the children of former high-ranking communists. There were times inside this bar when I was reminded of Márai's description of the AVO officers on the balcony.

The Tilos Az Á had closed down when I went back to Hungary in the summer of 1996: its closure was interpreted by some cultural commentators as bringing to an end the initial phase in Hungary's transition to democracy. The FIDESZ itself had lost much of its former popularity, and had fared disappointingly in the national elections of June 1994, when the Democratic Forum was decisively defeated by a Socialist party led by Gyula Horn, a former communist foreign minister. Under this new socialist government, devaluations and drastic cuts had been made in an attempt to stabilize the economy of a country in which the gap between rich and poor was continuing to widen. I discovered that the fashionable meeting-places of the moment—such as the Incognito and the Café Mediterrán on the formerly quiet Liszt Ferenc tér—no longer cultivated the anarchic, experimental look of the Tilos Az Á but aimed instead to appeal to the more conventional, comfort-loving tastes of a new Hungarian elite comprising mainly entrepreneurs or those working for Western employers.

Western art galleries and publishers provided the main financial support for many of the dissidents from the days of *Mozgó Világ*, several of whom had acquired once again the status of political opponents. Some of them had joined an alternative Hungarian Academy founded by the architect Makovecz in a building of his (in Óbuda) that incorporated Renaissance capitals from the time of Matthias Corvinus. I attended one of its meetings—held under a huge painted ceiling of the zodiac—and was relieved to find that in the changing Hungary of today there were places where traditional Hungarian generosity and love of the good life had remained undiminished: a conference table groaning as this one was under pastries, wine, and spirits would have been difficult to conceive anywhere else.

Frequently in the course of this last visit to Budapest, I thought back to the city I had first known, and became increasingly conscious that these memories were of a period that already seemed like distant history to a young generation of Hungarians. The first doctoral dissertations on *Mozgó Világ* were beginning to appear, I was told by Réka Szabó, a 22-year-old editorial assistant who came with me one morning to the Új Köztemető cemetery to see the ultimate symbol of the new Hungary— György Jovánovics's memorial to Imre Nagy and the victims of 1956. Réka's boss handed me a CD-Rom summarizing the complex history of this monumental abstract work. He himself had been present at Nagy's reburial—a momentous historical event that Réka had apparently missed out on. 'She was too young at the time,' he said with an ironic grin. 'Instead of joining the large queues in the cemetery, she was out hunting for food for her hamsters.'

In this Hungary where memories even of the recent past were fast fading, I sometimes regretted not having spent more time in the company of elderly witnesses to the war and the uprising. I was hoping in 1996 to go and visit Árpád's Scottish mother, but she had died a few months before my arrival. Instead I paid my pilgrimage to the past by going to the parental home of Árpád's sculptress wife Ildikó Várnagy, who had been brought up in a part of Budapest that evoked for me more than any other the troubled history of twentieth-century Hungary—'Red Csepel'.

The district's high-tech monument glorifying the Soviet Union had been ingeniously transformed into a Volkswagen salesroom; but the place seemed otherwise the same as ever, only more polluted and decayed. Ildikó's parents had lived since their marriage in a one-storeyed home whose prewar landlords had recently reacquired the freehold. The parents were now being charged a hugely increased rent for a house that was rapidly falling down through rot and neglect. Over the years Ildikó had stored in its rooms her remarkable sculptures, which were disintegrating at the same pace as their surroundings, and now were barely indistinguishable from the chaos of rotten floorboards, damp-destroyed plaster, and musty furniture.

I stepped into the wasteland of a garden to pay my respects to Ildikó's father, a philosopher; but he just sat there silently, an overcoat over his dressing-gown, staring towards an abandoned railway track. Gestures from the mother indicated that his mind had gone completely since the last time I saw him.

Then she took me back inside to show me a sight of almost unbearable poignancy: stacked in neat bundles between the fridge and the remains of the ceiling were literally hundreds of notebooks containing a lifetime of her husband's philosophical reflections. Written as if in a secret code, unpublished, and now bound together by a grey film of grease, they conveyed through their appearance alone the collected memories of the Hungary through which he had lived.

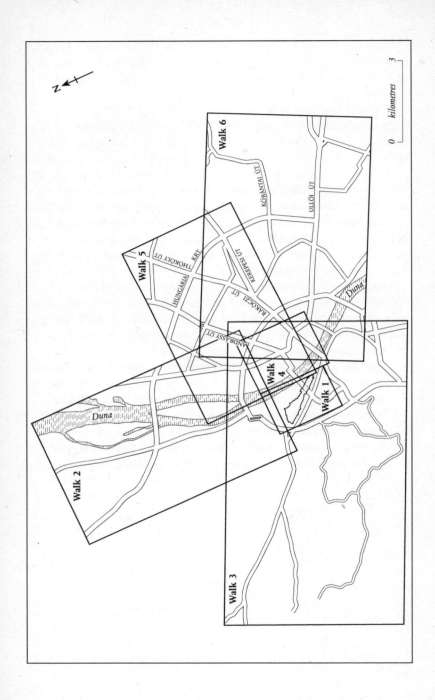

Walk 6

Walk 5

HUNGÁRIA KRT

THÖKÖLY ÚT

KÖBÁNYAI ÚT

ÜLLŐI ÚT

KEREPESI ÚT

RÁKÓCZI ÚT

ANDRÁSSY ÚT

Duna

Walk 4

Walk 1

Walk 2

Duna

Walk 3

N

0   kilometres   3

Part Two: *Walks*

The time has now come to take the reader on a tour through each of the city's main districts, stopping to look not only at all the major monuments but also at a personal selection of lesser-known sights. Among these are a number of bars, restaurants, and hotels that I have chosen mainly for their historical, architectural, or sociological interest (one or two of my favourite eating and drinking establishments have also slipped in, but not, unfortunately, the remote and isolated Sport vendéglo (Csömöri utca 198), where you can eat such exotic specialities as frog-leg stew with gnocchi in a setting of barn-like simplicity). The information given is intended to supplement that of the main body of the text (to which numerous cross-references are made), and has also been arranged in such a way as to provide a roughly chronological account of the city's development, beginning with the First district and proceeding in numerical order to the Ninth district and beyond. Although these itineraries are labelled 'walks', the distances are at times so great that you will have to resort to Budapest's cheap and excellent public transport system. This will take you to within one hundred metres or so of almost every place mentioned below (the transport details given in the text can be supplemented by one of the city maps or atlases published by Cartographia; anyone staying in the city for more than three days should also purchase a weekly, fortnightly, or monthly travel-pass).

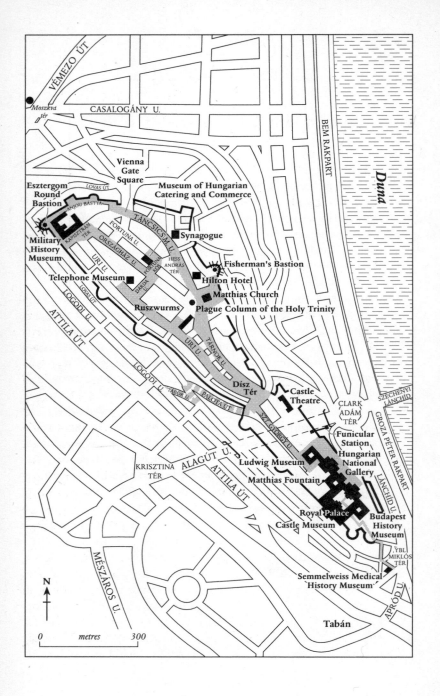

VÉMEZŐ ÚT

Moszkva tér

CASALOGÁNY U.

BEM RAKPART

Duna

Vienna Gate Square

Esztergom Round Bastion

LOVAS ÚT

ANJOU BÁSTYA

Museum of Hungarian Catering and Commerce

TÁNCSICS M. U.

Synagogue

KAPISZTRÁN TÉR

FORTUNA U.

Military History Museum

ORSZÁGHÁZ U.

HESS ANDRÁS TÉR

Fisherman's Bastion

DARDA U.

FORTUNA U.

URI U.

Telephone Museum

Hilton Hotel

LOVAS ÚT

Matthias Church

LOGODI U.

Ruszwurms

Plague Column of the Holy Trinity

ATTILA ÚT

URI U.

TÁRNOK U.

LOGODI U.

Dísz Tér

TÁBOR U.

PALOTA ÚT

Castle Theatre

CLARK ADÁM TÉR

SZ. GYÖRGY U.

SZÉCHENYI LÁNCHID

Funicular Station

KRISZTINA TÉR

ALAGÚT U.

Ludwig Museum

Hungarian National Gallery

ATTILA ÚT

Matthias Fountain

GROZA PÉTER RAKPART

LÁNCHID U.

Royal Palace

Budapest History Museum

Castle Museum

MÉSZÁROS U.

YBL MIKLÓS TÉR

Semmelweiss Medical History Museum

APRÓD U.

N

Tabán

0   metres   300

❧❧ Walk 1 ❧❧

The Castle Hill

Buda's Castle district or **Vár** rises up above its ring of parkland and battlements to present a picturesque profile uniting baroque grandeur and Gothic fantasy. The most memorable feature on the Budapest skyline, this is the obvious starting-point for any sightseeing tour of the city, not least because of the all-embracing views from its terraces and bastions.

Forming today the nucleus of the city's First District, and containing nearly all Budapest's surviving medieval monuments, this was the Buda that Béla IV had created in the wake of the Mongol invasion of 1241. With the emergence of the nineteenth-century metropolis, it was known for its conservative, traditional character, and for harbouring a high proportion of the city's fast-diminishing German population; it would also have seemed increasingly rustic, dirty, and old-fashioned in relation to the rapidly developing township on the other side of the river. The streets of Buda, wrote the French traveller Victor Tissot in 1880, had a 'rural aspect. Large carts incessantly pass, yoked to oxen or horses with grey harness, ornamented with crescents and figures of copper. The courtyards of the inns are full of these rustic vehicles, which carry corn, wine, fruits, and tobacco.' Despite this evident quaintness, and the place's enormous historical importance, the district as a whole did not as yet appeal greatly to tourists, most of whom were drawn instead to the city's smarter and more modern aspects.

One of the first foreigners openly to prefer the shabby, modest architecture of the Castle district to the fashionable eclecticism so prevalent elsewhere in the city was Jerome Tharaud, a French visitor of 1899. In this district's 'sleepy old streets', with their tastefully simple 'old yellow houses', and decaying courtyards with 'rusted wells', Tharaud found that he could 'hear the murmuring of history' better than he could amidst all the city's 'neo-medieval sham'. This opinion would be shared by the

British travel-writer Patrick Leigh Fermor, whose fairy-tale memories of Budapest in the 1930s were greatly conditioned by his having been put up in a house in the Castle district exuding faded gentility.

By Leigh Fermor's day the romantic potential of the district had given it a reputation as 'Hungary's Faubourg Saint-Germain', according to the writer Sándor Márai. But the place's present showpiece character does not date until after the Second World War, when extensive bomb damage not only initiated a major programme of restoration but also revealed many of the medieval elements underlying the baroque and rococo façades. Cars and coaches were later excluded from its streets, which came increasingly to be lined with restaurants, souvenir shops, and art galleries. A Hilton hotel was created in 1976 on the ruins of a Dominican monastery; and there was even talk in the mid-1980s of selling off some of the houses for conversion into luxury apartments for the Japanese market. Commercialization increased with the collapse of communism, and has given to the district some of the phoney, stage-set quality that Tharaud had criticized in other parts of the city.

Anyone visiting the district for the first time should try now and come here as early as possible in the morning, when the 'murmuring of history' still stands a chance of being heard over the chattering of tourists. The usual approach by public transport is from Buda's Moszkva tér, where you can catch the small 'Vár' bus, which departs at regular short intervals on a circular route around the district; but a more special journey is by the No. 16 bus, which departs from Pest's Erzsébet tér, and provides a wonderful introductory glimpse of Budapest as you cross the Danube on the Chain Bridge, and then climb up the Castle Hill from the Clark Ádám tér. Those wishing to walk to the top—'a very precipitous approach', in the words of Julia Pardoe in 1840—should alight at the latter square, and make their way up the steep parkland that lies off the Hunyadi János utca. From this same square you can also reach the Vár by using the world's second oldest funicular service, which was built in 1870 on the initiative of Count István Széchenyi's son Ödön. Victor Tissot travelled in this 'tooth-wheeled, almost perpendicular railway' in 1880, and likened the sensation to 'being let down in a basket from a tower by a crane'. The original funicular, which functioned up to the Second World War, was replaced in 1986 by an electrically operated copy that does the journey in just under a minute; the turn-of-the-century fittings are very much in the ersatz spirit of the district you are about to visit.

The No. 16 bus will leave you at the narrow **Dísz tér**, which marks the northern and main approach to the enormous Royal Palace complex, where the funicular terminal is to be found. The square itself, and all the narrow streets to the north, constitute the part of the Castle district known as the Polgárváros or 'Citizens' Town', which retains its medieval street plan, as well as the cheerful rows of steep-roofed, pastel-coloured houses that were rebuilt over medieval structures after the departure of the Turks in 1686. The wealth of thirteenth- to fifteenth-century detailing uncovered during the Second World War include a total of sixty-three niches attached to the portals: the purpose of this peculiarly Hungarian feature has been much debated, one bizarre suggestion being that they were used as stalls by broadcloth tailors.

If you head north from the Dísz tér along the Tárnok utca (which is named after the court functionary who dealt with royal revenues), you will be following the street where the German burghers once held their weekly market. The street, with its charming mid-eighteenth-century pharmacy at No. 18 (now a museum), broadens out into the square named after its baroque 'Plague Column' of the Holy Trinity (Szentháromság) and dominated by the extravagantly pinnacled Church of Our Lady, which had originally served as the parish church to the Germans. Popularly known as the **Matthias Church** (see p. 6), and today the main focus for sightseers in Budapest, this building in its present state has perhaps a greater historical and symbolical value than it does a structural or artistic appeal. Great historical events have taken place here— the coronation of Charles of Anjou in 1309, the two marriages of Matthias Corvinus, and the crowning in 1867 of Franz Joseph as king of Hungary (the occasion for which Liszt wrote his famous Coronation Mass). But the vicissitudes of taste and Hungarian history have not treated the structure kindly. Begun by Béla IV on the site possibly of a romanesque foundation destroyed by the Mongols, the church became the first important example in Hungary of the French Gothic style. Remodelled as a hall church under Louis the Great and Sigismund of Luxemburg, and then further altered by Matthias Corvinus, the building was turned afterwards into a mosque by the Turks, who whitewashed the painted walls and removed all its furnishings, including two richly ornamented chandeliers that hang today in Santa Sofia's in Istanbul. After 1686 the church was entrusted first to the Franciscans and then to the Jesuits, who enlivened it with baroque trappings and erected alongside it a college and a seminary building. All these additions were stripped away at the end of the nineteenth century by Frigyes Schulek, who, after considerable archaeological and archival research, created a free-standing Gothic structure incorporating as much as possible of the original medieval features and masonry. This in turn suffered extensive Second World War damage that was only fully repaired in 1970.

Among the genuinely medieval parts of the church's exterior are the base of the south tower (which was rebuilt during Matthias's reign) and much of the adjoining Mary portal (on the south side of the building), which retains most of its naturalistic fourteenth-century carvings representing Christ in majesty, the death of the Virgin, and the eleventh-century Hungarian kings SS. Stephen and Ladislas. Once inside the church (the usual entrance is through the Mary portal), the task of sorting out the medieval from the eclectic is made difficult by the overall gloom and the dense covering of turn-of-the-century painted decorations, including many uninspired historical scenes by the prolific Károly Lotz. The double sarcophagus of King Béla III and his wife, Anne of Châtillon, can be seen in the second chapel on the north side of the building; and there is a crypt featuring fragments of the original building, as well as a red marble sarcophagus containing bones found in the royal tombs at Székesfehérvár. But the interior is perhaps best enjoyed if you come here primarily to attend either a concert or else one of the choral and orchestral masses that are held here every Sunday at ten in the morning (the church, with its excellent acoustics, has enjoyed a reputation for music since Matthias's day).

The extent to which Schulek became lost in his world of medieval make-believe is revealed as you leave the building and walk east past the limestone plinth he designed for Alajos Stróbl's impressive bronze equestrian **statue of Stephen I** (the king who brought Christianity to Hungary in the early eleventh century): a relief at the back of this plinth shows the bearded Schulek presenting the king with a model of his church. The statue itself, combining baroque monumentality with a stylized, finely detailed medievalism, is similarly free in its rendering of history: Stephen's crown, copied from an actual one in the National Museum, is much later in date than the one he would have worn.

Schulek seems better as an architect the less he attempts blindly to imitate the past, as in his endearingly imaginative **Fishermen's bastion**, which runs behind the apse of the church, and provides the building with a wonderfully theatrical terrace. Though a replacement of the original medieval ramparts (which were traditionally said to have been defended by members of the Fishermen's Guild), Schulek's extraordinary neo-romanesque structure bears no relation to any known medieval defence system, and is merely a decorative flight of fancy commanding outstanding views over the Danube to Pest. Understandably, this was once a favourite nocturnal spot for lovers, who could hide among the romanesque nooks and crannies while enjoying a panorama of the city's lights. However, the recent introduction of an entrance fee has turned this into a domain solely for tourists, who have now to endure the continual and competing strains of violin and piano music.

The northern end of the bastion adjoins the **Hilton Hotel**, which has been variously described as a successful blending of the old and the new, and a hideous modern intrusion that has dropped on medieval Buda like a Martian spaceship. Occupying the site of a mid-thirteenth-century Dominican monastery appropriated later by the Jesuits, it brings together such disparate architectural elements as an eighteenth-century façade, the enormous ruins of a Cistercian Gothic church, and great sheets of tinted plate glass: this potentially explosive mixture is tempered by an overall atmosphere reminiscent of an airport lounge.

In earlier times the only lodging-house in Buda had been the Red Hedgehog inn, which stands adjacent to the Hilton's main entrance, at the junction of the Táncsics Mihály utca and the Hess András tér. Originally a private house dating back at least to 1390, this was converted in 1686 into an inn where occasional balls and theatrical events were also held. The building, with its neo-classical main façade, and Gothic side-entrance and window (on the Fortuna utca), typifies the architectural palimpsest that is Buda. A similar mixture of the medieval and the neo-classical is also evident in the neighbouring house (now a restaurant) at No. 4 Hess András tér, where, on entering the gateway, you will find some fine examples of the district's mysterious wall-niches; beyond is an especially attractive courtyard that has now lost its former quiet charm thanks to the creation right in the middle of it of a tourist bookshop and cafeteria.

A contrast to the toy-like, medieval-based architecture that occupies so much of the Castle district is the grand and wholly baroque mansion at No. 7 Táncsics Mihály utca, just to the north of the Hilton. This former private residence of the Erdődy family was built in the mid-eighteenth century by the minor Viennese architect Mátyás Nepauer, who gave the building additional prominence by using a forecourt to set it back from the narrow street. Presumably on the basis that Beethoven had once stayed here, the mansion was turned in the mid-1980s into a **Music History Museum**. Anyone visiting this museum in the hope of seeing an atmospheric baroque interior will be disappointed, for the rooms have been starkly modernized and whitewashed; none the less the present light and airy setting, with its enchanting views down to the Danube, makes for an excellent, clear display of the old Hungarian instruments that form the nucleus of the collections.

From Hungary's musical past you move on into its Jewish past as you continue walking north along the Táncsics Mihály utca, and enter what had been the heart of Buda's sixteenth- and seventeenth-century Jewish quarter. Large numbers of Jews had settled in Buda after 1251 on the invitation of Béla IV—the first Hungarian monarch to show any degree of tolerance towards them: predecessors of his had passed laws preventing Jews from marrying Christians, engaging in agricultural activities, and holding public office. The first Jewish quarter had grown up almost on the threshold of the Royal Palace, around what is now the Fehérvári Gate (formerly the 'Jewish Gate'), off the southern corner of the Dísz tér. In the early fourteenth century, however, this first community was driven out of Buda by a combination of plague and enforced conversions. Returning to the town soon afterwards to find that their properties had been confiscated, the Jews founded a new quarter for themselves at the north-eastern corner of the Castle district. During the reign of the enlightened Matthias Corvinus, who established the titled position of *Prefektus* or 'principal of all Jews', this new community became the centre of Hungarian Jewish life, with an estimated population of around 500. It continued to flourish under the Turks, and indeed became in the seventeenth century the most important such community in the Ottoman empire; but the protection of the Turks meant also having to share the latter's fate in 1686: many of the Jews were massacred, and the rest were taken captive.

The properties at Nos. 23, 26, and 28 of the Táncsics Mihály utca belonged to the Mendel family, whose members held the title of *Prefektus* of the Jewish community from the time of King Matthias up to 1539. In the courtyard of No. 23, the foundations were discovered of a large synagogue dating back to 1461. Excavations carried out in the 1960s seemed to indicate that this had been one of Buda's finest late Gothic structures; but lack of funds later led to the reburial of the ruins. Anyone interested in the history of Jewish Buda has at least the satisfaction of being able to see at No. 26 the fascinating **Small Synagogue**, a whitewashed, cellar-like space in which a tiny Jewish museum has been laid out. There are tombstones and inscribed steles from the medieval Jewish cemetery, as well as a number of liturgical and everyday objects that have been bequeathed by Buda's Jews. But the interest of the museum is essentially the space itself, which functioned as a house of prayer during the Turkish occupation, and has curious drawings and inscriptions on its ceiling testifying to the Jews' constant state of alertness during this period as a result of the frequent Christian assaults on the town: 'Heroes might break their bows, but those who fall will gain new strength.' At the end of the Táncsics Mihály utca is a reminder of another troubled period in Jewish history: attached to the wall of the turn-of-the-century Lutheran Church is a bronze plaque commemorating Pastor Gábor Sztehlo, who, during the Second World War, saved 2,000 persecuted children, many of whom were Jewish. In 1984 an olive tree in his honour was placed in Jerusalem's Grove of the Faithful.

The Táncsics Mihály utca emerges into the Bécsi Kapu tér (the Vienna Gate Square), which had once been known as Jewish Street. The present gate, together with the statue of an angel in front of it, was erected in 1936 on the occasion of the 250th anniversary of the recapture of Buda by the Christians. Those wishing to spare a thought for the defeated Turks should go to the nearby **Esztergom round bastion**, which can be reached by walking west along the attractive promenade that follows the whole length of the northern and western ramparts, with their views towards the Buda hills. The bastion, at the north-western corner of Buda, has a symbolic tomb recording (in Hungarian and Turkish) that the last Turkish ruler of the town, Abdurrahman Abdi Aranaut Pasha, 'fell close to this spot in his 70th year on the afternoon of 2 September, 1686'. The memorial, curiously enough, was paid for in 1932 by the descendants of a young Hungarian soldier who had been killed on the very same day as Abdurrahman.

As a brief distraction from the theme of war you can peer from the northern ramparts down to the so-called '**Open Air Public Lighting Exhibition**', which is administered by the excellent 'Hungarian Electrotechnical Museum' in Pest (see pp. 186–7). This extensive collection of old street lamps dating from 1884 to 1944 is arranged in the parkland between the ramparts and the Lovas utca. It was formed at a time when the elegant and often exquisitely wrought examples of lighting on display here were being replaced throughout Budapest by more functional designs.

Continuing to walk around the tree-shaded ramparts, you will reach the main entrance to the **Military History Museum**, which was opened in 1937 in a grim late nineteenth-century barracks. The character of a barracks still survives in this drably old-fashioned institution, with its echoing corridors and large, little-visited rooms that tell the military history of Hungary from the War of Independence onwards; even the recent installation of a 1956 display fails to redeem the place's moribund atmosphere. Leaving the museum and the ramparts and turning left into the Kapisztrán tér, you are offered a further reminder of war in the surviving foundations and medieval tower of the former parish church of Buda's Hungarian community, the **Church of Mary Magdalene**: bombing in 1944 brought to an end a complex structural history dating back to the 1250s (see p. 7).

The main thoroughfare of medieval Buda, the Országház utca, connects the Kapisztrán tér with the Szentháromság tér to the south: named after the former Parliament building at No. 28, it features the Castle district's finest group of medieval houses (Nos. 18, 20, and 22), the central one of which has a delightful trefoil-arched cornice of the fourteenth century. The parallel street to the west is the long Úri utca—'a waving street of jutting windows, tiled roofs and arched doors with coats of arms', in the words of Patrick Leigh Fermor, who stayed here in 1933. The former telephone substation at No. 49 was turned in 1991 into the **Telephone Museum**, the popularity of which is due almost entirely to its being one of the few Hungarian museums where visitors can activate the objects on display: children reputedly love the opportunity to send faxes to each other or else to dial up a terrible Hungarian pop song of 1970. Another, longer-established museum is housed in a former late eighteenth-century inn at No. 6 of the nearby Fortuna utca (which runs to the east of the Országház utca and was originally called French Street after the French craftsmen who worked here in the Middle Ages). This is the **Museum of Hungarian Catering and Commerce**, which belies its unappealing name with an evocative display of reconstructed interiors ranging from coffee-houses to dining rooms: the elderly women who work here seem of an age comparable to much of what is on show, and reinforce the overall nostalgic atmosphere (which has miraculously survived the museum's recent revamping).

The history of Hungarian confectionery (so well documented in the museum) is likely to stimulate an interest in the actual eating of cakes and pastries. The Café Miró, at the corner of the Úri utca and the Szentháromság utca (which leads to the square of that name) is one of the smartest and most successful of the city's recently opened cafés; as its name suggests, its decor owes nothing to Hungarian tradition but everything to the work of the Catalan artist Joan Miró. Traditionalists will prefer the enchanting **Ruszwurm's** (at Szentháromság 7), which is a better example of a Biedermeier confectioners than the reconstructed one from Miskolc in the Museum of Catering and Commerce. The oldest surviving place of its kind in Hungary, Ruszwurm's was founded in 1827 by a Viennese confectioner called Franz Schwabl, who died three years later, leaving a widow who then married the court confectioner to the palatine Joseph, Leonard Richter. It was Richter who commissioned the mahogany-inlaid cherrywood furniture that still decorates the two barrel-vaulted rooms that make up this tiny establishment. Said by some to be the birthplace of the 'Linzer torte', Ruszwurm's was once popularized by aristocrats, army officers, and high-ranking officials, and could even boast as one of its apprentice confectioners a certain Baroness Blanka Korányi, a daughter of a minister of finance. The clientele had changed by the 1920s, according to a book written during that decade by Nándor Szücs and Jenö Komlós: 'Now grey-haired ladies from Buda and lovers from Pest while away the time at the tables. There is more talk of love in this confectioners' than in all the English novels.' Today the place is constantly crowded by tourists anxiously waiting for a table.

After being fortified by cakes and coffee, you may feel that the time has finally come to move towards the **Royal Palace**. There is little else to distract you in the Castle district, especially now that the privately owned Wax Museum at the southern end of the Úri utca has been closed (the museum itself was almost comically bad, but it allowed you access into the 10-km. labyrinth of caves and manmade passages that have been used for defensive purposes at various stages of Hungarian history, most recently during the Second World War).

The Royal Palace, enticing though it might be from a distance, becomes an increasingly daunting prospect as you approach it from the Dísz tér. There is also the shock, immediately on entering its enclosure from the south-eastern corner of the square, of seeing to your right the shell-marked ruins of the former Ministry of Defence: the only building in the Vár to have been left as it was after the war, it gives a good idea of the extent of the wartime devastation. Other buildings were either pulled down completely after 1945 or else largely rebuilt, as was the case with the Castle Theatre (on the eastern side of the Ministry of Defence), which was given a marble and concrete interior by the time it was finally reopened in 1978: originally part of a baroque monastery that was dissolved in 1784, it is famous for having been the venue, in 1790, for the first performance of a play in Hungarian. Also heavily restored is the neighbouring building to the south, the Sándor Palace, once the official residence of Hungarian prime ministers: it was here in 1941 that the pro-British premier Count Pál Teleki shot himself rather than condone Germany's invasion of Yugoslavia through Hungarian territory. In front of the palace extends the now largely bare Szent György tér, where government buildings had once stood; at the square's south-eastern corner is the pastiche late nineteenth-century funicular station, and a giant bronze statue of the mythical protector of the Hungarian people, the Turul Eagle.

A neo-baroque wrought-iron gateway opens above the double flight of steps leading down to the magnificently situated terrace where the main entrance to the Royal Palace is to be found. The view from here down to the Danube was described in 1869 by the British traveller W. P. Byrne as 'perhaps the finest . . . in the world'. 'No conqueror who ever took possession of this portion of the Danube', he wrote, 'could have failed to cast an admiring eye on the bold and commanding height which overlooks an almost boundless expanse, and to exclaim, "What a spot for a palace!".'

Rather less enthusiasm has generally been shown for the palace itself, which impressed Byrne primarily for being 'grand and imposing'. The building that he himself saw (considerably less grand and imposing than it would shortly become) was the 203-room structure that the Empress Maria Theresa had built in the late eighteenth century over the ruins of the medieval and Renaissance palace. After the Compromise of 1867, the architect Miklós Ybl planned large-scale extensions, one of which—the western wing now housing the National Library—was completed by the time of his death. Work was resumed in 1893 under the direction of Alajos Hauszmann, who added to the north a replica of the Maria Theresa wing, and joined the two blocks together with a domed central section. Sándor Márai dismissed the overall result as 'tastelessly massive' and 'built without love'; and he found that the place did not gain in romantic stature even after it had been reduced to a burnt-out shell during the siege of Buda of 1944–5. The devastation of the palace prompted from 1950 onwards a reconstruction more in accordance with conventional architectural tastes of the time: the decorative frills, elaborate roof, and other flippantly eclectic elements of the late nineteenth-century building were removed in favour of a more sober and even duller structure, complete with a neo-classical dome and a pedimented, porticoed frontispiece. In the course of the reconstruction—which was not finally completed until the 1980s—much of the earlier palace was uncovered, and the whole was transformed into museums and a library. The modernized interiors have a marbled pretentiousness.

Byrne, after recalling what the palace must have been like during the days of Matthias Corvinus, complained that in 1867 the place could not claim to have a single picture, sculpture or 'article of *vertu* . . . to record the tastes and predilections of its occupants'. 'In this respect,' he concluded, 'the Palace of one of the Sovereigns of modern Europe is on a par with the hut of the humblest of his subjects.' Today the main block of the palace houses what is certainly the largest, and in many ways the most interesting, art collection in Hungary—the **Hungarian National Gallery**.

The idea for such a gallery was a consequence of the national reform movements of the first half of the nineteenth century. The precursor to today's institution was founded in 1851 and was later briefly amalgamated with what is now its rival establishment, the Museum of Fine Arts, which is devoted solely to foreign schools; it was transferred from Pest to its present location in Buda in 1975. Although some visitors might be dismayed by the vast number of mediocre works that are crowded into the museum's multitude of rooms, those who come here with an open mind will enjoy the excitement of discovering artists who are almost entirely unknown outside Hungary. Even the worst of the paintings—notably the bombastic nineteenth-century history scenes—can be not only entertaining but also fascinating for what they reveal about national preoccupations and myths. And there are undoubted revelations: the long hall room devoted to the Master M.S. and late Gothic winged altarpieces; the sombrely expressive works of László Paál and Mihály Munkácsy (see pp. 77–8); and the colourful, *plein air* landscapes and figure scenes of Szinyei Merse and the Nagybánya School (see pp. 79–80). The eccentric and visionary Csontváry (see pp. 80–1), not to everyone's taste, is relegated to the staircase well, while the works of contemporary Hungarian artists (including a fascinating symbolic work by Ildikó Várnagy) are displayed directly under the dome, in a part of the museum that is likely to be reached only by the most persevering of visitors.

The **National Széchényi Library** (which was founded in 1802 on the initiative of Count István Széchenyi's father, Ferenc), Alajos Stróbl's superb and enormous **Matthias fountain** of 1904 (depicting the king as a huntsman falling in love with the 'Beautiful Ilonka'), and the entrances to the **Ludwig** and **Castle Museums** are situated on the western side of the palace, the courtyards of which are connected to the eastern terrace by an arched opening. The former museum, donated in 1989 by the German collector Peter Ludwig and his Aachen-based foundation, houses a largely unexciting group of Hungarian and European works of art from the 1950s onwards, including a singularly bad Picasso. The Castle Museum, filled mainly with displays relating to the history of Budapest, allows access through its basement into the eloquent remains of the medieval and Renaissance palace (see pp. 7 ff.).

Throughout the summer months the visitor can leave the Castle district through a door in the Castle Museum that leads to the reconstructed thirteenth- to sixteenth-century bastions and courtyards on the palace's southern side. After going through a gate next to the so-called 'Wall Hammer Tower', you will enter the attractive parkland that forms today most of that part of Budapest's First District known as the **Tabán**. Deriving its name probably from the tanning workshops that existed here in Turkish times, the Tabán became after 1686 a place of refuge to large numbers of Serbian families fleeing the Turks. A densely populated slum area inhabited also by Greeks and gypsies when Lady Mary Wortley Montagu visited Buda in 1717 (she described the homes as closely packed rows of hovels that appeared 'at a little distance like old-fashioned thatched tents'), the Tabán was devastated by a serious fire in 1810. By 1908 plans were already afoot to pull down much of what was left of this picturesque but largely insanitary and insalubrious district, which was notorious by now for its gambling dens and cheap prostitutes; these plans were finally carried out by the 1930s. The only remaining testimony to the Turkish occupation is a tiny group of gravestones in the south-eastern corner of the park: these mark the burial ground of the Turks killed in 1686. Just below this, at Nos. 1–3 Apród utca, is a surviving early nineteenth-century example of one of the wealthy merchants' houses that grew up on the southern fringes of the Tabán after 1767, when a boat bridge was made linking this part of Buda with Pest. This house was the birthplace in 1818 of the pioneering Hungarian doctor **Ignác Semmelweiss**, in whose honour the present medical museum was created (a recent director was the late Hungarian premier József Antall). The museum, with its attractive old interior, and reconstructed pharmacies, has a number of compellingly gruesome exhibits, such as a mummified head (sitting on top of a box of 'mummy powder') and some realistic seventeenth- and eighteenth-century models of dissected women. Across the road from this, on the Ybl Miklós tér, is the elegant colonnaded kiosk that Ybl built between 1874 and 1879 to pump water up to the Castle district; in 1992 it was transformed into a casino.

It was the north-western edge of the Tabán, directly below the Dísz tér, that became especially popular early this century with writers such as Kosztolányi, Márai, and Babits, who enjoyed its self-contained, quasi-rural character. Descending from the square down the Palota utca, you will reach the short Tábor utca, where, on a modern block at the bottom of the street, is a plaque marking the site of the house where Kosztolányi lived for much of the latter part of his life (see p. 87). The quiet, steeply sloping Tábor utca emerges on to the pleasantly verdant Logodi utca (Babits briefly had a house here), which runs parallel to the ramparts and leads into the third and final part of the First District—the Krisztina. This area, once extensively covered in vines, has been entirely transformed in modern times. The Southern Station (Déli pályaudvar), which rises above bleak parkland and a busy network of roads, is a character-less modern replacement for the train terminal once used by newly-wed Hungarians departing for Venice on their honeymoons.

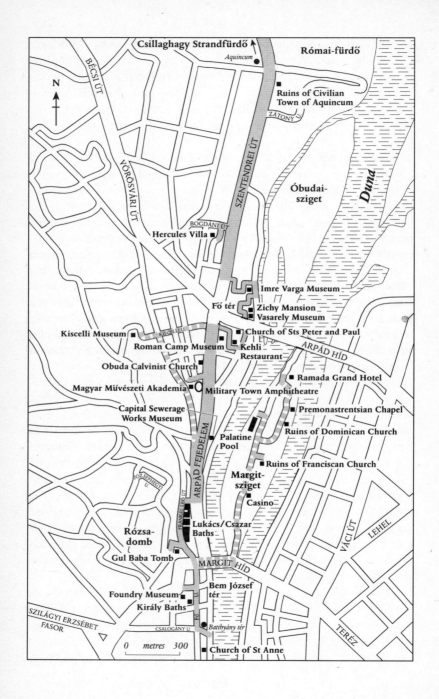

N

Csillaghagy Strandfürdő

Aquincum

Római-fürdő

Ruins of Civilian
Town of Aquincum

ZÁTONY

Óbudai-
sziget

Duna

Hercules Villa

BOGDÁNI ÚT

Imre Varga Museum

Fő tér

Zichy Mansion
Vasarely Museum

Kiscelli Museum

Church of Sts Peter and Paul

Roman Camp Museum

Kehli
Restaurant

ÁRPÁD HÍD

Obuda Calvinist Church

Magyar Művészeti Akadémia

Ramada Grand Hotel

Military Town Amphitheatre

Capital Sewerage
Works Museum

Premonastrentsian Chapel

Ruins of Dominican Church

Palatine
Pool

Ruins of Franciscan Church

ÁRPÁD FEJEDELEM

Margit-
sziget

JÓZSEFHEGY U

Casino

Rózsa-
domb

Lukács/Csazar
Baths

Gul Baba Tomb

MARGIT HÍD

Foundry Museum

Bem József
tér

Király Baths

SZILÁGYI ERZSÉBET
FASOR

Batthyány tér

CSALOGÁNY U

VÁCI ÚT

LEHEL

TERÉZ

BÉCSI ÚT

VÖRÖSVÁRI ÚT

KISCELLI U

0   metres   300

Church of St Anne

❧❧ Walk 2 ❧❧

North along the Danube

From the Víziváros to Óbuda and Beyond

OUTSIDE the compact and now toy-like Castle district, the important pre-nineteenth-century monuments on the west side of the Danube are mainly scattered over a long, narrow area extending north from the Castle Hill all the way to the northern reaches of Óbuda. Two of the finest of Budapest's Turkish monuments, the oldest of its medieval remains, a remarkably well-preserved group of baroque buildings and streets, and Central Europe's most extensive Roman ruins will all be seen as you meander north along the river, following an itinerary that also includes in abrupt succession industrial museums, bleak stretches of modern development, and idyllic rural enclaves.

This itinerary corresponds roughly to the HÉV suburban railway line, which has its terminal in the Batthyány tér, in the heart of the district known since the Middle Ages as the **Víziváros** or 'Water Town'. Formerly surrounded by walls, this small and narrow riverside district in between the Chain and Margaret bridges was like a poorer version of the Vár, with a social makeup diametrically opposed to that of the predominantly prosperous, Jewish, progressive and Hungarian district tauntingly situated on the opposite side of the Danube—the Lipótváros. The Víziváros was a largely German and very conservative district composed not only of artisans but also of fishermen, whose former presence here is attested by an excellent and homely fish restaurant called the Horgásztanya or 'Angler's Hut' (at Fő utca 27), which has a large fishing-net suspended above its long tables and benches.

Though the Víziváros lost its small-town character in the early years of this century, something of its original appearance can be gleaned from the **Batthyány tér**, which is dominated by late eighteenth-century buildings. Two of these, sunk slightly below street level on the western side of the square, are the former White Horse Inn (which has today a nightclub named after Casanova, who reputedly stayed here) and the adjoining house (at No. 3), built in the 1790s as the home of an architect. Next to these, at the south-western corner of the square, is a covered turn-of-the-century market (now a supermarket) that replaced the open-air one that had been held in the square since at least the eighteenth century. The animation that the Batthyány tér must have had when packed with market stalls returned after 1972 with the arrival here of the Red Metro line, which linked the place directly to Pest. Today the square's crowds of commuters are joined by numerous tourists, who linger here to enjoy the dramatic vista across the Danube to the Parliament building, to visit the daily if rather desultory flea market, and to relax at a wonderful café (the Angelica) attached to the square's culminating eighteenth-century monument—the twin-towered **church of St Anne**. One of the most impressive of Budapest's baroque churches, this church was begun in 1740 by an unknown architect and consecrated in 1805: the liveliness of the exterior sculptural decoration is complemented by the richness of the interior furnishings, which include a blue and gilded pulpit and a theatrical high altar of St Anne and the Virgin. The presbytery on the building's Danube side was originally an inn that had been adapted for ecclesiastical use in the early eighteenth century; appropriately enough, in view of the presbytery's former status, the ground floor was converted in the early 1970s into the now enormously popular **Café Angelica**, which has an elegant outdoor terrace (frequented mainly by tourists) and an atmospheric interior with stained-glass windows, and a regular crowd of elderly Buda ladies.

The long and narrow Fő utca, which runs down the western side of the Batthyány tér, is the main artery of the Víziváros, and passes to the south a neo-Gothic Calvinist church (1892–6) adorned with a colourful skyline of Zsolnay tiles. Walking instead north along the street, and passing to your right the recently restored early eighteenth-century Church of the Elizabeth Nuns, you will soon be offered to your left a rather incongruous oriental vision comprising four low-lying domes and a central crescent moon. You have reached the famous **Király or 'King' baths**, which were built by the Turks in the late 1560s; so that the bathers would not be caught unawares by Christian invaders, the place was constructed within the district's defensive walls, a kilometre away from the outlying thermal springs whence the water had to be pumped (these are directly below the present Lukács baths). The original Turkish structure, after being hidden by baroque remodelling (removed in the 1950s), became incorporated in the early nineteenth century within a neo-classical complex named, not after a monarch, but after a nineteenth-century owner called König (later Magyarized to Király). The darkly inviting Turkish pool can only be seen by those intending to use it: men are allowed in on Mondays, Wednesdays, and Fridays, women on Tuesdays, Thursdays, and Saturdays.

Immediately beyond the Király baths, the Fő utca comes to an end at the architecturally uninspiring Bem József tér, which had been the starting-point for the 1956 uprising (see pp. 95 ff.): the modern statue at its centre shows the eponymous 1848 hero commanding his troops to attack the bridge at Pilski ('If we do not have the bridge,' the inscription reads, 'we do not have the country'—a rather ironic statement, given that the country was lost even though the bridge was recaptured). A fascinating detour into Hungary's industrial past can be made from here by heading west up the Bem József utca to see (at No. 20) the country's oldest steel foundry. Established here in 1844 by a Swiss steelworker called Abraham Ganz, it continued to function as the Ganz machine works right up to 1964: though converted subsequently into a **Foundry Museum**, it still retains its ladles and jib cranes in their original setting, and gives an overall impression less of a museum than of an actual factory whose workers have mysteriously disappeared.

The northern continuation of the Fő utca is the Frankel Leó utca, which goes through the underpass of the late nineteenth-century Margaret Bridge. Anyone visiting Budapest in the past would not have left the city without making a special journey to the **Margaret Island**, which is accessible from the Margaret Bridge by a small connecting bridge dating back to 1900. 'The Pearl of the Danube', as this island was once called, had been popularized by the Romans, who exploited the thermal waters in its northern half, and who are thought to have joined the place to Buda by a tunnel. Used as a hunting-ground by the first of the Hungarian kings, the island then became a home to various monastic orders, including the Dominicans, whose convent was founded here by Béla IV, who had reputedly vowed during the Mongol invasion to bring up his daughter Margaret as a nun. Under the Turks the island was depopulated, its buildings were destroyed, and its holy associations—in particular with the saintly Margaret—were desecrated with the decision of one of the Turkish pashas to set up his harem here. Although the island was later for a short period the home of nuns of the order of St Clare, it would live on after the Turks essentially as a place of pleasure rather than religion. In 1795 the palatine Joseph planted it with vines and rare trees and turned the place into a public promenade, access to which was restricted after various outbreaks of vandalism: for a while no one was allowed here from Pest, or indeed anyone whose appearance—in the words of the British traveller Julia Pardoe—suggested 'wanton mischief'. Miss Pardoe visited the island in 1840 and found it 'as sweet a spot as ever gemmed the bosom of a river', and 'enough to turn even the most sober pilgrim for the time being into a day-dreamer; and to exalt every enthusiast into a poet'. Enhanced afterwards by the creation of a luxurious spa hotel and accompanying recreational facilities, the place also drew regular crowds of Sunday trippers. Tissot in 1881 described the island as having the 'thick vegetation, shady alleys, velvety lawns, and large leafy trees' of an English park but with 'something which recalls to mind France rather than England; gaiety . . . merry laughter, bright sun-light, dance music'.

The presence today of large sports complexes, bleak playing-fields, a new bridge at the island's northern end, and a huge water tower have helped to diminish somewhat the place's resemblance to paradise; but a lazy day or afternoon can happily be spent here during the spring and summer months, especially if you enjoy what Stendhal considered the ultimate traveller's pleasure—watching the inhabitants of a city at play. The Ybl-designed Casino, one of the island's most popular spots from the late nineteenth century up to the 1930s, is the first old landmark you will reach on walking north from the southern connecting bridge; it is now a much-altered structure housing a restaurant and terrace bar. Further north, also to the right of the broad central thoroughfare, are the shaded ruins of a thirteenth- to fourteenth-century Franciscan church, with a particularly eloquent Gothic window with tracery. Higher up still, on the opposite side of the promenade, is the island's main summer attraction—the Olympic-sized **Palatinus swimming-pool**, and adjoining thermal pools, where you can indulge in a warm, open-air bath in the company of hundreds of other people. The important ruins of the thirteenth-century **Dominican church and convent** (see p. 6) where St Margaret spent most of her life lie to the east of here, a few hundred metres below the rebuilt eleventh-century **Premonstratensian chapel**—Budapest's oldest monument. Much of this northern part of the island is adorned with busts of the many artists, writers, musicians, and actors who have found rest and inspiration here, including the poet János Arany, who stayed for long periods in the former sanatorium hotel, which was destroyed during the Second World War and recently rebuilt as the Ramada Grand in a way intended to recall its late nineteenth-century splendour.

Back at the Margaret Bridge and continuing to head north through Buda along the Frankel Leó utca, you leave the Víziváros and skirt to your left the slopes of the leafy, suburban district of the **Rózsadomb** or Rose Hill. Roses were another legacy of the Turks, one of whose officials planted this hill's eponymous rose garden: today this man, Gül Baba (which means in Turkish the 'father of roses'), is the only Turk after whom a Budapest street has been named. The Gül Baba utca is a steeply ascending cobbled alley that you will find immediately to your right on turning into the Török utca or 'Turkish Street'. It leads to one of the spots in Budapest that has most enchanted romantic visitors to the city— the **tomb of Gül Baba**. Gül Baba was a Muslim Dervish who took part in the capture of Buda in 1541 but died later in that same year. His tomb—a heavily restored octagonal chapel with a hemispherical dome— was built by the third Pasha of Buda, Yahjapashazade Mehmed; though still a place of worship for Muslims, it is officially a tiny museum that contains inside a number of exhibits relating to the so-called 'whirling dervishes'. The beauty of the place lies in its superb views over the Danube, its setting of roses, and the peace that envelopes it—the din of coach parties has yet to reach here. Its character was excellently evoked by the Italian writer and scholar Claudio Magris in his magisterial book *Danube* (1989): 'It looks down upon Budapest not ... with the proud glance of the dominator of yore, but with that serene distance of one who rests in Allah. Before this tomb and amid this tranquillity death has no fears for us. It is rest and repose, an oasis reached after crossing the desert.'

Most of the Rózsadomb seems in fact like a green and tranquil oasis in the middle of the noisy and polluted city. Filled with grand villas from the turn of the century onwards, it has long been a favourite residential area for the city's more privileged citizens: popular now with *nouveaux-riches*, it was famous earlier for having been the home to a high proportion of the country's communist hierarchy, including Kádár himself, who lived after 1956 at No. 21 József hegyi út (now a children's 'rehabilitation centre'). An unwilling neighbour of Kádár's was the populist poet and writer Gyula Illyés, whose house was further down the street, at No. 9. Though of impeccable working-class credentials (he was of landless peasant stock), and the most respected Hungarian writer of the communist era, Illyés refused to commit himself to the postwar Communist cause and was an outspoken critic of Kádár and his regime. His grandson, who showed me around the house, made it quite clear that the place had been bought long before Kádár had moved into the area; he also pointed out how some of the villas that the communists had built for themselves in the 1960s and 1970s had destroyed some of the beautiful Danube views to be had from his grandfather's top-floor study, which is still lined from floor to ceiling with his books.

Continuing north along the Frankel Leó utca you seem to be entering an early nineteenth-century spa town as you pass alongside a melancholy small park frequented by the elderly and infirm (some in their dressing-gowns), and a group of tall and elegant buildings forming part of the Lukács thermal complex, which incorporates both the **Csaszar** and the **Lukács baths** (see pp. 29, 32). A large shaded courtyard marks the entrance to this complex, which retains on the outside many of its neo-classical elements. The Csaszar or Imperial baths, now part of the National Institute of Rheumatism and Physiotherapy, had been the most extensive of Buda's Turkish baths, and still feature the magnificently domed and arched Bath of Veli bey—the finest of the city's Turkish *ilidjes*. After being rehoused in the mid-nineteenth century in a neo-classical building designed by József Hild, these baths became a favourite venue for Buda's fashionable society. In contrast, the Lukács baths, in the words of a physician writing in 1859, were 'visited by lower-class people only'. These baths—the only part of the complex freely open today to the public—have been completely modernized inside, and have a strong medicinal character, which extends even to their two outdoor pools. An evocative if rather offputting account of a visit to them is included in the German poet Franz Fühmann's *Twenty-two Days or Half a Lifetime* (1973) (see pp. 33–4).

The dank odours from the Lukács baths might help to put you in the right frame of mind for the next attraction on your walk north into Óbuda—the **Capital Sewerage Works Museum**. The name alone of this museum has ensured that it has never ranked high on any list of Budapest's tourist sights; but the place itself is an engagingly eccentric relic of the city's industrial past. To an even greater extent than the Foundry Museum, this is a museum that exudes the atmosphere of an abandoned factory. Entering the place from the Zsigmond tér, you pass through a black ironwork gate into an overgrown yard, where a bearded man in blue overalls will show you into a large brick building com-

prising a pumping plant built between 1912–17. 'Dear Visitors,' reads a
notice in English attached to the entrance, 'Welcome to pumping
plant on behalf of the Metropolitan canalization and draining works.'
Inside are numerous photographs and panels relating the history of
Budapest's sewerage from Roman times up to 1917, with a particular
emphasis on the major sanitary reforms carried out in the early nineteenth century on the initiative of the enlightened palatine Joseph. But
all this information is of subsidiary interest to the space itself, which is
like a futurist vision straight out of H. G. Wells: sinister rows of black
pumping engines are lined up below an upper control room featuring a
Siemens switchboard full of clocks and handles that you can imagine
under the control of some demented scientist. 'Have a nice day on
the Canalization Historical Collection!' runs the museum's cheery last
message to its visitors.

Tourists with more conventional sightseeing tastes can catch a No. 17
tram from directly outside the museum and make a detour up the Bécsi
út to see one of the most beautiful of the city's baroque complexes—
the former Trinitarian monastery now housing the **Kiscelli Museum**.
Alighting at the Kiscelli utca, you walk up through a wood to a group
of light ochre buildings standing amidst green meadows. The history of
this former monastery has its origins in a pilgrimage made in 1691 by
palatine Pál Esterházy to the votive chapel of Mariazell in Styria, which
had been founded in the fourteenth century by the Hungarian king Louis
the Great. Taking part in this gesture of thanksgiving to the Virgin for
having helped in the recent victory over the Turks was the newly
appointed feudal lord of Óbuda, Péter Zichy, who decided afterwards to
found a votive chapel of his own on the hill above his fiefdom. Completed in 1724, 'Little Mariazell' and its surrounding land were acquired
nearly twenty years later by the Trinitarians, who developed the site as
a monastery and hospital, which they commissioned from the Viennese
architect Johann Entzenhoffer. Dissolved by the palatine Joseph, and
then left for many years as a ruin, the place was turned at the end of the
nineteenth century into the private residence of the Viennese collector
and furniture manufacturer Maximilian Schmidt, who bequeathed it to
the city of Budapest on his death in 1935. Recently modernized with
tasteful simplicity and bare floorboards, this now houses a mixed group
of spaciously displayed collections ranging from baroque statuary and
early printing presses (you can even have a copy of Petőfi's *Arise
Hungarians!* specially printed for you on one of these machines) to a

representative selection of twentieth-century Hungarian art. The former monastery church, heavily damaged during the war, has an excellent ceiling painting (by Johann Gell) inspired by the perspectival illusionism of the Italian Padre Pozzo. The building itself is used for daringly presented modern art exhibitions.

The Kiscelli utca leads all the way down to the Flórián tér, at the heart of Óbuda—an area messily strewn with flyovers, grey apartment blocks, extensive remains of the Roman military settlement of Aquincum, and prettily restored stretches of the baroque township. Recently, some of the offending modern buildings have been pulled down to make way for Biedermeier pastiches and reconstructions, as you will notice if you come here directly from the Zsigmond tér, following initially the Lukács utca. At No. 46 Lajos utca is a rebuilt early nineteenth-century inn occupied by one of the district's famous old landmarks, the **Sipos Restaurant** (Lajos utca 46): this wonderful fish restaurant was founded in 1930 by Károly Sipos, whose best-known speciality was a boneless fish soup; reopened in 1995, it has revived its reputation both for its fish soup and for its literary and intellectual gatherings. Further north along the street, at No. 163, is Óbuda's former synagogue (now a television studio), a large pedimented building designed in 1769 by Mátyás Nepauer and inaugurated in 1821, when it was acclaimed as the finest 'among all the synagogues within the Austro-Hungarian monarchy'.

Your first sight of Roman Óbuda will come at the very end of the Lukács utca, when there opens up to your left the neatly landscaped square in which are set the ruins of the **Military Town Amphitheatre**, which was in use between the second and fourth centuries AD, and probably served later as a fortress. The low-lying ruins, unimpressive when seen from a passing car or bus, only begin to convey the amphitheatre's enormous dimensions (greater than those of the Colosseum in Rome) once you have started walking through them. Another reason for crossing this square is to go on afterwards to the extraordinary **Magyar Művészeti Akadémia**—an alternative art academy founded by the visionary architect Imre Makovecz at Zápor utca 9 (almost immediately behind the amphitheatre). The building, designed by Makovecz himself in 1995, is a statement of his nationalist and architectural beliefs, and has a façade combining elements from the traditional wooden architecture of Transylvania with some recently discovered Renaissance capitals from the royal palace at Buda. A great hero to Makovecz and his followers is the Transylvanian-inspired architect Károly Kós, one of whose

rare Budapest works is the nearby church house next to the Óbuda
Calvinist Church (at the junction of the Selmeci utca and the Lukács
utca's northern continuation, the Pacsirtamező utca).

As you near the Flórián tér along the Pacsirtamező utca, the remains
of Aquincum become ever more numerous. In the basement of the grim
1950s block at No. 63 is a museum (the **Roman Camp Museum**) built
to display the foundations of a second-century dwelling house that was
turned into a bathing establishment in the third or fourth century AD.
The ruins of further baths, and other fragments from the Roman military camp, can be seen in the equally dispiriting setting of the huge
underpass below the Flórián tér and the adjoining Árpád Bridge.

For all the archaeological interest of these ruins, you will probably be
pleased to reach afterwards the provincial-looking group of charming
cobbled streets and stuccoed buildings that cower behind the towering
housing schemes and scar-like excavations. This is the Óbuda that grew
up after 1686 under Count Péter Zichy, who invited here numerous
German settlers. The town, with its population of shipwrights, fishermen, craftsmen, bootmakers, and cobblers, retained the atmosphere of
an old-fashioned Danubian community up to the days of Gyula Krúdy,
who famously described the place as an 'antique town' where the streets
were 'as bent as old people, huddling like tramps in the merciless wind
on the high road'. The one-storeyed Biedermeier-style inn that Krúdy
so regularly frequented lies a few hundred metres to the east of the
Roman Camp Museum, at No. 3 of the cobbled Mókus utca (now the
Kehli restaurant). Just to the north of this, in pathetic isolation below
the Árpád Bridge (the construction of which led to the pulling down of
the surrounding houses), is the charming mid-eighteenth-century parish
church of Sts Peter and Paul, where Count Péter Zichy is buried.

The best preserved part of eighteenth- and early nineteenth-century
Óbuda is a small and largely traffic-free zone extending north of the
Árpád Bridge, and resembling a lovingly constructed film set that has
been taken over by museums and country-style restaurants. The area is
centred around the Fő tér, which is dominated on its eastern side by the
mid-eighteenth-century **Zichy mansion**, where you will find a cultural
centre, a local history collection, and a small memorial museum devoted
to the avant-garde poet, writer, and artist **Lajos Kassák** (who lived in
the industrial district of Angyalföld, directly across the river from
Óbuda). On the eastern side of the square, at No. 4, is an attractive late
eighteenth-century house that belonged to a recent collector of Hun-

garian folk art, **Zsigmond Kun**; his house, now a museum of folk art, has been little altered inside, and makes for a far more appropriate setting for traditional Hungarian ceramics and other craft objects than the pretentious neo-baroque building in which Pest's Ethnographic Museum is housed.

In the adjoining Szentlélek tér, and on the cobbled Hajógyár utca, are museums dedicated respectively to **Victor Vasarely** and **Imre Varga**—the two most famous Hungarian artists of today. Vasarely, the self-styled father of Op Art, is the only Hungarian artist after Moholy-Nagy to have made a major international impact this century. A waiter's son from the southern Hungarian town of Pécs, Vasarely lived almost all his life in Paris, where he developed an enormous talent for making influential friends and convincing them of his genius. The Óbuda museum, the most recent of no fewer than four institutions devoted to his work, has at least the dual virtue of being attractively set in a two-storeyed white house and having a large amount of empty space. It contrasts markedly with the more crowded and homely Imre Varga Museum, which spreads out from a pastel-shaded Biedermeier house into a delightful garden that stretches out towards the Danube. Varga, though little known internationally, has been Hungary's most prolific creator of public memorials since the 1960s; his figurative sculptures may be slick and undemanding, but they are also accessible, entertaining, and occasionally moving. Though now in his late 70s, he still continues to visit his museum on Saturday mornings.

The ruins of the civilian town of Aquincum, and some pleasant open-air pools, are the main incentives for persevering further north into Óbuda. Outstanding third-century Roman mosaics are to be seen (through a window) at the **Hercules Villa**, which is almost completely hidden by the surrounding high-rise dwellings; the villa, named after the subject of its mosaics, is at Meggyfa utca 19–21, about a twenty-minute walk north-west of the Flórián tér. From this point you would be best advised to continue north either on one of the three buses that run along the Szentendrei út (No. 34, 42, or 106), or else on the HÉV (which ends up at the much-visited and commercialized small town of Szentendre). You should certainly try and make the effort to stop off at the **Aquincum Museum**, a small classical-style museum of 1894 that sits like an authentic Roman building in the middle of the excavated foundations of the civilian town. Wandering around this extensive open-air site on a hot summer's day, you can almost convince yourself that you are in Italy. However, if it is too hot, you might be better off continuing further north to the Római Strandfürdő—a very popular complex of open-air pools occupying the site of Roman baths, and set amidst flat, grassy lawns. Better still, and certainly quieter, are the pools of the Csillaghegy Strandfürdő (the next stop on the HÉV), which have a wooded, hilly setting, and an atmosphere redolent of the 1920s.

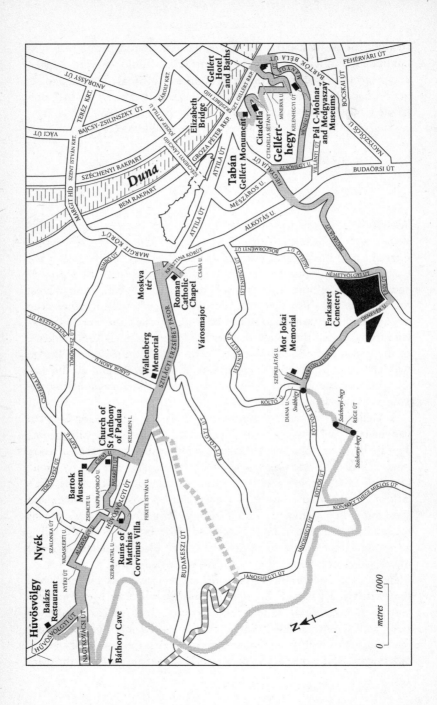

❦❧ Walk 3 ❦❧

Southern and Western Buda

From the Gellért Hill to the Moszkva tér

SOUTH of the Castle district, the most prominent landmark on the Buda skyline is the **Gellért Hill** with its crowning citadel. A climb to its summit has been a prerequisite of any visit to Buda since at least the early nineteenth century, when the hill was covered partly by vineyards and partly by the hovel-like houses of the southern Tabán. Though most tourists today do this either by taxi or coach, an enjoyable if rather steep 20–25-minute walk to the top can be made through the wooded parkland that replaced the vineyards after the European phylloxera epidemic of the 1880s and 1890s. A stepped path behind the Elizabeth Bridge will lead you up the most dramatic side of the hill, passing on the way an artificial waterfall and colonnaded monument commemorating the saint after whom the place is named.

St Gellért, an eleventh-century German bishop whom King Stephen had invited to Hungary to help convert the country to Christianity, appears as a ferocious bearded figure in Jankovits's monument of 1904 (this was one of Budapest's ten public memorials paid for by Franz Joseph in response to the German Kaiser's complaints about the city's lack of them). Faced with such a man as this brandishing a crucifix and speaking with a German accent, it is no wonder that Hungary's pagans reacted by nailing him inside a barrel and throwing him down the hill— an incident that probably contributed to the place's reputation in the Middle Ages as a home of witches and other evil spirits.

In 1851 the Gellért Hill acquired further unpleasant associations when the Austrians celebrated and strengthened their victory over the Hungarians by building at its summit the present thick-walled **citadel**. In 1947, as if to ensure the citadel's continuity as a symbol of oppression, the Hungarians built here a monument glorifying the Soviet 'liberation' of Hungary. This work, depicting a 14-m.-high woman holding the palm

139

of victory, was by Zsigmond Kisfaludi-Stróbl, who had earlier designed a near-identical work honouring the dead son of General Horthy. After 1990, the sculpted Soviet soldier at its base (which was regularly defiled with graffiti) was removed, thus liberating the work from all remaining political content. Now that the citadel has been reduced to a popular tourist complex (with a hotel, restaurant, and café), you can shamelessly enjoy from here a panorama of the Danube that has inspired even more superlatives than the one from the Castle Hill. Julia Pardoe, standing here transfixed in 1840 as the sun set and the moon rose, believed that neither words nor paintings could ever do the scene justice. Forty years later, the ever-imaginative Victor Tissot opined that the steepness of the climb was well rewarded by a 'marvellous panorama' that made the buildings of Pest seem like the palaces along Venice's Grand Canal. Today this is a view that can only be fully appreciated on one of those increasingly rare days when the sky is not obscured by a polluted haze.

Steps directly below the monument will take you down the hill's southern slopes, where you will glimpse to your left the dome of a Pauline chapel excavated out of the rock in 1931. You will emerge on to the Kelenhegyi út, where, at Nos. 12–14, is the art nouveau Atelier-Mietshaus, a three-storeyed studio-apartment house designed in 1903 by the architect/painter Gyula Kosztolányi Kann, and still used today by artists. This makes a good introduction to a district rich in monuments from the early years of the century, notably the extraordinary **Gellért baths** and **Hotel**—a gigantic, multi-domed apparition rising up above the busy riverside square at the very bottom of the hill (see p. 33). The many visitors wishing today to see but not to swim in the dazzlingly decorated indoor pool may now officially do so on purchase of a ticket from the baths' echoing vestibule (entry to which is from the Kelenh-egyi út).

The broad and noisy Bártok Béla út, on the southern slopes of the Gellért hill, is the main artery of a part of Buda (the Lágymányos) that had been almost entirely rural up till the end of the nineteenth century. It was around 1900 that the architect József Fischer began implement-ing here an ambitious, American-style town-plan involving enormous round intersections linked with parallel and diagonal avenues. Although a relatively small part of this scheme was actually carried out, Fischer left here numerous examples of his own architecture, including two of the many imposing turn-of-the-century buildings lining the upper part of the Bartók Béla út (Nos. 43 and 49). Among these other buildings is an important if now sadly dilapidated work (at No. 40) by the greatest architect of the Hungarian art nouveau, Ödön Lechner: built in 1898–9 as a house and studio for his brother Gyula, it has an interesting asymmetrical plan, with the studio placed on the fourth floor, next to a roof terrace; typically for Lechner, the façade combines ochre plasterwork with rococo detailing in pale green.

A number of other impressive tall buildings from this period are to be found on the adjoining streets, including, at Orlay utca 2B, an apartment block built by **István Medgyaszay** in 1909–10 for the St Gellért Cooperative: Medgyaszay's only surviving work in Budapest from before the First World War, this building characteristically combines folkloric motifs (for instance in the balconies) with a use of steel and concrete derived from his Viennese master, Otto Wagner. If you are interested in finding out more about Medgyaszay, you should turn left at the top of the Orlay utca into the long and quietly suburban Ménesi út, where, at No. 59B, you will see a sign in French reading '*Lieu d'Hommage Medgyaszay*', which marks the entrance to the tiny overgrown alley where the architect lived after 1921. His modest, ivy-covered brick and wood house at the top of the alley was designed by himself in a 'Hungarian-Indian style', to use the words of his devoted son-in-law, who still lives here and takes on the role of both guide and proselytizer. You have to listen to an impassioned exposition of Medgyaszay's mysticism and fascination with folklore and the Orient as you walk around a dark, atmospherical interior where present-day domestic objects have slipped into rooms that would otherwise be shrines to the architect and his work. After an hour or so of looking at old photographs and albums, you might find it necessary to make your excuses and leave. This is a course of action that might also have to be adopted if you decide to visit afterwards the nearby studio-museum of the painter **Pál C. Molnár** (at No. 65), where you are shown around by the artist's charming and loquacious daughter, Éva Csillag. Her late father (1894–1991) is sometimes described as Hungary's leading surrealist painter and graphic artist; but the crudely executed and conceived works on show in this single-roomed museum would barely deserve more than an amused glance were it not for the daughter's long, uncritical commentaries. Among the many other intellectual and artistic residents of this street were the marxist art historian and 'Sunday Circle' member Arnold Hauser, and the prominent historian of Hungarian medieval art and architecture Géza Entz, whose rambling old house, with its unkempt garden, Transylvanian souvenirs, and background strains of piano music had struck me during the Communist period as an enclave of a bygone Hungarian world.

The Ménesi út, after skirting the southern slopes of the Gellért Hill, ends up near the busy thoroughfare of the Hegyalja út, where you can begin a tour of Buda's hilly and verdant western suburbs by taking a No. 8 or 8A bus to the **Farkasrét Cemetery**. Unless you are a Stalinist sympathizer anxious to pay your respects to the tomb of the notorious Mátyás Rákosi, the interest of this cemetery lies largely in the extraordinary Mortuary Chapel (just to the right of the main entrance), which was designed in 1975 by the most controversial Hungarian architect of today, Imre Makovecz: this relatively early work exemplifies his belief in 'organic architecture' in its predominance of undulating wooden forms, and in its rib-like interior that gives the visitor the impression of being inside a human body; the rather mannered, Secession-inspired furniture (a rather less fortunate feature of the work of Makovecz and his numerous followers) is by Gábor Mezei.

To continue from here to the **Mór Jókai Memorial Museum** and into the Buda Hills, you can either walk north along the Denevér utca or else descend by a No. 59 tram to the Southern Station, and from there take a No. 21 bus up to the top of the long and winding Istenhegy utca. The once internationally famous novelist Jókai lived during the last years of his life in a house situated just to the west of the latter street, off the tiny Tücsök utca (see pp. 61–2). The extensive wooded grounds remain, and include the writer's stone bench and table, where he sat working during the summer months, stopping periodically to observe the magnificent panorama of the distant city. However, his baronial-style country mansion was burnt down this century, and has been replaced by the modern headquarters of Hungary's Forestry Commission; a surviving window from the old house, incongruously attached to the new concrete building, marks the outer wall of the tiny memorial room containing some of the writer's belongings. The museum's elderly caretaker, fast asleep in the Forestry Commission's reception area, was woken up to show me inside this room. I was his only visitor in the month.

The journey up into the **Buda Hills** can be completed from here by cog-wheel railway. This railway, dating back to 1873 and the third of its kind in the world, runs between the Szilágyi Erzsébet fasor (see below) and the top of the Széchenyi hegy; one of its stops is almost directly in front of the Tücsök utca. From near its upper terminus you can continue into the densely wooded Buda Hills by taking the **Children's Railway**, which (with the exception of the driver) is run entirely by officious children, who, during the communist era, were members of the Pioneer corps. A fifteen-minute walk from the train's fourth stop will take you to the highest point in Budapest, the **János-Hegy** (527 m.), which is crowned by a neo-Romanesque lookout tower designed in 1908–10 by Frigyes Schulek, the architect of the Fisherman's Bastion and the remodelled Matthias Church. If you want now to go back into the city you can do so by chairlift, which will leave you at the Zugliget utca, whence you can catch a No. 158 bus to the Moszkva tér (see below). If instead you continue to meander by railway along the ridge of the Buda Hills, your next stop will be the Szépjuhászné, next to which is a garden restaurant that was much frequented by Gyula Krúdy. On the stretch of wooded hillside in between here and the railway's final stop, the Hüvösvölgy, is the cave where an eccentric seventeenth-century member of the Báthory family lived for many years as a hermit.

The **Hüvösvölgy** became an especially popular place for Sunday excursionists from the nineteenth century onwards, particularly after the establishment of what is now the 56 tram route (which begins in the Moszkva tér). Picnickers continue to frequent the grassy clearing of the Nagy-rét (to the east of the station and the adjoining Hüvösvölgyi út), where there is also a small fairground and ferris wheel. At 207 of the Hüvösvölgyi út is one of the oldest of Buda's garden restaurants, the Balázs, which was owned from 1838 up to the 1940s by six generations of the Balázs family. Middle-class families and members of workers' choral societies came out here to drink, eat, and listen to gypsy music under the trees and wooden canopies of the restaurant's courtyard; though the place was destroyed by fire in 1979, it has been restored to its original state. On the opposite side of the street is the entrance to the Ördögárok, where, at No. 80, is another popular garden restaurant, the Náncsi Néni, which is known for its excellent reasonably-priced food and lively atmosphere.

The Hüvösvölgy, south of the Balázs restaurant, is a district steeped in literary and artistic associations, as I discovered one afternoon when visiting one of the many beautiful old villas lining the quiet street that runs parallel to the Hüvösvölgyi út, the Alsóvölgy út. I was talking to a formidable academic, Mihály Szegedy-Maszák, from whose encyclopedic mind information flowed in a near-continuous stream, interrupted only by the odd value judgement ('very superficial' was one of his favourite comments) and forays into his crammed bookcases. His own house, near the corner of the Nyéki út, has itself played an important role in the district's cultural history: Csontváry, one of his ancestors, lived here, as did Nijinski, who during his last years was married to a Hungarian woman, with whom he later moved to a house opposite, at No. 12, half-way between the Nyéki út and the Vadaskerti utca. The philosopher Ernst Bloch had a house just to the east of the Vadaskerti utca (on the Szalonka utca) that was a popular meeting-place for members of the Sunday Circle; Ady spent much of his final illness in the sanitorium at the western end of the Nyéki út. Two writers of completely opposed political tendencies to both Ady and the Sunday Circle were also residents of this district—the romantic novelist Cecile Tormay (see p. 84) and her husband, Ferenc Herczeg, who wrote Jókai-inspired novels recording the plight of Hungary's decaying aristocracy, as well as a work of memoirs entitled *Hüvösvölgy*. Appropriately enough, their home here (at No. 87 Hüvösvölgyi út) was a picturesquely gabled example of nostalgic, Transylvanian-style architecture specially built for them in 1912 by Károly Kós's pupil and collaborator Dezső Zrumeczky.

Lower down this same street, at the junction with the Szerb Antal utca, you will come across a wooded, densely overgrown plot of land ringed with barbed wire and containing the excavated foundations of two adjacent structures, the broader of which is protected by a wooden covering that has half-rotted away. Though unmentioned in any of the foreign guidebooks to Budapest, these ruins are among the city's few architectural remains associated with Matthias Corvinus—they represent all that is left of the first Italian-style Renaissance villa north of the Alps. The former medieval township of **Nyék**, where these are situated, had flourished in the fifteenth century thanks to the frequent sojourns here of Matthias Corvinus, who favoured the area as a hunting-ground. The function of the narrower of his two excavated buildings here—a Renaissance pavilion built over a fourteenth-century structure—is unknown; but the building on its eastern side, which seems to have had a colonnaded façade, was certainly the king's hunting seat. Traces of gilt tiling and some exquisite limestone carvings were found here (the latter are now in Buda's Castle Museum), indicating that the villa had been as lavish and sophisticated in its architecture as Matthias's palaces at Buda and Visegrád.

Further down the Hüvösvölgyi út, almost at the point where it is joined by the Alsóvölgy utca, you skirt to your left a short valley that was built

SOUTHERN AND WESTERN BUDA

up in the first three decades of the century with houses and villas for well-to-do families with often progressive architectural tastes. At the northern end of this small district, the Pasarét, is the curious **Napraforgó utca**, which was built between 1931 and 1932 as an experimental show-case for modern, Bauhaus-influenced design: remarkably, this project, devised by leading Hungarian modernists such as Lajos Kozma, József Fischer, and Farkas Molnár, and featuring twenty-two houses of differ-ent design, was sponsored by the municipality, which had generally regarded this type of architecture as being decadently cosmopolitan. At the centre of the district, on the Pasaréti tér, is another major example of 1930s architecture—the **Franciscan church of St Anthony of Padua**. Designed by Gyula Rimanóczy in 1934 and possibly the finest of Budapest's modern churches, this white, geometrical structure, with its elegant, tall bell-tower, lives up to Franciscan ideals of simplicity.

At the time of all this exciting architectural activity in the Pasarét, the composer **Béla Bartók** settled in the district, where he bought a 1920s villa at 27 Csalán utca (a short walk north from the Pasaréti tér up the Csévi utca). Bartók moved to this most luxurious of his Budapest homes in 1932 from an apartment in the Third district, where he had become increasingly disturbed by the noisiness of his neighbours. At first his new home, with its large garden and leafy surroundings, had all the tran-quillity that he had long been searching for. Later he found out about the annual 'Gugger Hill Motorcycle Race', and the training sessions that preceded this, all of which took place directly below his home. His new-found peace was finally shattered once and for all after 1936, when construction was begun on two houses on either side of his: he used earplugs, and even tried to forget the noise outside by creating a small machine that made a continual monotonous hum; but to no avail. Then the war broke out, providing him with greater distractions, and forcing him eventually to leave for America in 1940. His Pasarét house was com-pletely modernized inside on being turned into an informative if not especially characterful museum, where you can see such items as his folk-crafted desk from the Transylvanian region of Kalotaszeg, and the phonograph he used for his famous recordings of Hungarian folk tunes; occasional concerts are put on here (see p. 76).

At its lowest end the Hüvösvölgyi út turns into the Szilágyi Erzsébet fasor, where, at the junction with Nagyajtai utca, the saviour of so many of Hungary's Jews during the Second World War, Raoul Wallenberg, was belatedly commemorated in 1987 by a statue by Imre Varga (an earlier memorial to him had disappeared as mysteriously as the man himself): recent evidence suggesting that Wallenberg had been working as a spy for the Americans has helped partly to explain the official silence that has long surrounded his fate.

Shortly before joining the Moszkva tér, the Szilágyi Erzsébet fasor is bordered to the south by formal gardens and to the north by numerous impressive turn-of-the-century apartment blocks that extend into the adjoining streets. On the eastern side of the gardens (at Csaba utca 5) is a delightful Roman Catholic Chapel by Aladar Árkay—a rather late example (1920) of the blend of English Arts and Crafts, Finnish, and, above all, Transylvanian elements that went into so much Hungarian architecture of the early years of the century.

Arriving at the ugly and perpetually busy **Moszkva tér**, you return to an urban scene more usually associated with Pest than with Buda: a terminal of Buda's transport system, with a battered central terrace full of improvised-looking kiosks, this place draws numerous gypsies and Romanians (who gather here in search of work), as well as a colourful crowd of costumed Hungarian peasant women, selling vegetables and lace tablecloths. To ease yet further the transition from Buda's green suburbs to the polluted and bustling world of urban Pest, you should have a meal in the nearby **Szent Jupát restaurant** (on the Retek utca), where you can eat huge plates of goose and other filling Hungarian specialities in a lively, smoky cellar that remains open throughout the night.

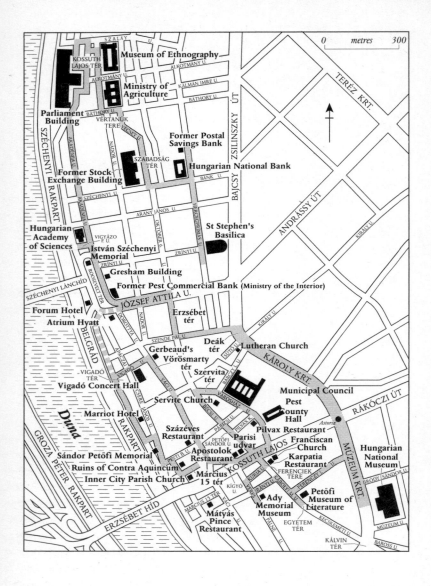

KOSSUTH
LAJOS TÉR
Museum of Ethnography
SZALAY U.
ALKOTMÁNY U.
ALKOTMÁNY U.
KÁLMÁN IMRE U.
Ministry of
Agriculture
BÁTHORY U.
Parliament
Building
BÁTHORY U.
VÉRTANÚK
TERE
VÉCSEY U.
SZÉCHENYI RAKPART
AKADÉMIA U.
NÁDOR U.
SZABADSÁG
TÉR
Former Postal
Savings Bank
BAJCSY ZSILINSZKY ÚT
TERÉZ KRT.
0   metres   300
Former Stock
Exchange Building
SZÉCHENYI U.
Hungarian National Bank
BANK U.
HERCEGPRÍMÁS U.
ANDRÁSSY ÚT
KIRÁLY U.
ARANY JÁNOS U.
Hungarian
Academy
of Sciences
VIGYÁZÓ
F.U.
OKTÓBER 6.
ZRÍNYI U.
St Stephen's
Basilica
István Széchenyi
Memorial
ZRÍNYI U.
ROOSEVELT TÉR
Gresham Building
SZÉCHENYI LÁNCHÍD
Former Pest Commercial Bank (Ministry of the Interior)
JÓZSEF ATTILA U.
Forum Hotel
Atrium Hyatt
DOROTTYA U.
NÁDOR U.
Erzsébet
tér
BELGRÁD
RAKPART
APÁCZAI CSERE JÁNOS U.
SZENDE PÁL U.
Gerbeaud's
Deák
tér
SÜTŐ U.
Lutheran Church
KIRÁLY U.
KÁROLY KRT.
VIGADÓ
TÉR
Vörösmarty
tér
Szervita
tér
VIGADÓ U.
VÁCI U.
DEÁK FERENC U.
BÁRCZY U.
VÁROSHÁZ
RÁKÓCZI ÚT
MÚZEUM KRT.
Vigadó Concert Hall
Servite Church
Municipal Council
VÁROSHÁZ U.
Pest
County
Hall
Duna
Marriot Hotel
RAKPART
VÁCI U.
VÁCI U.
PÁRIZSI U.
Pilvax Restaurant
Astoria
Hungarian
National
Museum
Százéves
Restaurant
Parisi
udvar
Franciscan
Church
PETŐFI
SÁNDOR U.
GROZA PÉTER RAKPART
Sándor Petőfi Memorial
Apostolok
Restaurant
PESTI B. U.
Karpatia
Restaurant
FERENCIEK
TERE
BRÓDY SÁNDOR U.
Ruins of Contra Aquincum
KOSSUTH LAJOS
KÁROLYI M. U.
Inner City Parish Church
Március
15 tér
KIGYÓ
U.
Ady
Memorial
Museum
Petőfi
Museum of
Literature
ERZSÉBET HÍD
MÁRCIUS 15 TÉR
VÁCI U.
Mátyás
Pince
Restaurant
PILNE U.
EGYETEM
TÉR
KECSKEMÉTI U.
MÚZEUM U.
KÁLVIN
TÉR
BAROSS U.

⟐ Walk 4 ⟐

The Inner City and the Lipótváros

Two concentric rings of boulevards spreading out from the Danube, and pierced by the great arrow of the Andrássy út, define the general layout of Pest, and are expressive of an energy and purpose lacking in the more leisurely and meandering plan of Buda. The smaller of these rings, the Kiskörút, contains most of the Lipótváros and all of the district that enshrines Pest's early history—the Belváros or Inner City.

Historical logic compels the visitor to start a tour of Pest besides the sad remains of Roman **Contra Aquincum** (see p. 4), which are displayed in a concrete depression at the centre of the Március 15 tér—a square named after the momentous March day (in 1848) whose course will be followed later during this walk through the Belváros. Masonry and works of art from every period in Pest's history, from Roman times up to the late twentieth century are present in the fascinating **Inner-City Parish Church** (see p. 4), which stands in front of the modern bridge-head that cuts through the southern half of the square. Important and rare medieval, Renaissance, and Turkish fragments belie the building's twin-towered baroque façade, including (in the nave) two exquisite Renaissance wall-tombs, and (in the sanctuary), a Turkish prayer-niche or *mihrab*, and Gothic sedilia partially frescoed with the remnants of Italian-influenced fourteenth-century works.

Neither this church nor the ruins of Contra Aquincum seem to appeal much to tourists, who are drawn instead to the **Mátyás Pince Étterem**, on the square's southern side. More memorable for its history and appearance than for its food, this was built in 1904 as a brasserie for the Dreher brewery, who owned the apartment house above. Enjoying an instant success, it attracted a large cross-section of Budapest society, from industrial magnates to artists, who formed their own drinking clubs here. After its dining-room had been expanded three times in only twenty-five years, the place was remodelled in 1937 and given its present decoration of mock medieval chairs, wooden-beam ceilings, and frescoed and stained-glass scenes from the life of Matthias Corvinus. Another restaurant popular today more with tourists than with gastronomes is the **Százéves Étterem**, which is situated off the north-eastern corner of the square, in one of Pest's oldest surviving non-ecclesiastical buildings. Built in 1755 for Baron János Péterffy, this elegantly pedimented structure was turned shortly afterwards into an inn, whose taproom appears to have been frequented by boatmen. In 1831 this inn reopened as the Hasslinger restaurant, one of the most popular specialities of which was a beer soup made unappetisingly with beer, cinnamon, lemon-peel, eggs, sugar, and sour cream. Functioning as a restaurant ever since, it is the oldest such establishment in Budapest (its misleading name, meaning 'One Hundred Years Old', was given to celebrate its centenary in 1931). Among its remaining early nineteenth-century furnishings are a Transylvanian stove, a carved bar counter, and a painted musical box.

The north-western corner of the Március 15 tér adjoins the landscaped **Petőfi tér**, which is named after its statue of the revolutionary poet, shown here with one hand holding a scroll and the other raised as if exhorting the crowd with his famous poem 'Arise Hungarians!': the sculpture, designed by Miklós Izsó in 1882, was Budapest's first public memorial to this inflammatory writer, and became from 1942 onwards a rallying-point for opponents to dictatorial regimes. An inappropriate accompaniment to this patriotic monument is the half-heartedly neo-classical monument popularly known as the '**Greek Church**', which dominates the western side of the square. Commissioned in 1786 by Greek and Macedonian merchants who had settled in Pest in the eighteenth century, it was inaugurated in 1801, and has been since then Hungary's largest house of worship serving the country's Greek Orthodox community. Although this community has been officially Hungarian-speaking since 1931, some of the prayers are still said in Greek on important liturgical occasions.

From the Petőfi tér you should head northwards on the pedestrianized upper embankment known as the **Corso**, which runs all the way to the Chain Bridge and provides a magnificent (and now Unesco-protected) panorama across the river to Buda. The embankment, raised in the late nineteenth century so as to enable the construction of store-houses below the tramway, was a favourite promenade for Budapest society until its destruction during the Second World War (its only prewar building to survive is the one immediately to the north of the

Vigadó ter). Strollers (mainly tourists) have now begun returning in growing numbers to the Corso, which has also revived its reputation for luxury hotels: three enormous modern hotels owned by American chains (the Marriot, the Forum, and the Atrium Hyatt) have risen up in replacement to Anglophile establishments worthy of the Côte d'Azur of old. In between the Petőfi tér and the Vigadó tér once stood the neo-Renaissance Grand Hotel Hungaria, which, when opened in 1871, was the first five-storey building in Pest and a place considered as the last word in luxury, having as it did such facilities as a conference room, a hairdressing salon, and a postal and telegraph office: Gyula Krúdy remembered the days when its elegant society women were wooed in the Winter Garden by the music of the greatest violinist of his age, Antal Kóczé. The **Marriot**, formerly the Intercontinental, now occupies the site of both the Hungaria and the adjoining Bristol: built in 1969 as the first of Budapest's large hotels in modern times, it has recently become a popular meeting-place for the city's American residents, who gather here on Sundays for a copious brunch in the glass-fronted restaurant overlooking the Danube. The **Forum**, with its dark-glass frontage, is a high-rise 1980s building standing just to the south of the Chain Bridge, near the site of a nobleman's mansion that was transformed in the early nineteenth century into the first of Pest's luxury hotels, the Queen of England: Julia Pardoe, who stayed there in 1840, praised the place for having 'removed from Pesth the hitherto well-merited reproach of affording worse accommodation to travellers than any city of its size in Europe'. Adjacent to the Forum, and similarly insensitive to its architectural surroundings, is the tall block of the **Atrium Hyatt** (1981), the rooms of which are arranged hive-like around an atrium hung with a life-size reproduction of Hungary's first aeroplane.

Much of the promenade's previous animation had been centred around its cafés, such as the Szidon café, which had opened in 1870 on the corner of the Corso and the shaded Vigadó tér; this was turned later into the Dunacorso Café-Restaurant, the modern replacement to which has bright red awnings promoting Coca-Cola. From the Dunacorso's outdoor tables you can catch a glimpse through the trees of the Gothic and Turkish-inspired façade of Feszl's pioneering **Vigadó Concert Hall** (see p. 64), one of the most exciting of Budapest's nineteenth-century buildings. After being badly damaged by fire during the Second World War, the façade was restored to its original state, but the interior was totally changed and given a bland modern look. The Vigadó restaurant, which takes up part of the building, is a successor to a famous café commonly called the 'Hangli' after the man who was granted the lease of the place in 1871, on the recommendation of the liberal politician Ferenc Deák. The enormously successful 'Hangli', with its tables that covered most of the square in front, was described in 1889 by Fővárosi Lapok (in the book *Kiosk beside the Danube*) as a place that had miraculously maintained its appeal for over twenty years: 'The Budapest public still frequents the "Hangli", visitors from the country arrange to meet in the "Hangli", and foreigners are also sent to the "Hangli". Because almost everyone meets up there.' Although popular at first primarily for its panorama of Buda, it remained fashionable, according to Lapok, simply for being fashionable: 'The fact that people also take coffee and ice-creams here is of secondary importance. The two main things are: to see and to be seen.'

The Vigadó utca, which skirts the northern side of the Concert Hall, will take you into the **Vörösmarty tér**—the focal point of a large pedestrian area crowded with shops, tourists, and buskers. The Vörösmarty tér, despite its tourist fame, is as unappealing architecturally as London's Leicester Square, and has not exactly been enhanced by the severe 1970s office block that dominates the western side of the square, where once stood the city's German Theatre. In the centre of the square is an entertaining statue of 1908 to the early nineteenth-century poet Vörösmarty, who is portrayed surrounded by people reciting his patriotic words, 'Be always faithful to your country, O Magyar!' Below the inscription is a dark spot supposed to be a lucky coin donated by a beggar towards the erection of this monument; this spot is often difficult to find among the graffiti, while the statue itself tends to disappear under a canvas awning during the winter months, thanks to the lack of foresight of the sculptor, Ede Telcs, who carved it in a marble that tends to crack under icy conditions. Fortunately the square has one dependable attraction in the enormous café and confectioner's situated on the ground floor of the former bank building designed by Józef Hild in 1861 for the northern side of the square. Occupying this site since 1870, this establishment is named after the Swiss-born **Emil Gerbeaud**, who acquired the place in 1885, and exported from here (in elaborate wooden boxes of his own design) French-style cream pastries, cognac cherries, chocolate dragées, and other specialities of his to places as far away as South America and the Far East. The beautiful if over-restored interior, with its vitrines, chandeliers, wooden panelling, and marble fireplaces, is a mixture of neo-rococo and Empire, and dates back to renovations carried out by Gerbeaud in 1885. A booklet of 1910 entitled *The Secrets of the Gerbeaud* described the establishment as 'the most elegant public place in Budapest, where Archduchesses and ordinary ladies take their tea in identical cups, with cream, or rum, dark or light, depending on whether their mothers had brought them up well or badly.' Ordinary Hungarians are put off today by the high prices, and the place has come to appeal principally to tourists, whose demands for better service have apparently led to the import of German waitresses.

The strolling crowds from the Vörösmarty tér are channelled to the south into the **Váci utca**, which was established as Pest's most fashionable shopping street in the late eighteenth century, and was praised in 1835 by the Austrian painter F. S. Chrismar, who delighted in coming here at midday, when you could observe all 'the beauties of the country' filing past the 'tastefully arranged windows'. The height of the street's reputation for elegance and luxury was reached during the decades leading up to the First World War, as is evident from the many sumptuous turn-of-the-century buildings that line the street, including structures by Ödön Lechner (the Thonet House at No. 11A) and Imre Steindl (No. 28). Unfortunately the drastic and insensitive modernization of the shop-fronts from the 1970s onwards has detracted from the buildings above and given to the whole the garish character of a modern German or Austrian town (the only shop to have kept its original interior is the art nouveau Philantia florist at No. 9). Among the shops to have survived the end of communism is the Folkart Centrum at No. 14, still Hungary's largest emporium of modern folk and craft objects, even if most of the goods on sale reflect the appalling recent decline in taste and craftsmanship. Remarkably, in a street largely given over now to chain stores, eateries, and expensively priced food and tourist shops, the Váci utca had also retained until as late as 1996 its various bookshops, including, at No. 10, the Gondolat (frequented by the writers Attila József and Lajos Kassák), and, at No. 22, the Studium Akadémia, which still keeps the lugubrious wooden shop-front that it had when occupied by an undertaker.

Once you have reached the end of the pedestrian part of the Váci utca, you should turn left into the short Kígyó utca, where you will pass, at Nos. 4–6, the **Apostolok restaurant**, which was opened as a beer hall in 1902, and was once the only place in Hungary where Löwenbrau beer on tap could be found; today a popular tourist venue, it has kept its elaborately carved wooden alcoves and furniture of 1913, as well as its mosaics and stained glass of the Apostles that were installed in 1927, when the rules of the house called for 'silence and sobriety'. Alongside the restaurant is the office building of the former Downtown Savings Bank, which was designed in 1909 by Henrik Schmahl, and is studded with playful late Gothic detailing; cutting through its eastern corner is a dark shopping arcade, the **Párisi udvar**, where the Gothic style is entwined with the neo-Moorish.

You emerge from the Párisi udvar on to the Petőfi Sándor utca, which runs parallel to the Váci utca, and was known as the Herrengasse at the time when the poet Petőfi began frequenting the Café Pilvax. This famous revolutionary café was situated at what is now No. 7 of this street; but before visiting the restaurant that has replaced this (at Pilvax köz 3) and immersing yourself in Petőfi's world, you should continue north to the Szervita tér, where you will see to your left three major buildings exemplifying the transition in Hungary between the Secession and modernism. The most progressive of these, No. 5, was built by Béla Lajta in 1912 as the home and premises of the music publisher **Rózsavölgyi**, whose music shop can still be found here, albeit without the original ornaments and fittings by Lajta's pupil Lajos Kozma. This revolutionary building, which is like a more ornamental version of works by the Viennese architect Adolf Loos, alternates decorated and plain surfaces, and is divided into bold horizontal bands: the stressing of the horizontal rather than the vertical elements in a building of this height is unusual, as is the ornamentation, which reveals Lajta's geometrical transformation of traditional Hungarian folk motifs. The next building, at No. 3, is a more blatantly transitional structure than Lajta's: designed by Henrik Böhm and Ármin Hegedűs in 1906, and originally the headquarters of the Turkish Bank, its largely glass, functionalist façade explodes three-quarters of the way up into a burst of eclectic and art nouveau forms framing a giant mosaic by Miksa Róth. The mosaic, by an artist steeped in the Arts and Crafts ideals of the Gödöllő community, seems to defy the building's Turkish patronage by representing the heroes of Hungarian history paying homage to Our Lady of Hungary. The final building, No. 2, is the former Szénássy and Barczai department store, built c.1908 by Dávid and Zsigmond Jónás: both in its geometric motifs and in its use of decorative studs to hold the stone tablets of the façade in place, it reveals the strong influence of contemporary Austrian architecture.

The time has now come to cast your mind back to the Pest in which Petőfi had lived—a township centred around his beloved **Café Pilvax**. Among the surviving buildings that he would have seen on his daily visits to the café is the tall baroque church (built between 1725 and 1732 for the recently founded Florentine order of the Servites) at the eastern corner of the triangular Szervita tér. Adjacent to this, and with a main façade that runs half the way down the Városház utca, is Budapest's largest eighteenth-century monument—the former **hospital** for veterans of the war against the Turks. Serving now as the municipal council building, this was designed at the beginning of the eighteenth century by the important Viennese architect of Italian origin, Anton Erhard Martinelli: its monotonous severity is explained by the destruction of its original ornamentation during the Second World War (the sculpture of Pallas Athene inside the southernmost gateway is an Italian work of 1785 that was transferred here from Buda). More impressive today is the adjoining Pest County Hall, which takes up the southern half of the Városház utca: a majestically porticoed neo-classical work by Pollácks' follower, Mátyás Zitterbach, this was completed in 1842, at a time when the nearby Café Pilvax was embarking on one of the liveliest periods in its history.

In 1842 this recently founded café was purchased by Károly Pilvax, under whom the establishment became a favourite meeting-place for radical youth, as well as a principal home to Petőfi, who advised the poet Arany to send him letters here rather than to his actual home, where he was almost never to be found. Although the name of Pilvax was removed from the café's signboard after the revolution of 1848–9, it was brought back in 1870. In 1911 the building housing the place was demolished, but a new café bearing the same name was later set up in the large block that replaced the old structure. This new establishment, with its entrance near the junction of the Városmajor utca and the newly created Pilvax Köz, was turned in the late 1960s into the present Pilvax restaurant, an *ersatz* early nineteenth-century interior, complete with archive material relating to Petőfi and his times (see p. 58).

When Petőfi and his fellow conspirators set off on 15 March 1848 on their eastward march towards the National Museum, they would have emerged from the Herrengasse at a point directly in front of one of Pest's oldest churches, the **Franciscan Church** (9 Ferenciek tere). Founded in the 1250s just outside the town walls, this church was burnt down by the Turks in 1526, and then rebuilt by the Franciscan friars just in time for the Turks to use the building as a mosque after 1541. Nothing from these earlier structures can be seen in the present church, which was erected between 1727 and 1743 and given a more lavish interior (complete with ceiling frescoes by Károly Lotz) in preparation for the millennial celebrations of 1896. One of the pews, carved in the carpentry workshop of the Franciscan order, is marked as having been the seat of Franz Liszt, who stayed in the presbytery of the by now dissolved monastery in 1869 and again in the winter of 1870–1, when he established his legendary fame in Hungary with a series of thirteen 'musical mornings' given in the Franciscan Church by him and other musicians. In 1877 ground-floor premises in the presbytery were leased out to a restaurant, which was renamed in 1934 as the **Kárpátia**: this much-frequented tourist establishment (at Nos. 4–8 Ferenciek tere) has a striking neo-Gothic interior with elaborate wooden alcoves and painted vaults and lunettes, which partly compensate for the bad food and unfriendly service.

Continuing towards the National Museum, you should head south from the Franciscan Church down the Károly Mihály utca, in the direction of the **Petőfi Museum of Literature** (at No. 16), which also administers the nearby memorial museum to the poet **Endre Ady** (at Nos. 4–6 of the parallel street to the east, the Veres Pálné utca). This latter institution consists of the small fourth-floor apartment where Ady moved in 1919, near the very end of his short life (see pp. 83–4). The old woman who looks after the place strongly advised me, after my visit here, to use the ancient-looking lift rather than walk down the shabby old stairwell, which she described as 'not nice'. The apartment itself has been arranged to look exactly as it appears in old photographs, and includes most of the original furniture, as well as a handful of personal items such as his railway pass and hat and tie. With its tiny rooms and sparse furnishings, this modest apartment forms a complete contrast to the building housing the main body of the Petőfi Museum of Literature—a grand aristocratic mansion built between 1759 and 1768 for the Károlyi family, and containing a number of gilded and mirrored rooms lavishly ornamented with both rococo and neo-classical elements (the place was substantially remodelled in the nineteenth century). The literary exhibits, displayed in a modernized part of the mansion, are summarized in a minutely printed hardback book (available at the ticket desk) only one and a half inches square—not perhaps the most likely format in which to persuade foreigners of the importance of Hungarian literature. The writers best represented (with items ranging from Transylvanian chairs to typewriters and reconstructed studies) are Mór Jókai, Zsigmond Móricz, Attila József and, of course, Sándor Petőfi, whose life and times are concisely conveyed by the combination of his travelling-case and one of the tables from the Café Pilvax. Ironically, given the presence today of these and other Petőfi memorabilia, the mansion served during the 1848–9 revolution as the headquarters of the Austrian general Julius Haynau, who put under arrest here the first prime minister of an independent Hungary, Count Lajos Batthyány.

From the former Károlyi mansion it is but a short walk east along the Ferenczy István utca to the Múzeum körút, with its dominating **neoclassical museum** where the revolution broke out on 15 March 1848 (see pp. 58–9). In Petőfi's day the museum stood outside the city's boundaries, in surroundings so rural that cattle from the market held in what is now the Kálvin tér were sometimes known to have strayed into the grounds. In view of all the romantic mythology that has grown up around Petőfi's revolutionary address on the museum's steps, it is interesting to note the phlegmatic response to the occasion on the part of the museum's then director: 'A noisy mob was stirring up trouble outside, preventing me from working. So I went home.' The museum, though largely taken up today by objects and information panels telling the history of Hungary from 1000 to 1990, is mainly visited for its dramatically lit display of Hungary's ill-fated and much-travelled medieval **crown jewels**, which finally came here in 1978 after spending thirty-four years in Fort Knox. From the pleasant garden outside, laid out in 1856, you can glimpse the Radio Building (on the Bródy Sándor utca), from where the first shots of the 1956 Uprising were fired. Heated political discussions can be imagined as having taken place in the adjoining **Múzeum coffee-house** (at the junction of the Bródy Sándor utca and the Múzeum körút), which dates back to 1875 and was once a favourite haunt of students, writers, and politicians: though recently revamped as a smart restaurant, it has kept much of its late nineteenth-century interior, notably its wooden panelling, Zsolnay tiles, and fresco by Károly Lotz.

On retracing Petőfi's steps to the National Museum, you will have crossed the eastern boundary of the Belváros and seen most of the surviving Pest monuments that the poet would have known. Now is the time to move into a later period of Pest's history, and head north again towards the Lipótváros, which you can easily reach from the museum by taking one of the frequent trams or buses that run between the Múzeum körút and the great transport terminus of the Deák tér.

The **Deák tér**, with its multitude of metro entrances and untidy range of surrounding buildings, is a hectic and confusing space that has played a central role in the modern metropolis, having been, among other things, the site of the city's first public toilet (opened in 1883) and the starting-point (after 1866) of the third horse-drawn tram in Europe. The tram stop was situated just outside the **Lutheran Church**, where, before entering the Lipótváros, you can bid a final farewell to the neo-classical Pest in which Petőfi was brought up: the first Hungarian commission of Mihály Pollack, and erected between 1799 and 1809, this simple, spire-less structure, with an interior spartan even by Protestant standards, has a plaque inside recording that the 'romantic poet Sándor Petőfi was educated here'.

It says much of Pest's late nineteenth-century development, and of the Lipótváros in particular, that most of the striking and truly noticeable buildings you will pass as you walk north of the old town are the head-quarters of banks and insurance offices. Of the buildings surrounding the Deák tér itself, the one that sticks most in the memory is not the Lutheran Church but the massive and slightly preposterous former **Anker insurance company building**, which stands off the square's north-eastern corner, on the Bajcsy-Zsilinszky út. Featuring a raised neo-classical temple below a steeply roofed medieval-style tower, this is the work of Ignác Alpár, who is best known for his fantastical 'historical ensemble' in the Városliget: when completed in 1907, the building inspired a shocked reaction not only from the Budapest public but also from Alpár's wife, who, on being taken by her husband to see the work, is reported to have exclaimed, 'Oh, what a shame!'

Adjacent to the north-western corner of the Deák tér is the enormous Erzsébet tér, which is adorned in its verdant centre by a Bernini-inspired sculpture personifying Hungary's four main rivers (designed by Ybl in 1879 for the Kálvin tér, this was restored and brought here following extensive damage in the Second World War). The square is flanked to the east and south by examples of the worst extremes of twentieth-century architecture: the 1948 bus station on the square's eastern side is a work of dreary functionalism, while the luxury Kempinski Hotel (opened in 1992) is a fussy and brash post-modernist work. More enter-taining is the interior of the former **Domestic Bank** (now the British embassy) at the square's south-western corner: the former cashier's hall in the building's covered courtyard (which is used for occasional public exhibitions) has been preserved virtually intact from 1913, and has a superlative glass ceiling in a proto-Art Deco manner.

From the northern side of the square you can walk west down the broad József Attila utca into the riverside Roosevelt tér, where two of Pest's more spectacular commercial buildings await you. The first building to your right, at Nos. 3–4, is the former **Pest Commercial Bank** (now the ministry of the interior), begun in 1906 by Alpár and completed by him in 1918, with an interim period of several years in which he was replaced by Zsigmond Quittner, who, like him, was also forced to resign after quarrelling with the bank's director. Quittner was responsible for much of the interior, notably the three-storeyed covered courtyard, which, with its coloured glass dome, green marble balusters, simple arcading, and suspended ceremonial staircase, is a wonderfully theatrical space. While engaged on this building, Quittner was supervising next door the construction of his best-known work—the former headquarters of the **London Gresham Life Assurance Company**. The English sixteenth-century financier Sir Thomas Gresham, founder of London's Stock Exchange, appears in Elizabethan ruff at the top of a richly carved and moulded main facade that is flanked by cupolas and articulated by raised, giant-order columns: the overall energetic and massively swollen effect is truly expressive of the economic power of the company. The eloquence of this exterior was not simply a sham, as was the case with so many of Budapest's grandiose turn-of-the-century façades: behind were superlative stained-glass windows by Miksa Róth, and luxury apartments that had originally boasted an early form of central heating and a pioneering dust-extraction system. In recent years, however, the whole building has gone evocatively to seed, as will become apparent if you walk through the main portal, and into the T-shaped glass-roofed shopping arcade that lies behind, where you will find domed skylights thick with dirt, and sad-looking shop and office-fronts cowering in the gloom. A reminder of this arcade's former glory is the sinuous wrought-iron entrance gate on the Zrínyi utca, which is decorated with peacocks. For many years there has been talk of transforming the whole building into a hotel.

Although commerce is the principal force celebrated in the Roosevelt tér, the narrow northern side of the square is taken up by a building testifying to the more patriotic and less materialistic elements that went into the making of late nineteenth-century Budapest—the **Hungarian**

Academy of Sciences. Both Ybl and Feszl submitted plans for the design of this building, but, controversially, the commission eventually went in 1859 to the German architect August Stüler, whose neo-Renaissance structure—the first of its kind in Budapest—sparked off a heated debate as to whether this style was more suited to a Hungarian national institution than a neo-medieval one. The institution itself, dedicated to the development of Hungarian arts, science, language, and literature, was founded in 1825 by the dynamic Count István Széchenyi, whose presence is particularly strong in this square. Széchenyi lived between 1827 and 1835 in an apartment on the site of the former Pest Commercial Bank; and within days of his lonely death in 1860 a decision was made by the Academy of Sciences to erect in the square a statue to his memory. This work, delayed for political and other reasons until 1880, rises directly in front of the Academy, on a plinth with mythological personifications of Széchenyi's main spheres of activity—navigation, agriculture, industry, and commerce: the Italian writer and scholar Claudio Magris found it symptomatic of this period's 'pompous elevation of the world's prose to the status of poetry' that commerce should be personified here by Minerva, a goddess normally associated with thought and the intellect. But the square's principal memorial to Széchenyi is the bridge that is officially referred to now as the **Széchenyi Chain Bridge**, which was built between 1842–9 and was not only the first permanent link between Buda and Pest but also one of the largest suspension bridges of its time. Designed by the English architect William Tierney Clark (who was also responsible for the similar Hammersmith Bridge in London), it was erected under the supervision of the Scottish engineer Adam Clark (no relation), who even imported from England the iron that was used for it. Small fragments of the original structure—which was completely rebuilt after the Second World War—can be seen in the Transport Museum behind the Városliget Park (see pp. 179–80).

The Lipótváros or Leopoldstadt—epitome of the prosperous Budapest that developed after the Chain Bridge was built—stretches north of the Roosevelt tér across an area of formerly marshy land that was reclaimed in the mid nineteenth century. Its principal monument, Imre Steindl's **parliament building**, outshines even the Gresham palace as the most dramatic landmark along the Pest embankment (see pp. 71–2). The interior, as exciting as its fantastically pinnacled exterior might lead you to expect, is well worth visiting, even though this entails paying a large fee and participating in an interminable guided tour. Your guide is likely to assail you with statistics that emphasize the almost ridiculous lavishness and size of a structure whose 691 rooms make this one of the largest parliament buildings in the world, as well as a place that has never been fully utilized, even during the period when Hungary was a country of formidable proportions. Begun in 1885, it was completed seventeen years later with the aid of a daily workforce of about 1,000 labourers, and at a total cost that escalated from an estimated 18.5 million to 35 million gold crowns: large enough to contain fifty five-storeyed apartment buildings, its construction and decoration involved 40 million bricks, half a million ornamental stones, 40 kg. of 22–3-carat gold, and 242 statues. The main entrance, on the Kossuth Lajos tér, leads to a monumental staircase whose neo-Gothic vaulting has classical-style ceiling frescoes by the prolific Károly Lotz, including a central panel representing Hungary flanked by Széchenyi and Petőfi. At the top of the stairs, you come out into the circular central hall (used today for ceremonial occasions), which is surrounded by pyrogranite statues of all the Hungarian kings ('misshapen figures with parrot colours', grumbled one of the deputies in 1902) and covered with an elaborately vaulted dome that is like an explosion of gold. The Deputy Council Chamber, to the south of the central hall, was originally decorated behind the speaker's lectern with a large canvas by Mihály Munkácsy representing Árpád's troops conquering Hungary with an ease that was criticized by some of the painter's contemporaries (this painting—the most important single work of art in the whole building—was later transferred to the president's office). On the lectern itself a bullet-hole bears witness to one of the more exciting moments in the chamber's history, when the then speaker, István Tisza, was shot at in 1912 by a man who disagreed with his policies; after the bullet had become lodged in the lectern, the would-be assassin turned the gun on himself. The Old Upper House, to the north of the central hall, is an almost exact replica of the Deputy Council Chamber, and is now used for conferences.

Facing the Parliament across the rather bleak Kossuth Lajos tér are two imposing, classically inspired public buildings that in any other location would have dominated their surroundings: the one to the south is the ministry of agriculture (1885–7); the other is the former Palace of Justice. It is certainly revealing of Hungarian attitudes towards folklore that the latter building, at the governmental and symbolical heart of the country, should now be occupied by the **Museum of Ethnography**. The building itself, erected by Alajos Hauszmann between 1893 and

1896, must have struck fear in the hearts of all those who had approached it during its days as a Supreme Court, with its giant-order façade, pedimented frontispiece, crowning chariot of justice, and flanking towers that resemble ancient lighthouses. Even more intimidating and impressive is its vestibule, an echoing marbled space whose multitude of steps and columns, and high-flown frescoed allegory by Károly Lotz, successfully conveyed the overblown Belle Époque architecture of Buenos Aires in Alan Parker's recent film version of the musical *Evita*. However, few places are quite as unsuitable as this one is for a display of Hungarian folk traditions, unless the intention was to illustrate exactly the sort of pretentious cosmopolitanism that the upholders of Hungarian folklore were rebelling against.

Further monuments of hollow eclectic grandeur are to be found on the nearby Szabadság tér, which can be reached from the ministry of agriculture by walking south-east along the short Vécsey utca. Empty at night, like most of the Lipótváros, this has also by day a stranded, stage-set quality, thanks to being bypassed by all major streets, and by having been laid out in a remarkably short space of time (between 1901 and 1905) over what had been a military barracks and prison. The square represented a personal triumph for Ignác Alpár, who won commissions to design its two major buildings. The former **stock exchange building** (now the headquarters of Hungarian television), on the western side of the square, is the more interesting of the two, with its admixture of ancient Greek and Assyrian elements; but it was the **Hungarian National Bank** opposite (formerly the Austro-Hungarian Bank) that earned Alpár his short-lived reputation as the most successful Hungarian architect of his day. Such leading contemporaries as Ödön Lechner, Otto Wagner, and the prolific Viennese theatre designers Fellner and Helmer were among the many distinguished architects from Austria and Hungary who were invited to take part in the competition to design this bank. The unanimous decision to award the first prize to Alpár was regarded at the time as a great victory for Hungarian architecture; today it can also be seen as a victory of conservative, historicist tastes over the more progressive tendencies of the age. Wagner's design, which was later re-adapted as the pioneering Vienna Postal Savings Bank, was curtly dismissed by the *Budapesti Hírlap* as being a 'fanciful' work resembling 'a huge dovecote': 'If this is what modern architecture means,' it concluded, 'then we have a long way to go until we can cherish modernity.'

Lechner, though failing to win even the third prize, had at least the consolation of receiving almost contemporaneously the commission to build another major bank immediately behind the Hungarian Bank, to which it is now joined by modern corridors. This work, the recently restored former **Postal Savings Bank** (see p. 74), is one of the most playful and striking examples of Hungarian art nouveau, though sadly its exterior is difficult now fully to appreciate owing to its cramped position on the narrow Hold utca. Begun in 1900 and completed a year and a half later, the building aroused an inevitable mixture of intense admiration and mockery: 'It is not so much small investors who visit the Postal Savings Bank', wrote the critic Ödön Gerő in 1908, 'but rather its supporters and opponents, its enthusiasts and mockers. I can hardly think of any other building in the architecture of Hungary that has been the subject of so much feverish interest as this one has.' The brickwork exterior, with its flat composition and absence of historicist elements, has a daring simplicity that is partly mitigated by a use of colour and ceramic ornamentation which climaxes in a Hungarian-oriental roofline of Gaudí-like imagination: some of the ornamental forms have symbolical significance, such as the bees making their way to the hive-shaped finials, and the roof-top bull-heads copied from those discovered in a major turn-of-the-century archaeological find known as 'Attila's Treasure' (these heads, furthermore, flank that ultimate symbol of Hungarian folklore—the sheepskin waistcoat or *cifraszűr*; see p. 73). The interior, which has now been restored to its original state, is particularly notable for the ironwork detailing on its staircases, and above all for its glass-domed former cashier's hall. Unfortunately this is no longer open to the public.

The Hold utca is itself one of the more interesting streets in the Lipótváros. In its descent south towards the former Postal Savings Bank it passes an 'eternal flame' commemorating the assassinated 1848 hero Lajos Batthyány, and (at No. 13) a covered 1890s market that lends the street much of its daily animation. On either side of the market (at Nos. 11 and 15) are two cheap and popular restaurants that fall into the now threatened category of a *kisvendeglő*: the **Csarnok Étterem** (frequented by many of the stall-holders) specializes in lamb and mutton dishes, while the nocturnally more animated **Tüköry söröző**, which is perpetually crowded with students, is famous for its steak tartare and draught Dreher beer.

Continuing south of the Hold utca on the Hercegprimás utca (which will take you back to the Deák tér), you will soon pass to your left the west façade of Budapest's largest but not most beautiful church—**St**

Stephen's Basilica. This gloomy, domed structure has a suitably dismal history dating back to 1805, when a church on this site was conceived as part of the plans for the development of the Lipótváros. It was not until 1845 that a design for the building was actually made—by the neo-classical architect József Hild. Most of the walls and much of the dome had been completed by the time of Hild's fortuitous death in 1867; only a few months before he would have had the humiliation of seeing much of the structure collapse in so spectacular a fashion that a good 300 windows were destroyed in the vicinity. Miklós Ybl, who had already been appointed Hild's successor, was doubtless delighted by this accident, which gave him an opportunity to replace the original neo-classical design (comparable to that of the cathedral at Esztergom) with a marginally livelier, neo-Renaissance one. He too failed to see the completed church, dying in 1892, fourteen years before the building's inauguration. Even his structure, built with better materials than Hild's and with more careful engineering calculations, failed to withstand Second World War bombing; intensive restoration and rebuilding has been continuing since the 1980s. The lugubrious marble interior has some impressive sculptures by Alajos Stróbl, including one of St Stephen (behind the high altar); but your most lasting memory of a visit inside is likely to be the sight of **St Stephen's mummified right hand** (Hungary's holiest relic), which is kept in a chapel behind the chancel, and needs a coin to be illuminated.

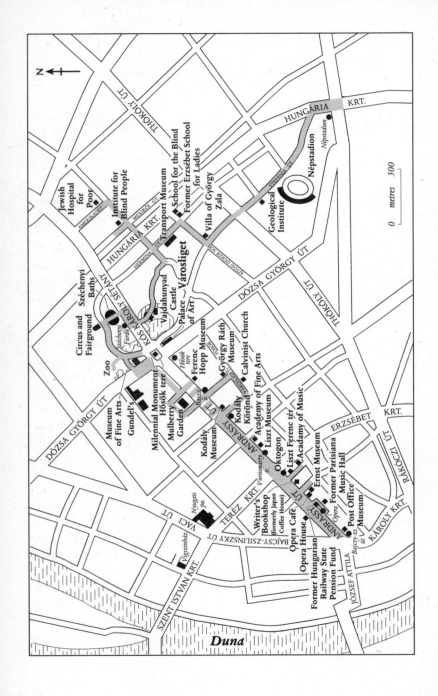

Duna

❧❧❧ Walk 5 ❧❧❧

The Andrássy Út and the Városliget

An excellent idea of the pride and jingoism affecting Budapest in the years leading up to the millennial celebrations of 1896 (see pp. 68 ff.) can be obtained by walking the whole length of the avenue that became the great showpiece of the modern metropolis—the **Andrássy út**. Almost as wide as the Champs-Elysées, and extending in a straight line for two and a half kilometres through the district of the Terézváros, it was born out of the new wealth and spirit of urban renewal generated by the Compromise of 1867. Begun in 1872, and known originally as the Sugár út or 'Radial Avenue', it was completed twelve years later, shortly before being renamed after the one-time Hungarian prime minister Gyula Andrássy (in 1990 it reverted to this name after having been called during the communist period the Sztálin út and then the 'Népköztársaság útja' or 'Avenue of the People's Republic'). H. Ellen Brown, the author of *A Girl's Wanderings in Hungary* (1896), stayed in this street in the 1890s, at the height of its popularity, in a 'charming town house' rented by an aristocratic couple 'in preference to their own gloomy family palace in an old-fashioned and duller part of the city'. The house, and the street itself, quite overwhelmed her: 'Situated in one of the finest streets of Europe, and "replete with every modern convenience", as the house-agents would say, it required some degree of effort on my part to remind me that I was still actually living in a "land of barbarism".'

The avenue, which projects north-eastwards from the edge of the old town, is divided into three distinct sections of near equal length, the first of which is closely packed mainly with offices and public buildings. In the metro terminal below the Deák tér, where you could begin your walk, you will find displayed several of the original carriages from the pioneering underground railway that was opened in 1896 directly underneath the Andrássy út. The British traveller Forster Bovill, writing in 1908, described this railway as 'a most serviceable system', while adding that 'travelling is not so luxurious underground as in London'. The railway, which originally ran from the Vörösmarty tér to the middle of the Városliget (in 1973 it was extended to the Mexikói út), functions like an underground tram, and forces you to choose your station entrance according to the side of the street you wish to go down.

The avenue's first attraction is the unpromising-sounding **Postal Museum**, which you will find to your right (at No. 3) almost immediately on entering the avenue from the Bajcsy Zsilinszky út. Though the history of Hungary's postal service might not be one of major interest to most visitors (although some people will undoubtedly enjoy operating the early telegraph tape machine), you should come here if only to look inside one of the avenue's grand private apartments from the late nineteenth century. Created between 1884 and 1886 for the wealthy builder András Saxlener, this seven-room apartment has kept much of its original decoration, including ceiling frescoes (above the staircase) by the ubiquitous Károly Lotz, Carrara marble fireplaces, and Murano chandeliers. The postal equipment, reconstructed post office, life-sized models of postal employees, and other such exhibits that have now been placed here curiously do not detract from this splendid setting, but instead evoke aspects of the everyday world that the room's former inhabitants would have known. The reason for establishing here such an apparently unsuitable museum goes back to the early communist days, when the house was taken over as the 'Centre of the National Association of Stamp Collectors'.

The most sumptuous building on the Andrássy út, if not in the whole of Budapest, is further up the street, on the left-hand side. Work on this building, the **Opera House**, was begun in 1875, and, though largely funded by the emperor Franz Joseph, was protracted until 1884, owing to constant financial problems. The architect, Miklós Ybl, was so meticulous in his attention to detail that he reputedly checked every cartload of bricks that was brought here: his close supervision of the construction is revealed in the overall liveliness and jewel-like ornamentation of this neo-Renaissance structure. Regular guided tours are conducted daily around the fabulously rich interior, the recent and extensive restoration of which entailed the use of 300,000 small pieces of 23-carat gold leaf, and has given a glittering vitality even to the frescoed dome of Parnassus by Károly Lotz, normally not the liveliest of artists. But this is a setting that only comes fully to life in the context of one of the ballets or operas that are put on here (the tickets for these, though difficult to obtain, are still remarkably cheap by the standards of other major opera houses). Gustav Mahler, Hans Richter, and Otto Klemperer have all been musical directors of this theatre—a theatre whose audiences were already known by 1900 as among the most critical and demanding in Europe. A curious anomaly of this place today is that foreign operas are often performed here in Hungarian but with the guest singers from abroad responding in their native languages. Ideally you should come here to see one of the works by the theatre's first musical director, Ferenc Erkel, who was Hungary's greatest operatic composer of the last century; his operas, undeservedly little known abroad, deal with the same themes from Hungarian history and mythology that inspired so many of the country's nineteenth-century artists and writers.

Before crossing back over the road to see a major early work by Lechner, you should peer into the Opera Pharmacy at No. 26 to admire its well preserved neo-Renaissance interior of 1888; on the way to the pharmacy you will pass (at No. 24) the site of the Three Ravens Inn, which was one of Ady's favourite places for indulging his love of drink. The Lechner building, which is directly in front of the Opera House, was the one he designed in 1883 as the **Hungarian Railway State Pension House** (see p. 73). Counteracting Ybl's Italianate palace opposite with a steep-roofed structure inspired by a French Renaissance château, Lechner's building is a wonderful mixture of Gothic and Renaissance detailing. Turned during the architect's lifetime into the Bokros Hotel, it houses today the State Ballet Institute, which is entered through the side-entrance in the Dalszínház utca; the high points of the interior are the large, elegantly detailed courtyard and the upper part of the main staircase, which is colourfully lit by stained-glass windows. The pavement below the beautiful arcade of the main façade was once laid out with tables belonging to one of the Andrássy út's most popular if also ill-fated cafés, Drechsler's, which eventually closed down after six successive owners had either committed suicide or gone bankrupt. György Klösz, Budapest's most famous photographer during the period of the Compromise, captured the habitués of the café in a photograph that is now frequently used to evoke the heady atmosphere of the turn-of-the-century city.

Directly behind Lechner's building, on the Paulay Ede utca, is one of the city's strangest structures from the early twentieth century, the former Parisiana music-hall (now the **Új Színház** or New Theatre). Designed by Béla Lajta in 1909 but drastically transformed at various times this century, it was painstakingly restored to its original state between 1988–9, on the basis of old photographs, documents, and samples of masonry. A key work linking the art nouveau manner of Lajta's youth and the modernism of his later years, its façade is in a style that 'can't be categorized', to use the unhelpful words of János Gerle, author of a guide to the city's turn-of-the-century architecture. Completely unlike any other building by Lajta, it is perhaps best described as a proto-Art Deco futurist fantasy, with a simplified neo-Egyptian portal, bold areas of undecorated wall, and a crowning, tightly packed row of angels resembling the elaborate wrapping around a birthday cake.

Returning to the Andrássy út, and continuing north-east on the right-hand pavement, you will pass at No. 23 one of the city's few remaining pre-First World War cafés and confectioners to have retained much of its original decoration and atmosphere: while tourists favour its cramped outdoor terrace, its many regulars tend to gather in the smoky gloom of the neo-rococo back room, where I was once surprised by the writer Péter Esterházy while eating an Esterházy cake. Further up the street you cross the Nagymező utca, which is sometimes known as the Broadway of Pest thanks to its concentration of nightclubs and theatres. At No. 20 Nagyméző utca, off the northern side of the Andrássy út, is the lavish turn-of-the-century building that served as the home and studio of the Viennese society photographer Mai Mano; this is now being transformed into a photography museum. In its basement is the currently closed-down **Arizona**, which had been one of the most popular night spots of Budapest's interwar 'Silver Age'. An article in the *Pest Courier* of 1935 stated that 'anyone who visits Pest, whether it be the Prince of Wales or anyone else, first heads for the Arizona'—a statement borne out by the fact that even the normally effete Patrick Leigh Fermor went there (an experience he described, in his characteristically high-flown way, as a 'plunge into the scintillating cave of the most glamorous night-club I have ever seen').

Turning instead south-east down the Nagymező út, you will come at No. 8 to the so-called **Ernst Muzeum**, built in 1912 for the art critic and collector Lajos Ernst, and which now houses on its second floor a gallery for temporary exhibitions of modern art. The modestly sized entrance-hall and staircase has black wooden benches and banisters by Ödön Lechner, and a delightful stained-glass window of 1911 by Hungary's leading 'Post-Impressionist' József Rippl-Rónai, who clearly shows in this work the influence of the simple decorative forms of the French 'Nabis'.

Both Lechner and Rippl-Rónai were regulars at the nearby Japán coffee-house, the site of which you will pass as you continue walking up the right-hand side of the Andrássy út. Before getting there you should take a look at the neighbouring **Divatcsarnok** (at No. 39), which was opened in 1912 as 'the grand Parisian department store'. The first such store in Budapest, it had staff who were trained to smile, and a roof-top which served as a restaurant in the summer and a skating rink in the winter; despite modern remodelling, the interior retains ceiling frescoes by Károly Lotz from the late nineteenth-century gentleman's club or casino that preceded the store, while the exterior is still domi-nated by the 1912 building's most sensational and original feature—a giant parabolic arch. A characteristically ironic description of the store features in Péter Esterházy's generally impenetrable book, *The Glance of Countess Hahn-Hahn (down the Danube)* (1991): 'On the ceiling of the main hall is an allegory of the city of Budapest, surrounded by figures repre-senting the arts and crafts. Now they sell camping equipment and bed-linen here.'

The former Japán coffee-house, at No. 45, is today the **Writers' Bookshop**, which has recently installed among the books a small café with photographic souvenirs of its celebrated predecessor. The original café, which was popular above all with artists, was decorated in an entrancing Japanese style, featuring white majolica walls painted with bamboos, fantastical birds, chrysanthemums, and vases. The white-bearded Lechner presided over the artists' gatherings here, and was described by one of his contemporaries as having eyes constantly directed on the café window in seach of attractive women passing by. Csontváry, the eccentric loner, was keen to be accepted here, and, in the course of his travels around the world, sent postcards to the café addressed simply 'To the artists': 'My oriental journey has been fully suc-cessful,' went one of his typically cryptic cards, posted in this case from Constantinople. For the writer Ernő Szép the very existence of this café obviated the need for exotic journeys such as these: 'Those of us who frequented the Japán', he recalled in 1931, 'perhaps travelled even further than if we had been to Japan itself. This coffee-house was more remote and exotic than the world of white lotuses, green tea and golden Buddhas, because it was the home of the fairy of our youth.'

A favourite meeting-place of today, not so much for artists but for young foreigners and privileged young Hungarians, is the green and narrow **Liszt Ferenc tér**, which you will pass to your right immediately beyond the Writers' Bookshop. New life has been given to this once moribund space by the presence on the western and eastern sides respectively of the Incognito and the Café Mediterrán, both of which have loud music at night, perpetually crowded summer terraces, and a bland, cosmopolitan atmosphere. In between these two establishments is a lively modern statue of Liszt, who was the first president of Hungary's Academy of Music, now situated at the southern end of the square. The **Ferenc Liszt Academy of Music**, founded in 1875, has occupied since 1908 a heavy, eclectic structure whose pompous exterior is dominated by a bronze by Stróbl of the seated Liszt. Much more enjoyable is the building's richly decorated interior, which sparkles with gold and Zsolnay ceramics and has stained-glass windows by Miksa Róth. The decorative climax is the large painting in the upstairs vestibule by the greatest master of the Gödöllő School, Aladár Körösfői-Kriesch: conceived as an integral part of its gilded surroundings (Körösfői-Kriesch was as much a designer as he was a painter), the work comprises a Burne-Jones-like composition centred on stylized female nudes; entitled *The Source of Art*, it was featured in 1990 on the catalogue cover of an important travelling exhibition dedicated to Hungary's 'Golden Age'.

Beyond the Liszt Ferenc tér the Andrássy út crosses the largest of Pest's ring of boulevards, the Nagykörút. The octagonal point of intersection, known as the **Oktogon**, was taken up on its south-eastern side by the important turn-of-the-century café called the Abbázia, which was especially popular with politicians and liberal sympathizers: 'a black coffee sipped after lunch in the Abbázia shows that the person has plans for disrupting the city,' wrote Gyula Krúdy in a story in which he claimed that it was sufficient 'to ask someone from old Pest to which coffee-house he had his mail addressed to be able to form within minutes a clear picture of his social circle, ideals and view of the world'. Today the dominant presence in the Oktogon are American fast-food joints, notably what is reputedly the largest Burger King in the world (if you really are desperate for a hamburger at this point you would be better off walking north-west along the Nagykörút to the luxury McDonalds that now occupies the chandelier-hung restaurant attached to Gustave Eiffel's ironwork Western Station).

North of the Oktogon, the buildings along the Andrássy út remain as

closely packed as ever, but the avenue widens slightly to accommodate
the parallel rows of trees that had originally been planned to line its
entire length. Earlier this century, many of the pedestrians walking up
the left-hand side of the avenue would have felt a shudder on passing
next to the infamous **No. 60**, which served as the headquarters of the
secret police both under Horthy and the communists: political suspects,
arrested always in the middle of the night, began to fear the worst when
they were driven to this address, where, if not executed outright, they
could expect weeks of torture in freezing, cockroach-infested cells
described by Pálóczi-Horváth as measuring three yards by four, with a
plank of wood for a bed, a permanently lit bulb hanging from the ceiling,
and a spyhole that opened and closed every five minutes. In the meantime the dreaded Stalinist police force known as the AVO regularly gathered for cakes and coffee at the superlative café and confectioner's at No.
70 Andrássy út, which they confiscated from the family of the philosopher György Lukács. When this establishment, the Lukács Cukrászda,
was later reopened to the public, it became part of the Gerbeaud chain,
which furnished its entrance area with the exquisite fittings of a reconstructed 1930s café supplied by the Museum of Commerce and Catering; the long upper room, with all its chandeliers and gilded neo-baroque
panelling, was left untouched. The resulting café had all the elegance
and excellent confectionery of the famous Gerbeaud's on Vörösmarty tér
(see pp. 152–3), but without the tourists, and with an atmosphere of
smoke-fuelled melancholy. Sadly, the place has been recently closed
down, and faces an uncertain future.

Across the avenue, at No. 67, is the former seat of the Academy of
Music, a late 1870s structure decorated on the outside with reliefs of
famous composers, including Erkel and Ferenc Liszt, both of whom had
apartments in the building. Liszt, born in a Hungarian village that is now
in Austria, made frequent visits to Budapest from his childhood onwards,
and after 1869 divided his time between here, Weimar, and Rome.
Although he once insisted that 'the style of my abode must be simple
and comfortable, with no trappings', the Hungarian government took
every step to ensure that the four-roomed apartment prepared for him
in 1879 in the Academy of Music was as luxurious as possible; he was
to stay there every winter from 1880 until his death in 1886. This
first-floor apartment, with its windows over the Andrássy út, has now
been turned into the **Ferenc Liszt Museum** and Memorial Building,
the entrance to which is at Vörösmarty utca 35. A copper plate in the

grand entrance hall to the former Academy states in Hungarian and German that 'Ferenc Liszt is at home between 3 and 4 p.m. on Tuesdays, Thursdays and Saturdays'. The apartment itself contains not only numerous portraits and personal items of Liszt—ranging from his propelling pencil to his Chickering grand piano—but also many of the original heavy furnishings, including the French Renaissance-style furniture that was especially designed for the place by Sándor Fellner, a young architect who had recently returned from Paris. Adolf Lang, who was responsible for the building itself, was also the architect of the adjoining neo-Renaissance structure at No. 69 Andrássy út, built in 1877 as an exhibition hall for the National Fine Arts Society founded by Count Andrássy in 1863 with the aim of promoting Hungarian art; at the same time there was erected next door, at No. 71, a sgraffitoed building by Alajos Rauscher intended as the first permanent home of Pest's School of Design. The two institutions were later joined together as the **Academy of Fine Arts**, which, for all its innovative teaching methods, preserves some of the atmosphere of the grand art schools of the past. Renaissance Italy was the principal inspiration to Lang's building (as it was to Rauscher's), which has an echoing, gloomily lit vestibule and an upstairs series of gilded, frescoed galleries reminiscent of some of the *loggie* in the Vatican. The artist, needless to say, was Károly Lotz.

The Kodály Körönd, further up the Andrássy út, is a circular intersection that was originally known simply as the 'Körönd' or 'Circus'. At its four corners are near-identical four-floor apartment blocks based on the one by Gusztáv Petschacher at No. 3—yet another Italian Renaissance-inspired structure, this one erected in the early 1880s for the Railways Pension administration. Enormous plane and chestnut trees have grown up in front of these buildings, which have also attractive front gardens rich in plants and flowers. Behind one of these gardens, at No. 1 (at the north-eastern corner), is the ground-floor apartment that belonged to the composer Zoltán Kodály from 1924 to his death in 1967, and which is now a small memorial museum to him. The dining-room and sitting-room are still exactly as they appear in the various old photographs on display here, some of which feature Kodály in the company of guests such as Yehudi Menuhin. The relatively simple decoration, featuring numerous Transylvanian and other folk objects, reflects a different and less pompous mentality compared to that of the Renaissance-obsessed age in which the building itself had been erected.

From the Kodály Körönd all the way to its conclusion in Heroes'

Square, the Andrássy út is more verdant and residential in character, and lined mainly with detached villas. There is also a corresponding change in the architecture, with the eclectic neo-Renaissance structures giving way generally to lighter, less grandiose buildings in an art nouveau style. To see some of the finest buildings in this style you have to wander off into the neighbouring streets, beginning with the parallel Városligeti fasor, which you can reach from the Kodály körönd by turning south down the Felső Erdősor. The distinctive spire that you will see to your right as you near the juction of the Városligeti fasor and the Bajza utca belongs to one of Budapest's most beautiful and original churches from the early years of this century—Aladár Árkay's **Calvinist Church** of 1911–13. Apart from the stained-glass windows by Miksa Róth—an artist as ubiquitous as Károly Lotz—every detail of this building, from the ironwork gateways to the pews and lamps of the interior, was designed by Árkay himself. The overall result is a harmonious application of stylized Hungarian folk motifs to a pleasingly simple setting based largely on Protestant architectural models from Finland, Germany, and America.

Across the street, at No. 12, an opportunity to go inside one of this district's turn-of-the-century villas is provided by the **György Ráth Museum**, which is a small collection of Chinese and Japanese art beautifully displayed in the home of the eponymous Ráth, the first director of Budapest's Museum of Applied Arts; unfortunately, as with the nearby Ferenc Hopp Museum of East Asian Art, the interior has been almost completely modernized. Further up the street, at No. 24, is a virtuoso Parisian-style art nouveau building of 1901 by the versatile Emil Vidor, who also designed (for his father) the even more bizarre house across the street at No. 33, which is like a Swiss chalet as imagined by a deranged architect determined to incorporate fantastical decorative elements from all the main European art centres of the turn of the century; the porter will occasionally allow visitors to look around the well-preserved ground floor.

Returning to the Andrássy út along the Bajza utca, and then turning right, you will come at No. 103 to the collection of Indian, Indonesian, and Mongolian art installed in the former villa of **Ferenc Hopp**, a wealthy businessman who travelled five times around the world between 1882 and 1914. Afterwards you should cross the avenue and continue walking west along the Bajza utca, where, at No. 42, is the former Lederer apartment block of 1902, which has a mosaic frieze by Károly Kernstock, and finely carved windows emulating Italian ones of the early

Renaissance. This is the sort of finely crafted fifteenth-century pastiche that would have appealed to British Arts and Crafts artists such as Walter Crane, who indeed visited Budapest in 1900 and admired the adjoining building at No. 44—a work of 1898 by the same team of architects, Zoltán Bálint and Lajos Jámbor. Across the street is the so-called **Mulberry Garden** ('Epreskert'), a large green space that has been used since 1882 by the sculpture department of the Academy of Fine Arts. Alajos Stróbl, the most important of the many nineteenth-century sculptors to have had their studios here, devoted much time to embellishing this garden with copies of famous Hungarian sculptures. His principal achievement was to have brought here from the Kálvin tér a wonderful baroque **calvary chapel** that had been threatened with demolition; this crumbling structure, with its theatrical flights of steps, has often been attributed to the great Austrian architect Fischer von Erlach, but it was probably the work of the lesser-known András Mayerhoffer. The architect Frigyes Schulek, while rebuilding the Matthias Church, made his own contribution to the garden by placing here a medieval portal from the latter church, and then turning this into a Romantic-style ruin.

Running parallel to the Bajza utca on the northern side of the garden is the Munkácsy Mihály utca, where, at No. 23, there is a superb example of baroque influence on the art nouveau in the dynamic flowing portal forming the centrepiece of a house designed by Kálmán Körössy in 1904. Almost next to this, at No. 19B, is József Vágó's Schiffer Villa of 1910–12, a proto-modernist structure with a corner turret resembling a rather squat space rocket; the interior, which might one day be opened to the public, contrasts with the bare exterior by being decorated with colourful panels by such leading artists of the time as István Csók, Béla Iványi-Grünwald, and József Rippl-Rónai. Turning north from here into the Lendvay utca, you will pass at No. 28 the impressive Groedel Villa of 1900–1, which has a two-storey medieval-style hall, and all the grandeur of an aristocratic mansion. Appropriately it is the headquarters of the FIDESZ (Federation of Young Democrats), many of whose remarkably young members come from some of the city's most privileged families.

The Lendvay utca, which runs parallel to the Andrássy út, ends up in Heroes' Square, a monumental space of a kind that could have been dreamt up by an extreme totalitarian regime. As the centrepiece of the millennial celebrations of 1896, it would not have been nearly so severe as it appears today, the central area having been originally landscaped with trees and bushes and only covered in massive paving stones in 1938 in preparation for the 34th International Eucharist Congress. It has been used for most of the grand ceremonial occasions in the history of twentieth-century Hungary, from the burial of Munkácsy in 1900 to the reburial of Imre Nagy in 1989; and, in its paved state, it has served as the perfect stage for displays of tyranny and power. The central millennial monument, with its colonnade of sculpted kings by György Zala, and 36-m. column with the Archangel Gabriel, has adapted itself well to being draped both with swastikas and hammers and sickle; and, indeed, it must once have seemed an ideal companion to the huge statue of Stalin that stood on the north-western edge of the square.

The square's great paved expanse is today much appreciated by skate-boarders, who remind the visitor that this space is not just a repository of symbolism but is also the gateway to a part of the city largely given over to pleasure and the arts. The neo-classical temples that flank the square might have a fearsome, Speer-like look, but in fact they are art galleries, the smaller of the two (the Palace of Art or Műcsarnok) being a venue for temporary exhibitions, and the other being the home to Hungary's largest collection of foreign-school paintings. The latter institution, the **Museum of Fine Arts**, does not quite live up to the expectations raised by its enormous size. This is a museum with all the gloomy, marbled inhospitality of Vienna's Kunsthistorisches Museum, but without the latter's extraordinary succession of masterpieces; the conditions of display are admittedly improving in the course of the extensive restoration campaign that the building is now undergoing. The nucleus of the collection is a large group of works acquired from the Esterházys in 1870, and featuring especially rich concentrations of Italian and Spanish paintings. Raphael's 'Esterházy Madonna'—a delicate and luminous early work—crowns the holdings of Italian Renaissance art, which also include portraits by Raphael, Giovanni Bellini, Giorgione, Titian, and Veronese, a *Madonna and Child* by Crivelli and one by Correggio, and a version of Bronzino's erotic allegory *Venus, Cupid, and Jealousy*; the two Raphaels gained particular publicity in the early 1980s after being stolen with laughable ease by an Italian gang (the works later reappeared in a Greek monastery). The eighteenth-century Venetian school is also well represented, notably by a large painting by G. B. Tiepolo of *St James Conquering the Moors*—one of this artist's most stirring and eloquent religious pieces.

But in terms of sheer number of works the museum's greatest claim to fame are its Spanish paintings, one of the largest such groups to be seen outside of Spain. Most of these were brought together by Count Pál Esterházy after 1819, at a time when Spanish art as a whole was remarkably little known; his interest was initiated with the purchase of forty canvases from the former Danish ambassador to Madrid, Edmund Bourke. Especially impressive is the scope of this Spanish collection, which has examples of Spanish art from the late Middle Ages up to the early nineteenth century, and includes works by nearly all the famous Spanish artists, from El Greco to Goya. However, the quality of these paintings is very variable, with even the one work by Velázquez (a genre scene from his Seville period) having been probably executed partly by an assistant. In many ways the most exciting of the Spanish works are the Goyas, in particular his intimately observed portrait of the wife of the art historian Céan Bermúdez, and his two powerful genre portraits, *The Knife-Grinder* and *The Water-Carrier*.

Among the later holdings are a number of French nineteenth-century paintings, the most important of which is an enormous canvas by Courbet of *Wrestlers*—a work of intentionally provocative realism; also well known is Manet's portrait of his mistress, who looks here like a dis-carded and disgruntled doll. In addition the museum has an extensive print collection, and a small group of Egyptian, Greek, and Roman an-tiquities. Revealingly, the most popular part of the building today ap-pears to be the basement cafeteria and gift shop.

After leaving the Fine Arts Museum, a great range of pleasurable options await you in the **City Park** or Városliget, which has its origins in a marshy expanse that was slowly reclaimed and turned into parkland from the time of Maria Theresa. In the late nineteenth century, when the park was given its present English-style layout, the importance of the place was increased enormously not only thanks to its being chosen as the grounds for the millennial celebrations but also because of the dis-covery here some twenty years before of important mineral springs. Many of its attractions are to be found on the winding Állatkerti körút, which runs from the side of the Fine Arts Museum all around the north-ern half of the park. Immediately behind the museum is the former Wampetics restaurant, which was founded in the 1870s, when it was linked to the city by omnibus; famous politicians, writers, and artists gathered here long before the establishment was taken over by **Károly Gundel**, who turned it after 1910 into an internationally renowned centre of gastronomy—a reputation which the current owner, George

Lang, has successfully revived (see pp. 45 ff.). The sounds of fellow eaters both here and in the neighbouring, Transylvanian-style **Bagolyvár** are occasionally interrupted by the assorted noises coming from the **zoo** behind. More interesting for its architecture than for its animals, this zoo was laid out between 1908 and 1909 by Károly Kós and his architectural school friend Dezső Zrumeczky, both of whom devised extraordinary animal houses in which architectural elements from the exotic countries appropriate to the particular animals were linked with traditional Hungarian ones. Sadly, most of Kós's and Zrumeczky's own buildings were later pulled down, the main surviving one being the Transylvanian-style Bird House. However, there remain the Eiffel-designed Palm-Tree House, and Kornél Neuschlosz-Knüsli's extraordinary neo-Moorish Elephant House, which is decorated with giant elephant heads made from Zsolnay ceramics. Another relic from the turn-of-the-century zoo is Neuschlosz-Knüsli's entertaining entrance-gate, where elephants are employed once again, this time to support an enormous Gothic arch crowned by a ring of aggressive polar bears.

Continuing to walk around the Állatkerti körút you will pass to your left first a permanent circus dating back to 1891 and then a ramshackle old fairground, with a number of pre-First World War attractions including a recently restored neo-rococo carousel with carriages bearing trumpeting angels. The festive atmosphere extends across the road to the neo-baroque Széchenyi baths, which feature Budapest's most enjoyable and impressive open-air pools. To the south of here are the Városliget metro station, and the Kós Károly sétány, which divides the park into two, and crosses—immediately after leaving Heroes' Square—the large lake that provides the park with its main focal point. The skating pavilion on the lake's western side replaced an earlier structure by Ödön Lechner, who considered it 'for all its modest size one of my best achievements'. Rising above the opposite shore, like a turn-of-the-century Disneyland, is the main legacy of the millennial exhibition—Ignác Alpár's historical assemblage known as the **Vajdahunyad Castle** after the fantastical fifteenth-century Transylvanian structure (built for Matthias Corvinus's father) that was copied for its lakeside façade. A statue of Alpár dressed as a medieval guild master stands on the drive leading up to this fairy-tale historical world, which includes copies of Hungarian towers from what is now Slovakia, a life-sized model of the thirteenth-century Benedictine chapel at Ják, and a wing reproducing the Esterházy palace at Fertőd—a magnificent baroque structure that makes a wholly inappropriate setting for the Museum of Agriculture that has been installed inside since the communist period. From here you can walk to the south-western corner of the park to visit the interesting **Museum of Transport**, the oldest part of which occupies the remodelled, station-like 'Transportation Hall' of the millennial exhibition: the narrow central hall is crammed with old trains, planes, boats, and other displays relating to the history of transport in Hungary and Budapest; there are also fragments from the original Chain Bridge.

If you still have the energy for serious sightseeing, you will find a number of major turn-of-the-century buildings off the western and southern sides of the park. The western edge is marked by the Hermina út, which runs behind the Museum of Transport and has, at No. 47, a striking art nouveau villa, picturesquely asymmetrical and oozing with undulant forms; this building, formerly the Sipeki-Balázs Villa and now an old people's home, was designed in 1905 by Ödön Lechner and his two followers Marcel Komor and Dezső Jakab. Unusually for a work by Lechner and his circle, this building's art nouveau style has nothing specifically Hungarian about it. In contrast, Hungarian folkloric motifs abound in the two masterly works by Béla Lajta to be seen in the quiet residential streets that lie on the other side of the busy Hungária körút, which you can cross by following the Erzsébet királyné útja. At No. 60 Mexikói út (take the first turning to the left once you have gone underneath the Hungária körút), is Béla Lajta's former Jewish Institute for the Blind (1905–8), which combines English and Finnish influences in the overall design with a main portal decorated with stylized biblical scenes and copper reliefs in Braille. A yet grander portal, with simplified animal and vegetal motifs, can be seen two streets further on, at Amerikai út 57—it forms part of Lajta's Jewish Hospital for the Poor, which was built in 1909–11 in a style featuring strong Transylvanian elements.

Returning to the Városliget, you should walk down the Ajtósi Dürer sor, which follows the southern side of the park, passing to begin with two impressive and adjoining Lechner-inspired buildings—a School for the Blind (at No. 39) and the former Erzsébet School for Ladies (at No. 37). Lechner himself produced the initial design for a villa further down the street (at No. 25) that was commissioned in 1895 as the home of György Zala, the sculptor of the Millennial Monument in Heroes' Square. This villa, much altered when finally erected in 1900 (by Bálint and Jámbor), attracts attention principally for its powerful, deeply carved relief of female nudes by Zala himself.

If you want to end your walk by seeing one of Lechner's finest and best-preserved buildings in Budapest, you should leave the Ajtósi Dürer sor and head in a south-easterly direction along the Stefánia út (which will eventually take you to the Népstadion metro stop, whence you can return easily to the centre of the city). A third of the way down this street, at No. 14, you will be confronted with the enormous **Geological Institute**, the commission for which was won by Lechner in a competition held in 1897. Cheekily, Lechner's winning design was much less lively and more conservative than the building that was actually erected—a pale ochre structure enlivened by brilliant blue Zsolnay ceramics culminating in a variegated, celestially coloured roof-line crowned by Atlas figures supporting a huge globe. The interior, which can be visited by asking permission from the porter, has kept much of Lechner's original decoration, notably on the staircase, which has patterned floors and flowing decorations in paint, stucco, and ceramics.

In addition to Lechner's architecture, this still-functioning institute (founded in 1869) is fascinating for its associations with the eccentric, Transylvanian-born palaeontologist Baron Ferenc Nopcsa, whose life and achievements are recalled in musty displays arranged in vitrines on the staircase landings. Nopcsa, who served as director of the institute from 1925 to 1928, made his name with important dinosaur findings made in Transylvania in the 1890s (one of which ended up in the central hall of London's Natural History Museum). In later life his attention was increasingly diverted by his obsession with Albania: he wore Albanian costume, built up one of the largest libraries ever assembled on this country, and became a leading contender for the Albanian throne. Not surprisingly, he eventually succumbed to insanity, killing himself in 1933 with the same gun he had used minutes earlier to kill one of the two Albanian male companions of his lonely last years.

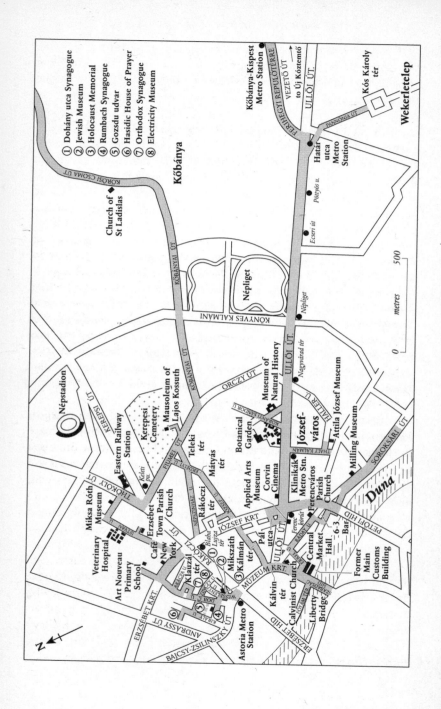

① Dohány utca Synagogue
② Jewish Museum
③ Holocaust Memorial
④ Rumbach Synagogue
⑤ Gozsdu udvar
⑥ Hasidic House of Prayer
⑦ Orthodox Synagogue
⑧ Electricity Museum

Kőbánya

KŐRÖSI CSOMA ÚT

Church of
St Ladislas

KŐBÁNYAI ÚT

Népliget

KÖNYVES KÁLMÁN

Népliget

KŐBÁNYAI ÚT

Kőbánya-Kispest
Metro Station

FERIHEGYI REPÜLŐTÉRRE
VEZETŐ ÚT
to Új Köztemő

ÜLLŐI ÚT

PANNÓNIA ÚT

Kós Károly
tér

Wekerletelep

Határ
utca
Metro
Station

Pöttyös u.

Ecseri út

500

metres

0

Népstadion

KEREPESI ÚT

THÖKÖLY ÚT

Eastern Railway
Station

Kerepesi
Cemetery

Mausoleum of
Lajos Kossuth

ORCZY ÚT

Museum of
Natural History

ÜLLŐI ÚT

Nagyvárad tér

HALLER U.

József-
város

Attila József Museum

SOROKSÁRI ÚT

Miksa Róth
Museum

Veterinary
Hospital

Art Nouveau
Primary
School

Café
New
York

Erzsébet
Town Parish
Church

ANDRÁSSY ÚT

ERZSÉBET KRT.

BAJCSY-ZSILINSZKY ÚT

Klauzál
tér

⑥

⑤

④

③

②

①

⑦

⑧

Mikszáth
Kálmán
tér

Blaha
Lujza
tér

Rákóczi
tér

Teleki
tér

Mátyás
tér

Applied Arts
Museum

Corvin
Cinema

Klinikák
Metro Stn.

Ferencváros
Parish
Church

Milling Museum

Central
Market
Hall

6-3
Bar

Former
Main
Customs
Building

Duna

Kálvin
tér

Calvinist Church

Liberty
Bridge

Astoria Metro
Station

ÜLLŐI ÚT

MÚZEUM KRT.

JÓZSEF KRT.

RÁKÓCZI ÚT

Pál
utca

Ferenc
körút

PETŐFI HÍD

ERZSÉBET HÍD

N

◈◈◈ Walk 6 ◈◈◈

From Jewish Pest to Industrial Pest

The Seventh, Eighth, and Ninth Districts,
and Beyond

WHEREAS the Lipótváros and the Terézváros are expressive of the commercial and civic greatness of turn-of-the-century Budapest, the remaining districts named after the Habsburgs featured on Pest's outer ring of
boulevards convey instead much of the city's dark, overcrowded, and
industrial reality. This is also a part of the metropolis in which you will
begin truly to appreciate the enormous contribution made by the Jews
to Budapest life, especially in the Erzsébetváros or Seventh District,
which has most of the city's surviving Jewish monuments, and has also
preserved—to an extent comparable to Prague's Old Town—the atmosphere of an old Jewish quarter.

A Jewish community, smaller than that of Buda, had been based in
Pest from at least the time of Béla IV right up to 1686, when Jewish life
in Hungary became concentrated in Óbuda and Pozsony (now Bratislava
in Slovakia). For much of the eighteenth century, fear of commercial and
industrial competition prevented the Jews from resettling in Pest,
where—in the words of a document of 1727—they were unable even to
stay after dark 'except when necessary, or if they are suddenly caught
out by the night, or if they have business at the imperial court'. This situation changed completely after 1783, when Joseph II issued his imperial edict of tolerance. Jews began settling outside the city's walls, on and
around what is now the Király utca, where they established a synagogue
as early as 1787. In the course of the nineteenth century, when the Jewish
community became widely dispersed throughout central Pest, considerable antagonism developed between the powerful and wealthy Jews
associated with Lipótváros and the humbler and generally artisan
Jewish community of the Erzsébetváros, where the city's main Jewish

183

institutions were situated. These tensions, which were reflected even in the discussions of the 'Sunday Circle', reached a head in the Second World War, amidst reports of Jewish betrayals and deals made with the Nazis.

The size of Budapest's Jewish community from the 1840s onwards will become apparent at the very start of this itinerary, when you leave the Astoria metro station and approach the massive twin-towered **synagogue** that rises to the north on the Dohány utca. The decision to create a large synagogue in which orthodox and reform tendencies would be combined was taken in 1845, but it was not until 1854 that work was actually begun. Leading architects were invited to submit designs, including József Hild, who planned a neo-classical structure, and Frigyes Feszl, who devised instead a neo-Byzantine one. The commission eventually went to the eclectic German architect Ludwig Förster, who had made his name in Vienna by designing the Ring, the main synagogue, and numerous public buildings. When completed in 1859, the Dohány utca synagogue was not only the largest synagogue in Europe, but also the second largest in the world. In addition it was 'among the finest specimens of architecture attempted by the Jews in modern times', according to the British traveller D. T. Ansted, who came to Pest in 1862. Its style, described by him as 'somewhat mosque-like and oriental', comprises a mixture of Byzantine and Moorish features, including bulbous domes on the towers, a basilica plan, and an interior replete with Alhambra-like detailing. The richness of the original structure has become fully revealed by the intense restoration programme begun after the Second World War, financed by Jewish organizations around the world, notably the foundation spearheaded by the film actor Tony Curtis, whose father was a Hungarian Jew called Kertész. The place seems set to become one of Budapest's greatest tourist attractions, to judge by the popularity of the adjoining **Hungarian Jewish Museum**, which has valuable liturgical items and much documentation relating to the history of Hungarian Jewry. Also commemorated here is Tivadar Herzl, 'the founder of Zionism', who was born in a house on this site and who was one of the Jews most opposed to the idea of Jewish assimilation into Hungarian life.

The Jewish quarter that extends behind the synagogue is still popularly called today the '**ghetto**', even though relatively few Jews still live here, and it only functioned as a ghetto for little more than a month during the Second World War. When the Germans occupied Budapest in April 1944, the authorities had decided at first to place the Jews in scattered, star-marked houses rather than concentrating them in a single area (which they thought would make the rest of the city more vulnerable still to Allied bombing). Not until early December of that year, with the taking of power by the Arrow Cross Party, were the city's remaining 70,000 Jews (mainly women, children, and the elderly) confined to a walled ghetto bordered by the Dohány utca, Király utca, and Kertész utca; by 18 January, when the ghetto was finally liberated, thousands had been killed by hunger, the cold, and marauding criminals. Behind the Jewish museum, on the side of the synagogue overlooking the Wesselényi utca, memorial stones mark the site of the common grave where many of the dead were buried. Beyond, past a small temple commemorating Jewish soldiers who died fighting for Hungary in the First World War, is a courtyard containing a **Holocaust memorial** created by Imre Varga in 1991. One of the more striking images by this most accessible of sculptors, the memorial features a broken marble slab inscribed with the word 'Remember', on top of which rises a silver weeping willow with leaves bearing the names of Jewish families massacred by the Nazis.

After taking the first turning to your left along the Wesselényi utca and then crossing the Dob utca, you will reach another magnificent **neo-oriental synagogue**, which, however, is still in the devastated condition in which it was left after the Second World War. Known commonly as the Rumbach, after the street on which it is situated, it was built in 1872 for those conservative Jews such as Herzl who were unhappy with the assimilationist tendencies of the time. An early work by the distinguished Viennese architect Otto Wagner (and his only building in Budapest), this lavishly ornamental 'neo-Moorish' structure can barely be imagined as being by the same man who pioneered modernism in Central Europe.

Turning now on to the Dob utca and heading north-east, you will find to your left (at No. 22) a friendly and evocatively decrepit survival of a Jewish café and bakery, the Fröhlich Cukrászda. Shortly before this (at No. 16), a portal marks the entrance to the extraordinary **Gozsdu udvar**—described by Péter Esterházy as 'one of the largest and most mysterious arcade buildings in Budapest', this is in fact a group of seven interconnected courtyards and apartment blocks extending all the way to the Király utca, and linked by a long covered passage-way large enough for cars to drive through. Emerging from the apartment block on the Dob utca into the first of the courtyards is like stumbling across a lost Jewish world that you can easily picture during its former days as a thriving labyrinth of workshops. The still lively Király utca, which had had a 70 per cent Jewish population at the turn of the century, leads north-east past the Vasvári Pál utca (to your left), where the small courtyard at No. 5 hides a **Hasidic house of prayer**. Before reaching the latter street, there opens to your right one of the more interesting and atmospherical streets of the Jewish quarter, the Kazinczy utca. On entering this street you will come at No. 41 to a narrow, cobbled courtyard containing a kosher butcher's, where excellent sausages can be bought. Further down, at the junction with the Dob utca, is the **Carmel Pince Etterem**, which puzzlingly promotes its 'non-kosher Jewish food': its particular speciality is its goose dishes—a great staple of Hungarian Jewish cooking. A true kosher experience awaits you in the courtyard of the **Orthodox synagogue**, the main entrance to which is at Nos. 29–31 Kazinczy utca. The synagogue itself, a Secessionist building of 1913 with elements of a Venetian palace, is closed to the public; but non-Jews are welcome into the Hannah kosher restaurant, where they often sit around with baffled expressions, observing the scene around them as if they were witnessing a sociological documentary. After buying your meal tickets from an understandably grumpy old woman (who has to put up with perpetual questioning from perplexed tourists), you wash your hands in the basin at the entrance to the long and simple dining-hall, where you will find yourself eating good (if expensive) food in the company of Budapest's orthodox Jewish community. This same community makes use also of the city's one remaining Mikvah or public ritual bath, which is situated almost directly in front of the synagogue, at No. 16 Kazinczy utca.

Alongside the synagogue, at Kazinczy utca 21, a distraction from Jewish Pest is provided by an electrical transforming station of the 1930s. Today the headquarters of the **Hungarian Electricity Board**, this houses a diffuse and virtually unadvertised museum dedicated to the history of the Hungarian electrical industry. Exuding an atmosphere reminiscent of that of Fritz Lang's film *Metropolis*, this is a fascinating and entertaining curiosity whose appeal is considerably enhanced by the charming, white-coated old man who leads you around the place, and supplies you with interesting information delivered in quaint broken English. The tour begins in the former director's office, with its original wooden furnishings; here you will be told about the life and work of the pioneering electrical engineer Ányos Jedlik, who began experimenting with electromagnetic induction in 1831 and who in 1858—six years before the German engineer Siemens—created the world's first electric dynamo. Your guide, who himself resembles an eccentric inventor, enjoys making explosions and flashes of lightning while demonstrating models of Jedlik's machines. Later in the tour, as he shows you a whole range of domestic electrical gadgets from the turn of the century onwards, he might even come out with the words 'At your service, Sir/Madam' as he activates a 1930s servant-calling system.

Returning to the Dob utca and turning right, you will reach the heart of the Jewish quarter—the Klauzál tér. This slightly decayed space, with its sparse central gardens, is fronted on its eastern side by a covered ironwork market: containing today a branch of an Austrian supermarket chain, it had been used at the end of the Second World War as a temporary storage place for Jewish corpses. The **Shalom Kosher Restaurant** at Klauzál tér 2 is a friendly, old-fashioned, and inexpensive establishment. But if you are looking for a wider choice of food you should continue walking for another block along the Dob utca and then turn right into the quiet Akácfa út, where you will find, at No. 38, the **Kispipa**: though much of the character of this popular and long-established restaurant has been lost in the course of recent refurbishments, it still offers one of the most extensive menus in Budapest.

Continuing along the Dob utca, you will leave the Jewish quarter (whose traditional eastern boundary is the Kertész utca) and come to the stretch of the Nagykörút named after the Empress Erzsébet. After crossing this major thoroughfare, you should stay on the Dob utca if you wish to see, at No. 85, a superb **art nouveau primary school** of 1905–6: this building, by Ármin Hegedűs, has a Lechner-inspired pale green and ochre façade that is adorned with a charming frieze of playing and studying children by Zsigmond Vajda; Hegedűs's extensive pedagogic researches informing his design of the interior included devising comfortable desks and chairs appropriate to the particular age group taught in each class.

Back on the Erzsébet körút, you are back once more in the bustling heart of metropolitan Budapest, whose ultimate symbol from the early years of this century is the **Café New York**, occupying the ground floor of the New York Palace—a grandiose eclectic structure built by Alajos Hauszmann in 1891–5 as the headquarters of an American insurance company. The building, which you will see to your left as you head south down the Erzsébet körút towards the Dohány utca, is recognizable from the outside not so much by its architecture (which is com-

pletely un-American) or even by its height, but by the wooden scaf-
folding that has been holding it up ever since a Soviet tank rammed it
in 1956. The extravagantly neo-baroque café, with its palatial fittings and
inevitable Károly Lotz frescoes, reputedly inspired, on its opening night
in 1894, a suitably imperial gesture on the part of the playwright Ferenc
Molnár, who threw its key into the Danube so that its doors should never
be closed. Open thereafter for twenty-four hours a day, and frequented
by all the many journalists in the area, the place soon became the leading
literary café in the city—a reputation that it maintained from about 1910
(when it was a popular meeting-place for the *Nyugat* Group) up into the
1930s. Closed for a period after the war, and then turned in 1954 into
the Hungária restaurant, the place miraculously maintained much of its
original interior, despite various design aberrations during the Communist period. Known once again as the Café New York, and covered with
photographs and drawings from its heyday, it caters today mainly for
foreigners affected by *fin-de-siècle* nostalgia.

Leaving the Erzsébet körút, and walking north-east along the Dohány
utca, you will emerge at the Rézsák tere, where Imre Steindl, of Parliament fame, created after 1895 one of the finer examples of neo-Gothic
ecclesiastical architecture in Hungary—the tall, slender-towered **Erzsébet Town Parish Church**. Crossing the Rottenbiller utca and continuing north-east on the Landler Jenő utca, you will skirt to your left the
mid-nineteenth-century Veterinary Hospital, one of the oldest such institutions in Europe (the oldest is in Vienna); its mustily old-fashioned grey-
green halls, in which the Habsburgs' horses were once treated, made a
suitably surrealistic setting for an operation I witnessed in 1996 on the
broken hip of an over-enthusiastic kangaroo. Turning right afterwards
into the Nefelejcs utca, you will come, at No. 26, to the early
nineteenth-century block where the prolific stained-glass and mosaic
artist **Miksa Róth** had his house and workshop. Róth inherited both
the place and his craft from his German-born father, who bought the
building in 1836; Róth, who was born in the house in 1865, continued
working and living here until his death in 1944, by which time he had
decorated an extraodinary cross-section of important Hungarian buildings, from the Parliament to the Basilica of St Stephen, from the
Széchenyi baths to the Dohány utca synagogue. An excellent new
museum has recently been installed in his well-restored living quarters,
which include an original gas-fired chandelier. Fragments of mosaics,
stained glass, and Tiffany glass are accompanied by drawings and studies,

as well as a portrait of him and his wife by his friend Zsigmond Vajda, the designer of the mosaics on the Dob utca Primary School.

The Nefelejcs utca comes out at its lower end in front of the chaotic and slightly seedy space embracing the late nineteenth-century **Eastern Railway Station**, where the British contribution to railway engineering is generously acknowledged in prominent statues to James Watt and George Stephenson. The station, with its interior of faded grandeur (epitomized in the barely visible traces of frescoes by Károly Lotz), overlooks a major intersection: the broad Rákóczi út heads off west towards the Astoria metro station and the Erzsébet Bridge, while the Fiumei út runs in a south-easterly direction past the **Kerepesi Cemetery**, where Lajos Kossuth, Ferenc Deák, Count Lajos Batthyány, and other major figures from Hungarian history lie buried in suitably grand mausoleums. The dilapidated part of town that lies between these two main streets forms the centre of the **Józsefváros** or Eighth District.

'The tourist who sets out to visit Budapest', wrote Giorgio and Nicola Pressburger in their autobiographical *Homage to the Eighth District* (1986),

could stumble upon the Eighth District only by mistake. Getting down at the East Station, he would have to meander along one of the narrowest and darkest ways, all cobbled with granite, which open off Rákóczi Avenue, to the left of those leading towards the city centre. There he will find no monuments, no famous sites, nor vivacious *quartiers* . . . This is no place to visit with a light heart, but with one full of suffering, of sadness, even of abjection.

Planned in the late nineteenth century as a spacious residential quarter, with large, green spaces, this district soon changed its character as a result of the enormous influx of gypsies, impoverished Jews, and countryfolk drawn both to the Eastern Station and to the bustling market on the **Teleki tér** (directly opposite the main entrance to the Kerepesi cemetery)—an important arrival and distribution point for provisions coming into the city. This square today, with its dirty confusion of stalls and kiosks, maintains its popularity with the Budapest underworld, who have infiltrated much of the area that extends between here and the József körút to the west. Ukrainians, Romanians, and Chinese shop-owners now live alongside the gypsies and remaining Jews; but the district remains outwardly much the same as the place remembered by the Pressburgers from the 1930s and 1940s—a place of cobbled granite streets, and grand peeling blocks divided up into tiny crowded apartments. Though there is nothing here of conventional tourist appeal, an interesting stroll into the past can be made by walking west from the Teleki tér, past the Mátyás tér and along the József utca towards the Rákóczi tér and the József körút. A certain decisiveness of step is required during the last stages of this walk, when you will pass right through the centre of what has become once again the favourite haunt of the city's prostitutes, many of whom now are from Romania and the former Yugoslavia. Gyula Krúdy, as much a lover of prostitutes as he was of food, was a regular visitor to this district, and his name has been given to what had originally been the western end of the József utca (beyond the József körút). Walking down this street you will enter the small and appealingly furtive **Mikszáth Kálmán tér**, once animated by the famous alternative nocturnal haunt of the early 1990s, the Tiloz Az Á. At the centre of the square is a bronze of the eponymous and corpulent Mikszáth, a late nineteenth-century novelist of rural themes who spent here the last years of his life, having obtained by then an international reputation so great that Theodore Roosevelt is said to have visited him in Hungary simply to express an admiration for his novel *St Peter's Umbrella* (1895).

Further west still you will emerge into the **Kálvin tér**, one of the major junctions of Pest's old town. Situated on the Kiskörút, and marking the site of a medieval gate that had been pulled down in 1796, this broad intersection made a surprisingly positive impression on the city-hating protagonist of Móricz's tale *The Caged Lion*: 'this was probably the first instance when one of the sights of Budapest struck him as beautiful,' wrote Móricz about a man who found Pest generally 'an unpleasantly over-sized city'. Deprived now of its central fountain by Ybl (now in the Erzsébet tér), and reduced to a busy traffic nucleus, this untidy space retains little of visual appeal apart from the neo-classical **Calvinist Church**, which was begun by József Hofrichter in 1816 and continued by József Hild, who embellished the severe main façade with a portico and tympanum; the domed and barrel-vaulted interior is notable for the monumentality of its proportions and the bold simplicity of Hild's organ loft and pulpit.

As you walk from the Kálvin tér down to the river (following the stretch of the Kiskörút known as the Vámház körút), you will skirt to your right the southern half of the Inner City, and pass (at No. 2) a supremely elegant Burger King installed in the ceramic-tiled premises of a former butcher's shop of the turn of the century. On the opposite side of the boulevard extends the Ninth District or **Ferencváros**—a once predominantly German district that was repeatedly destroyed by floods, culminating in one in 1838 that left only nineteen buildings standing. After being rebuilt, the district began slowly to lose its former reputation as a centre of the crafts industries, and came to be known instead as 'the stomach of Budapest', owing to the various mills, slaughterhouses, market halls, and canning and meat processing factories that were established here from the late nineteenth century onwards. Near the river end of the Vámház körút is the building that best epitomizes this district—the **Central Market Hall** of 1893–6. This superlative six-aisled structure in brick and ironwork, built originally as Budapest's main wholesale market, was the largest of the six covered halls erected in the city during the 1890s. Later given over to the retail trade (with the exception of the large flower gallery on the upstairs floor), the market soon became one of the city's liveliest and most colourful spectacles, ablaze with the vivid reds of its paprika stalls and bustling with countrywomen in long black skirts and multi-coloured headscarfs. For many years during the late communist era one of the stalls displayed a blown-up photograph recording the momentous moment in 1984 when Margaret Thatcher (then a great popular heroine in Hungary) visited the market and handed over a few forints in exchange for a paprika. Recent major restoration has thankfully rid the place of this embarrassing memento; but it has also deprived the market, at least for the time being, of most of its former rambling, folkloric, and exuberantly chaotic character: uniform rows of freshly painted stalls, run by smart small-time entrepreneurs, typify today's building.

In between the market and the river is the former main customs building, an enormous Palladian-style structure built by Miklós Ybl in 1870–6 and reconstructed after the Second World War to serve as the Budapest University of Economics. Displaying Ybl's neo-Renaissance style at its most austere, it has an ornamental restraint that contrasts with the richness of the **Liberty Bridge** beyond. This ironwork suspension bridge, popular with suicide victims, and crowned with gilded orbs supporting the mythical 'Turul' birds, was opened in 1896 by the Emperor Franz Josef, who left here a silver rivet inscribed with his initials (the original rivet, which the emperor hammered in by activating a mechanical tool, was replaced after the bridge's destruction in the Second World War by a non-silver one that is now displayed under glass). Looking north from the bridge, you can see the fifth-floor flat at No. 2 Belgrad rakpart where the marxist philosopher György Lukács spent the last years of his long life, faithful to the end to his socialist ideals, despite all that he and Hungary had suffered during the Stalinist years and their aftermath. His flat, now a library and research archive belonging to the philosophy department of the Hungarian Academy of Sciences, is described in Claudio Magris's *Danube* as the background to one of the last photographs of the philosopher who, aged 86 and suffering from cancer and sclerosis, is shown sitting in front of the 'huge library of his home', holding his 'famous cigar'—'a cigar that makes a fit companion and comforter to a long lifetime spent as a protagonist in the major events of our century'.

Turning back now towards the Kálvin tér, and entering the dark streets that run south of the Vámház körút, you will find yourself in a newly fashionable area of nocturnal bars. At No. 5 Ráday utca, which begins in the south-western corner of the Kálvin tér, is the Berliner, a lugubrious beer-hall with a large cellar that could be the setting of some chamber of horrors; its stylistic opposite is the Paris, Texas (at No. 22 Ráday utca), whose tasteful main bar, with its quiet background music and period photographs of Piaf and her like, is more Paris, France than its Texan namesake. A much older establishment than either of these bars is the **Voros Postakocsiház** restaurant (at No. 15), which is named after Krúdy's most famous novel but serves food that would probably not have appealed to that great literary gastronome. Further down the street, at No. 28, you can move back into a more spiritual world by visiting the large Calvinist library and record office that has its origins in a collection of books and incunabula acquired in 1861 from Count Ráday: among the many treasures to be seen here are a religious painting by Lucas Cranach and a 1608 bible that once belonged to Prince György Rákóczi. Further still, at the junction with the Bakáts tér, is the Ferencváros Parish Church—an impressively tall, neo-romanesque structure designed by Miklós Ybl in 1865, and with paintings inside by Károly Lotz.

Before heading north from here to see the Ferencváros's major architectural and artistic attraction (Lechner's Applied Arts Museum), you might wish to make a detour south into the district's industrial heart. From the Ráday utca you should turn right to join the parallel Lónyay utca, where, at No. 62, is a refreshingly down-to-earth bar (dark and very smoky) that will be of great interest to football enthusiasts: known as the **6–3**, it commemorates one of Hungarian football's greatest moments when the national team, led by Ferenc Puskás (photographs of them all decorate the bar's walls), defeated England at Wembley in 1953. The Lónyay utca comes out at the major traffic junction of the Boráros tér, just to the south of which is the broad Soroksári utca, which runs south through an area of large warehouses and factories adjoining the Danube. At No. 24 is the **Concordia flour mill**, which dates back to 1868, and whose five floors are now taken up by old machines and other exhibits relating to the history of the milling industry; at Nos. 5–7 of the adjacent Máriássy utca is the beautiful and enormous Gizella flour mill, a late nineteenth-century complex that is still functioning.

The remaining attractions of the Ninth District are mainly to be seen on and around the exhaustingly long thoroughfare of the Üllői utca (which is connected to the Boráros tér by the Ferenc körút), beginning with the **Applied Arts Museum** at Nos. 33–7. The most oriental and controversial building by Lechner, as well as the structure in which all the hallmarks of his mature style were developed (in apparent recognition of this a seated statue of him has been placed in front of the main entrance), this was also the second museum of its kind in the world (the first being London's Victoria and Albert). The once multi-coloured neo-Mogul interior is taken up mainly by temporary displays, the single permanent one being devoted to the arts and crafts of the late nineteenth and early twentieth centuries.

On the Mária utca, directly facing the museum's façade, is the lively basement bar and jazz venue, Big Mambo, directly behind which runs the short **Pál utca**, made famous by Ferenc Molnar in his classic children's tale, *The Paul Street Boys* (1907); needless to say, the boys' threatened playground is no longer there. Back on the Üllői utca, and heading east, you will reach the street's junction with the Nagykörút or Great Boulevard, where there took place some of the fiercest fighting in the 1956 uprising. The insurgents established headquarters at the former Kilián Barracks (an 1845 building at Nos. 49–51 Üllői utca) and in the **Corvin cinema** opposite (in the Corvin köz), a 1920s structure combining a modern plan with neo-baroque ornamental features incorporating references to Matthias Corvinus (the place was turned in 1996 into a six-screen complex). Memories of *The Paul Street Boys* will return as you continue walking down what Molnár described as 'that interminable thoroughfare known as the Üllői út' and reach the University's Botanical Gardens (the entrance to this is on the Korányi Sándor utca), which the boys visit to spy out the activities of their vicious rival gang: 'The wind blew hard among the tender leaves and, in the darkness, the boys' hearts thumped furiously at the sight of the sprawling Botanical Gardens, with their mysterious bolted gates and weird whisperings.'

Standing in between the gardens and the verdant late eighteenth-century park known as the Orczy-kert is the newly housed **Museum of Natural History** (at Ludovika tér 3), the ultra-modern interior of which is hidden behind a neo-classical façade by the pioneering Mihály Polláck, who designed the building in 1834 as the riding-school for the Ludoviceum Military Academy. As a final and more appropriate farewell to the Ninth District, you should walk south of the Üllői út to the Gát utca to visit, at No. 3, the birthplace of the working-class poet **Attila József**. The grey, drab façade of this former slum block shields a pleasantly flower-decked courtyard with balconies and green-painted doors and window-frames. An old and charming woman will take you to the tiny ground-floor apartment (now a memorial museum) where the poet was born on 11 April 1905. A minute reconstructed kitchen, with stove and cloth-covered table with bowl and coffee-grinder, conveys the cramped conditions in which József's mother brought up her three children, who were soon to be orphaned. Their Romanian father, a worker in a soap factory, abandoned his family when Attila was very young, forcing the mother to eke out a gruelling existence as a washerwoman, which undoubtedly contributed to her early death from cancer.

To have a further glimpse of a Budapest that lies well beyond the tourist track, you should continue further down the Üllői utca to see the neighbouring districts of Kispest and Kőbánya. If you do this journey by metro (the nearest station to József's birthplace is Klinikák, on line 3), you should alight at the penultimate stop, Határ utca, which is at the edge of Kispest, in the Nineteenth District. Though this is an area largely of high-rise housing estates (one of which is even named after Attila József), you will also find, immediately to the south of the Határ utca station, one of continental Europe's pioneering garden suburbs, the Wekerle estate. This public housing project, begun in 1908 and largely completed by the outbreak of the First World War, is a wonderful expression of that period in Hungarian architecture dominated by the influence of Transylvanian folk traditions. The landscaped central square, with its medieval-style gateways, high-pitched roofs, and extensive use of wood, is named after the principal architect behind this movement, Károly Kós, who is also commemorated here by a modern statue; the building at Nos. 2–3 is by Kós himself, while that at Nos. 10–11 is by his faithful colleague and collaborator Dezső Zrumeczky.

From outside the last station on metro line 3, Kőbánya-Kispest, you can take a 68 bus to Budapest's largest cemetery, the Új **Köztemető**, where you could begin your tour by visiting the adjoining but entirely separate Jewish section (the bus will leave you right next to the Jewish cemetery's entrance, which is 700 m. to the north of the main entrance, along a rather rural-looking street lined with statuary workshops). The **Jewish cemetery**, off the Kozma utca, is evocatively overgrown and neglected, though not quite to the extent as described in Giorgio and Nicola Pressburger's *Homage to the Eighth District*, in which the narrator, visiting a relative's tomb for the first and last time, is attacked by a fox that had made the monument his lair. Timid visitors do not have to stray far from the entrance to see (just to the right of the main path) the marvellous art nouveau mausoleum built in 1903 for Sándor Schmidl and his family: designed by Ödön Lechner and Béla Lajta, and currently undergoing major restoration, this work is notable above all for its floral mosaics in deep blue, gold, and white.

Though American families of Jewish-Hungarian origin can regularly be seen making their way to the Jewish cemetery, foreign visitors are much less in evidence in the main part of the cemetery, the interest of which to the sightseer lies primarily in György Jovánovics' superlative **memorial to Imre Nagy** and the victims of 1956—surely one of Europe's most outstanding funerary monuments in modern times. Nagy and his fellow 'martyrs', together with others executed earlier under Mátyás Rákosi, were buried in unmarked graves in a remote northeastern corner of this vast cemetery, the intention being that their memories should be entirely erased from history. The now well-signposted 2-km. journey across the cemetery to reach lots 298–301 is integral to an understanding of Jovánovics' memorial, according to the art historian and publisher András Rényi, whose CD-ROM entitled *Plot 301* (Ikon Publishers, Budapest, 1995) includes a video of a drive by car through this wooded cemetery, the appearance of which becomes ever more rural as you approach the once abandoned graves.

Rényi drove me here himself on a brilliantly sunny July morning that gave to the whole experience the poignancy of some pastoral idyll. We got out of the car at lot 298, which is occupied by the Rákosi victims and has been turned into a traditional Hungarian country cemetery, complete with carved wooden grave-posts and a Transylvanian-style entrance-gate inscribed with the words, 'You may enter here only with your Hungarian soul'. Whereas most conservative nationalists would approve of lot 298, many are doubtless appalled by the nearby lot 301, Jovánovics's avant-garde *Monument to the Martyrs of the 1956 Revolution* (1989–92). This landscaped plot, laid out with paths of stone slabs, was explained to me as being a 'deconstructed' early Christian basilica. The 'dome'—a circle traced in the ground—has at its centre an open grave, in the middle of which rises a black hexagonal column exactly 1,956 mm. high. The geometrical and mathematical precision of this section of the plot is balanced by the more haphazard-looking white stone 'altar', which is topped by a rectangular 'monstrance' rising up at a slightly irregular angle. Rougher still is the ancient boulder (about 20 million years old) that the executed István Angyvál had requested as his tombstone, and which has been placed behind the altar, thus emphasizing the tension between nature—as represented by this dark, rough-hewn stone—and art, which is epitomized elsewhere in the monument either by a drapery-like smoothness in the handling of the surfaces or else by a machine-made precision. The overall result is a modernist anti-memorial, which is both a commentary on the nature of myth-making and a thoughtful, abstract riposte to the totalitarian tradition of bombastic glorification.

Those of you who have conscientiously followed this itinerary to this extreme corner of Budapest can now return to the city centre by treating yourselves to one of the city's longest tram-rides (about 35 minutes). Tram No. 28 will take you back to the Nagykörút (next to the Blaha Lujza tér), and allow you to enjoy on the way such industrial attractions as the giant Kőbányai brewery, with its turn-of-the-century mosaics bearing the crest of Matthias Corvinus. You will even have a reminder of the architectural greatness of the city as you catch a glimpse of the shining Zsolnay tiles and soaring idiosyncratic forms of Kőbánya's **Church of St Ladislas** (on the Szent Lászlo tér), which Ödön Lechner designed in 1892—Lechner's architectural boldness was such that the patrons who commissioned the work took fright half-way through its construction, and entrusted the design of the interior to a conventional neo-Gothic architect.

Further Reading

Travellers' Accounts, Memoirs, and Novels

The lack of good general books on Budapest is extraordinary for a city of its importance. One of the very few modern works in English is Franz Fühmann's *Twenty-two Days or Half a Lifetime* (translated from the German in 1992), a self-indulgent, disjointed, but at times beautifully poetical account of a writer's stay in Budapest at a critical stage of his life. The French publishers Autrement, in their series 'Monde', have brought out a volume entitled *Budapest: Danube Blues* (1988, edited by Anne Losonczy) that comprises a series of texts by leading Hungarian writers and historians; however, as the subtitle indicates, the emphasis is on the city's more melancholy aspects.

Among the early travellers' accounts featuring Buda and Pest are Edward Browne's *A Brief Account of some travels in Hungaria, etc.* (1673), Lady Mary Wortley Montagu's *The Turkish Embassy Letters* (1716; republished in Virago paperback, 1994), Robert Townson's *Travels in Hungary, in the year 1793* (1797), Julia Pardoe's *The City of the Magyar* (1840), Arthur Patterson's *The Magyars, Their Country and Constitution* (1869), W. P. Byrne's *Pictures of Hungarian Life* (1869), and John Paget's *Hungary and Transylvania*. The most successful of the late nineteenth-century travel books on Hungary was Victor Tissot's *Voyage au Pays des Tziganes* (1880), which was translated into English as *Unknown Hungary* (1881); Paul Tabori, in his lively *The Real Hungary* (1939), wrote of this rather fantastical French book that 'it went into many editions and its scurrilous statements clung for a long time to Hungary and her people'. Other late nineteenth- and early twentieth-century accounts include Louis Felbermann's *Hungary and Its People* (1892), H. Ellen Browning's *A Girl's Wanderings in Hungary* (1896), and W. B. Forster Bovill's *Hungary and the Hungarians*. Especially entertaining, if no less far-fetched than Tissot's book, is Walter Starkie's *Raggle Taggle: Adventures with a Fiddle in Hungary and Transylvania* (1933), which paved the way for the gushing neo-romanticism of Patrick Leigh Fermor's *Between the Woods and the Water* (1986), a memoir of a journey by foot undertaken in 1933. A more recognizable Budapest is portrayed in Anthony Bailey's *Along the Edge of the Forest: An Iron Curtain Journey* (1983) and Stephen Brook's *The Double*

Eagle: Vienna, Budapest, Prague (1988). For sheer intellectual brilliance and stylistic panache, you have to turn to Claudio Magris's *Danube: A Sentimental Journey from the Source to the Black Sea* (English translation, 1989).

Hungarian memoirs featuring long descriptions of Budapest include Arthur Koestler's *Arrow in the Blue* (1952) and George Mikes's *How to be Seventy* (1982). More poetic are the evocations of Buda contained in the essays and fiction of Gyula Krúdy, such as the novel *The Crimson Coach* (1913; translated 1967) and the anthology of short stories entitled *Sunflower* (1918; translated 1997 with an excellent introduction by John Lukács). Among the other works of fiction set in this city are Cecile Tormay's *The Old House*, Deszö Kosztolányi's *Anna Édes* (1926; translated 1998), Ferenc Molnar's *The Paul Street Boys* (1907; translated 1927), István Örkény's *One-Minute Stories* (see the English anthology published by Corvina in 1996) and Tibor Fischer's *Under the Frog* (1992). Giorgio and Nicola Pressburger's *Homage to the Eighth District: Tales from Budapest* (1986; translated 1990) is essential and delightful reading for anyone interested in the Jewish life of old Pest. The simplicity of the Pressburgers' style contrasts with Péter Esterházy's semi-fictional *The Glance of Countess Hahn-Hahn (Down the Danube)* (1991, translated 1994), which is heavy going for the English reader but full of witty observations on the city.

Guidebooks

The most detailed cultural guide to Budapest is Bob Dent's *Blue Guide: Budapest* (1996), which is crammed with historical facts; though Dent's book is better on practical information than most other Blue Guides, it is not nearly so thorough in this respect as the lively and excellent *Time Out Guide to Budapest* (1996), which has the advantage of having been written by a team of authors. András Török, now a leading member of the Hungarian art establishment, is the dandyish, *bon viveur* author of *Budapest: A Critical Guide* (3rd revised edition, 1997), which is unsurpassed as an opinionated and often hilarious insider's view of the city; the new edition, more eccentric than ever, and even better than before in its gastronomic advice, is now published in Britain and the United States by the suitably idiosyncratic imprint Pallas Athene. The drawbacks of Török's book are the limited scope of the itineraries (Óbuda, for instance, is omitted entirely) and the bizarreness of the English translation.

Specialist architectural guides include Imre Makrovecz's and János

Gerle's outstanding *Turn-of-the-Century Architecture in Hungary* (1990), Támas K. Pinter's *Budapest Architectura 1900* (1987), Tamás K. Pinter's and Anna Kaiser's *The Churches of Budapest* (1993), and András Ferkei's *Buda építészete akét világháború között* (Budapest, 1995) (of interest for its photographs alone, which record every important building in Buda from the late nineteenth century up to the present day). The Budapest City Hall published in the early 1990s a series of slender and badly translated city guidebooks on themes ranging from *Springs and Fountains* to *Courtyards*.

History, Literature, Art, and Architecture

A good, readable history of Hungary from ancient times up to the last days of communism is provided by Peter F. Sugar *et al.* in *A History of Hungary*. Hungarian art and architecture is less well served by general histories, the most useful one in English being Antal Kampis's stodgily written and outdated *The History of Art in Hungary* (1966). For a lively brief introduction to Hungarian literature, see the one by George Cushing in *The Traveller's Literary Companion to Eastern and Central Europe* (edited by James Naughton, 1995); a far fuller account is Lóránt Czigány's stimulating *Oxford History of Hungarian Literature* (1984).

The history of the medieval period in Buda is covered in Martyn C. Rády's *Medieval Buda: A Study of Municipal Government and Jurisdiction in the Kingdom of Hungary* (1985). László Gerevich's dense *The Art of Buda and Pest in the Middle Ages* (Budapest, 1971) relates in barely comprehensible English the artistic and architectural history of the two townships from the eleventh century right up to the time of Matthias Corvinus. After a struggle with Gerevich's book, the overview of Hungarian culture given by Thomas DaCosta Kauffmann in *Court, Cloister and City: The Art and Culture of Central Europe, 1450–1800* (1995) comes as a pleasant relief. Better still, however, is J. Bialostocki's classic *The Art of the Renaissance in Eastern Europe* (1976). For a more detailed account of the art and culture of Matthias Corvinus's reign, see Jolan Balogh's 'Mattia Corvino ed il primo Rinascimento ungherese' in *Actes du XXII Congrès International d'Histoire de l'Art* (Budapest, 1969); Csába Csápodi's *Biblioteca Corviniana* (Budapest, 1969), and Rosza Feuer-Toth's *Art and Humanism in Hungary in the Age of Matthias Corvinus* (1990).

Some of the best books on Budapest are those chronicling the emergence of the nineteenth-century metropolis, notably John Lukács'

Budapest 1900: A Historical Portrait of a City and Its Culture (1988), which, though criticized by some academics for its unevenness, is a compelling read mustering a wide range of fascinating information. Of more specialist interest, and descending occasionally into abstruse academic jargon, are the two generally stimulating collections of essays comparing Budapest respectively with New York and Vienna—*Budapest and New York: Studies in Metropolitan Transformation, 1870–1930* (1994; edited by Thomas Bender and Carl E. Schorske) and *Vienne-Budapest, 1867–1918: Deux âges d'or, deux visions, un empire* (1996; edited by Dieter Hornig and Endre Kiss). Another commendable group of essays and texts is in the Italian exhibition catalogue, *Budapest 1890–1919, l'anima e le forme.* Mary Gluck's *Georg Lukács and His Generation, 1900–1918* (1985) elaborates further on intellectual life in early twentieth-century Budapest, as does the short but brilliantly argued essay by Mihály Szegedy-Maszák, 'Conservatism, Modernity and Populism in Hungarian Culture' in *Hungarian Studies,* 9/1–2 (1994).

Ferenc Kollin's *Greetings from Old Budapest* (1988) brings together a series of old postcards of the turn-of-the-century city, the look of which is further illustrated in *Budapest Anno . . .* (1984), consisting mainly of the works of the outstanding court photographer György Klosz. There are numerous glossily illustrated but poorly written and largely uninformative books on the art and architecture of this period, including Judit Szabadi's *Art Nouveau in Hungary: Painting, Sculpture and the Graphic Arts* (1989) and *A Golden Age: Art and Society in Hungary, 1896–1914* (1990, edited by Gyöngyi Éri and Zsuzsa Jobbágyi). Much better than either of these is the exhibition catalogue entitled *Standing in the Tempest: Painters of the Hungarian Avant-Garde, 1908–1930* (1991; edited by S. A. Mansbach), which successfully places the artists in their social and historical context. For a wider introduction to twentieth-century Hungarian art, the reader will have to make do with Lájos Németh's tedious and old-fashioned *Modern Art in Hungary* (1969), which is written from the ideological standpoint of the communist era. A completely different type of publication—short, well-illustrated, and entertaining—is Gyúla Ernyey's *Made in Hungary: The Best of 150 Years in Industrial Design* (1993), which chronicles such Hungarian inventions as the Biro and Rubik's Cube.

The history of Hungary in the 1940s and 1950s is vividly brought to life in the various memoirs described in Chapter 5; for an academic study of the 1956 uprising, see Bill Lomax, *Hungary 1956.* Two good eyewitness accounts of the collapse of Communism in Hungary are featured in Mark Frankland's *The Patriots' Revolution: How East Europe Won its Freedom* (1990) and Timothy Garton Ash's *We the People: The Revolution of 1989 Witnessed in Warsaw, Budapest, Berlin and Prague* (1990).

Spas and Gastronomy

For the history of Hungarian spas, see Mária Vida's *Spas in Hungary in Ancient Times and Today* (1992) and Andor Medriczky's far more readable *Ancient Baths of Budapest* (1943), which, despite its misleading title, relates the development of the city's spas right up to the early twentieth century.

A good short introduction to the history of Hungarian food, together with selected recipes, is to be found in Lesley Chamberlain's *The Food and Cooking of Eastern Europe*; but those with a deeper interest in the subject should purchase the scholarly and entertaining *The Cuisine of Hungary* by George Lang, who also wrote (with Zoltán Halász) *Gundel: 1894–1994* (1994), a lively history of the celebrated restaurant of that name (of which he is now the owner). Halász's other publications include *The 100 Most Famous Hungarian Recipes* (Budapest, 1991) and the well-produced and thoroughly researched *Book of Hungarian Wines*, which includes an excellent historical chapter on taverns and inns. Károly Gundel's own recipes are featured in the regularly reprinted *Gundel's Hungarian Cookbook*.

Turn-of-the-century nostalgia is catered for in *Restaurants of Days Gone By* (1995), a light-hearted picture-book that makes extensive use of contemporary quotations to record the history not only of Budapest's old restaurants but also of the city's old bars, cafés, confectioners, and hotels.

Index

INDEX

Esztergom (*cont.*):
  Garamszentbenedek altar 11;
  Renaissance culture 21;
  Romanesque castle chapel 8
ethnic minorities/communities 59,
  66; *see also* settlers
Evliya Çelebi 21, 27, 40

Fadrusz, János 3, 77
Falk, Miksa 68
Faludy, György 90, 94–5
Far East 75, 152
fascism 89
Fascists 91, 93, 185
fast-food chains 51, 107, 135
Fehérvári Gate (former 'Jewish Gate')
  118
Felberman, Louis 67
Fellner, Sándor 162, 173–4
Ferenc Liszt Academy of Music
  172
Ferenczi, Sándor 69
Ferenczy, István 55–6
Ferenczy, Károly 79, 80
Ferrara 15, 16, 39
Fertőd 69, 179
Feszl, Frigyes 63, 64, 72, 73, 151,
  160, 184
Ficino, Marsilio 16–17
FIDESZ (Federation of Young
  Democrats) 107, 176
Filelfo, Francesco 13
Film Academy 101
Finland 74, 175
Fioravante (architect) 15
First World War 84, 90, 104, 194;
  Jews who died fighting for
  Hungary 185
Fischer, József 140, 145
fish 40, 42, 44, 127, 134
Fishermen's Guild 117
Florence 16, 17, 19; architects 15;

artists 13, 19; Brunelleschi's
  Duomo 71; San Apollonia
  church 13
Florentines 155
flour mills 193
folk-ballads 61
folklore 70, 72, 73, 75, 76, 141, 174;
  building revealing of Hungarian
  attitudes to 161; stylized motifs
  175; ultimate symbol of 163;
  upholders of 162
food 24, 37–52, 187; bad 156;
  expensively priced 153; kosher
  186; non-kosher 186; reasonably
  priced 143; shortages 90; *see also*
  restaurants
football 104, 192
foreign investment 65
Forestry Commission headquarters
  142
Förster, Ludwig 184
Förster (Viennese architect) 74
Fort Knox 17
France 23, 62, 130; *cuisine* 38, 42;
  Gothic churches 6; Kossuth's exile
  in 60; *see also* Barbizon;
  Burgundy; Paris; Vaucluse
Franciscans 115, 130, 155–6
Frank, Káto 37
Franz Joseph I, emperor of Austria
  and king of Hungary 59, 68, 69,
  100; coronation 43, 115; Liberty
  Bridge opened by 191; Opera
  House largely funded by 168;
  public memorials paid for by 76,
  139
freedom 59; restricted 90
frescos: (Lotz) Academy of Fine
  Arts 174; Café New York 188;
  Divatcsarnok department store
  171; Eastern Railway Station 189;
  Franciscan Church, Pest 156;

Helmer (theatre designer) 162
Herczeg, Ferenc 144
Heroes' Square (Pest) 97, 174, 179;
  blatant symbolism 69; central
  millennial monument 176–7, 180;
  Munkácsy's funeral 78; neo-
  classical temples 177
Herzl, Tivadar 184, 185
Hild, József 31, 132, 152, 164, 184,
  190
'Hindu style' 73, 74
Hofrichter, József 190
Hollósy, Simon 79–80
Holocaust memorial 185
Homer 61
homosexuality 104; gay meeting-
  places 35
Hopp, Ferenc 175
Horn, Gyula 107
Horthy de Nagybánya, Miklós,
  regent of Hungary 84, 85–6, 90,
  91, 95, 140, 173
Hortobágy 38
Horváth, István 55
hospitals 26, 54, 155, 180; mental
  60; veterinary 188
hotels: Angol Királynő 43; Atrium
  Hyatt 151; Bokros 169; Bristol
  151; Forum 151; Gellért Spa 33,
  46, 140; Hilton 7, 114, 117;
  Hungaria Grand 151; István
  Főherceg Szálloda 44; Kempinski
  158; Marriot (formerly
  Intercontinental) 151; Palatinus
  90; Queen of England 151
housing: public 194; shortage 104
Hugo, Victor 60, 63
humanism/humanists, see
  Bandini; Bonfini; Buonaccorsi;
  Filelfo; Loschi; Marzio;
  Thuróczi; Traversari; Vergeiro;
  Vitéz

humour 87–8, 102; surreal 101
Hungarian Academy of Sciences
  159–60, 192
Hungarian Dance Academy 73
Hungarian Democratic Forum 106
Hungarian Electricity Board 186
Hungarian Liberal Party 64
Hungarian National Bank 162, 163
Hungarian National Gallery 11, 55,
  63, 77, 79; largest and most
  interesting art collection in
  Hungary 123
Hungarian National Library 9, 122
Hungarian Parliament building 80,
  96, 97, 160–1, 188; dramatic vista
  across Danube to 128; Feszl's
  competition-winning design 64;
  Gothic detailing 71
Hungarian Radio headquarters 96,
  97
Hungarian Revolution (1848–9) 57,
  59, 60, 62, 73; Jews' enthusiastic
  support of Kossuth 67; 'poet of'
  84
Hungarian Socialist Party 98, 106
Hungarian State Railway Pension
  House 73, 169, 174
Hungarian Theatre 67
Huns 5, 14
Hunyadi, János 12, 14, 18
Hunyadi, László 18
Hunyadi, Mátyás, see Matthias
  Corvinus
Hus, Jan 10
Hus, Saloun 77
Huszadik Század (journal) 81–2
Huszka, József 73

identity 54, 72, 75, 103
illuminated manuscripts 9, 19–20,
  23
Illyés, Gyula 86, 131–2

Impressionism, *see* Cézanne; Monet
independence 60, 61, 71; *see also* War
  of Independence
India 73, 74, 75
industrial development 65, 84
industrialists: Jewish 67; short-term
  interests 64
industrialization 3, 5, 88
industries 65, 129; textile and
  milling 68
Ingres, Jean A. D. 24
Inner City, *see* Pest (Belváros)
inns 37, 38, 40, 150; Kéhli 41, 135;
  Red Hedgehog 117; White Horse
  127–8
intellectuals 53, 55, 82, 95, 134; anti-
  fascist 90; communist 94;
  dissident 104; Jewish 68; main
  focus of interest 105
International Congress of Balneology
  (1937) 33
International Eucharist Congress
  (1938) 177
Isabella, queen of Castile 27
Islam 9, 24, 27, 41
Italy 19, 23, 40, 55, 64, 72, 136;
  cultural relations with 12, 16;
  emulation of Hungary 18;
  intellectual relations with 12;
  palazzi 9; Renaissance 71, 144,
  174, 177; *see also* Bologna;
  Constance; Ferrara; Florence;
  Lombardy; Milan; Naples; Rome;
  Turin; Tuscany; Urbino; Vatican;
  Venice
Iványi-Grünwald, Béla 176
Izsó, Miklós 150

Jacobins 55
Jakab, Dezsõ 180
Ják, Benedictine chapel 179
Jámbor, Lajos 176, 180

Jancsó, Miklós 101
Jankovits (sculptor) 139
János, Master (stonemason) 10
Jeanneret, *see* Le Corbusier
Jedlik, Ányos 186–7
Jerusalem 119
Jesuits 115, 117
Jews 85, 86, 92, 145; 'anti-semitic'
  91; bankers, doctors, intellectuals,
  journalists, lawyers 68; enormous
  contribution to Budapest life
  183; Hospital for the Poor 180;
  Institute for the Blind 75, 180;
  reports of betrayals and deals with
  Nazis 184; restricted freedom 90;
  tolerance towards 118, 183; *see also*
  Buda; Óbuda; Pest; synagogues
Jókai, Mór 60–1, 81, 142, 144, 157
Jónás, Dávid 154
Jónás, Zsigmond 154
Joseph II, Holy Roman Emperor 183
Joseph, Archduke of Austria and
  palatine of Hungary 56, 121, 130,
  133
journalists 82, 83, 85, 87–8, 90;
  Jewish 68
Jovánovics, György 108, 195, 196
Joyce, James 103
József, Attila 88, 89, 98, 153, 157,
  194
'Judapest' 68

Kádár, János 52, 99, 100, 105, 131;
  outspoken critic of 132
Kalocsa 12
Kann, Gyula Kosztolányi 140
Karinthy, Ferenc 48
Karinthy, Frigyes 87–8
Karlsbad 30
Károlyi, Mihály, Count 84, 85;
  mansion 156–7
Kassa/Košice 17

Marxism/Marxists 82, 88, 100, 141, 191

Marzio, Galeotti 39

Masaccio (Tomasso de Giovanni di Simone Guidi) 13

Masolino da Panicale 13

massage 26, 31, 35

Master M. S. (artist) 21, 123

Matthias I Corvinus, king of Hungary 3–23 *passim*, 26, 39, 56, 69, 71, 108, 116, 123; architectural remains associated with 144; marriages 115; mosiacs bearing the crest of 196; neo-baroque features incorporating references to 193; *Prefektus* title 118; stained-glass scenes from the life of 150; statue at Kolozsvár 3, 77; Transylvania's associations with 61

'Matthias Calvary' 10–11

Matthias Church (Church of Our Lady) 6, 68, 92–3, 115–17, 176; Fishermen's Bastion 116, 143

Mayakovsky, V. V. 85, 107

Mayerhoffer, András 176

Medgyaszay, István 75, 76, 141

Medici, Lorenzo de' 18

medieval architecture 10, 149, 194; churches 116, 117; palaces 8, 71; politics and 106; prominent historian of 141; townships 4

Mediterranean 10, 80

Meggyesi, Miklós 9

Mendel family 118

Menuhin, Sir Yehudi 174

Merse, Szinyei 79, 123

Mészáros, Márta 101

Mezei, Gábor 142

Mező, Imre 99

Michelozzi, Michelozzo di Bartolommeo 15

Middle Ages 7, 120, 127; Buda's reputation in 139; Spanish art 177; thermal bathing 25, 26

middle classes 41, 86, 143

Middle East 27, 40

Mikes, George 87

Mikszáth, Kálmán 45, 107, 190

Mikvah (public ritual bath) 186

Milan 15

millennial celebrations (1896) 12, 45, 69, 79, 179; central monument 176–7; jingoism 70, 167

Milton, John 62

mineral springs/water 31, 34

Mineu 23

minorities 106

Miró, Joan 121

Miskolc 15, 121

mistresses 48, 178

modernism/modernity: architecture 145, 154, 162, 185; art 72; literary 81, 82

Mohács 20, 60

Mohammed Pasha, first Pasha of Buda 27

Moholy-Nagy, László 85, 136

Molnár, Farkas 145

Molnár, Ferenc 47, 81, 188, 193

Molnár, Pál C. 141

monasteries 122; Dervish 21; Dominican 114, 117; Franciscan 156; Trinitarian 133

Monet, Claude 72

Mongol invasion (1241–2) 3, 4, 6, 39, 113, 129

Montagu, Lady Mary Wortley 21–2, 124

Monte Carlo 42

moral censure 25

Moravia 54

Móricz, Zsigmond 82, 83, 86, 190

mosques 4, 21, 28, 115, 156

Mozgó Világ (journal) 104, 105, 106, 108
Munich 78, 79, 80
Munkácsy, Mihály 44, 77–8, 123, 161, 177
museums 115, 131, 141, 157, 188–9; Applied Arts 74, 175, 192, 193; Aquincum 136; Buda Castle 15, 18, 124, 144; Capital Sewerage Works 66, 132; Ethnographic 136, 161; Ferenc Hopp, East Asian 175; Ferenc Liszt (and Memorial Building) 173; Fine Arts 15, 16, 69, 123, 177–8; Foundry 66, 129, 132–3; György Ráth 175; History 7–8, 63; 'house' 76, 85; Hungarian Catering and Commerce 120, 121, 173; Hungarian Electrotechnical 119; Imre Varga 136; Jewish 119, 184, 185; Kiscelli 133; Kunsthistorisches (Vienna) 77, 177; Literary 58; Literature (Petőfi) 156; Ludwig 124; medical 124–5; 'memorial' 75, 173; Military History 120; Milling Industry 65; Miskolc 15; Mór Jókai Memorial 142; music history 117–18; National 56–7, 58, 96, 105, 116, 155, 157; Natural History (London) 181; Natural History (Pest) 193; Óbuda 25; Postal 168; Roman Camp 135; Telephone 65, 120; Transport 160, 180; Victoria and Albert (London) 193; Wax 121
music 78, 154, 169; background 141; bar 107; continual and competing strains 117; folk 61, 76, 145; gypsy 41, 47, 50, 51, 143; history museum 118; jazz 52, 193; loud 53, 171; pop(ular) 41, 120; *see also* Academy of Music; Ference Liszt

Academy
musicians 70, 156; buskers 152; busts of 130; peasant 76
Musil, Robert 64
Muslims, *see* Islam; Turks
Mustafa Sokolli 27

'Nabis' 171
Nádas, Péter 103
Nagy, Imre 95, 97, 98, 100; execution 99, 103; Jovánovics's memorial to 108, 195; reburial 105–6, 108, 177
Nagybánya/Baia Mare 78–80, 123; *see also* Horthy
Nagyvárad/Oradea 13, 83; Hungary's first humanist library 18; *see also* Scolari (Andrea); Vitéz
Naples 8, 9
Napoléon III, emperor of France 42
National Fine Arts Society 174
National Guard 98
National Institute of Rheumatism and Physiotherapy 132
National Peasants' Party 93
National Song 59
National Széchényi Library 123–4
nationalism 3, 55, 59, 61, 72, 134; attitudes towards 82; conservative 68, 196; extreme 106; musical 76; obsessive 70; romantic 57; Spanish 95
nationalization 50, 85
Nazis 91, 184, 185
Necksei, Demeter (Necksei Bible) 9
neo-classical architecture 64, 158; baths 31, 33; churches 117, 150, 190; monumental and virtually unornamented 56; museums 157; temples 177
Nepauer, Mátyás 117, 134
Netherlands 11

Pest (*cont.*):
96, 105, 116; Nefelejcs utca 188,
189; Népstadion metro stop
180–1; New York Palace 187;
Oktogon 85, 107, 172; Orczy-kert
194; Pál utca 193; Párisi udvar
154; Parisiana music-hall 169–70;
Paulay Ede utca 169; Petőfi tér
150, 151; Pozsony út 90; Ráday
utca 192; Rákóczi utca/út 49,
189; Red Metro Line link with
Buda 128; Rézsák tere 188;
Romanians 189, 194; Roosevelt
tér 159, 160; Rottenbiller utca
188; Rumbach utca 185; School
of Design 174; Soroskari utca
65, 193; Stefánia út, Geological
Institute 74, 180–1; Súgar út 167;
Szabadság tér 162; Széna tér 99;
Szénássy and Barczai department
store 154; Szent Lászlo tér 196;
Szervita tér 154, 155; Sztálin út
(now Andrássy út) 167; Teleki tér
189, 190; Terézváros 167, 183;
Thonet House 153; Three Ravens
tavern 83, 169; Turkish Bank 154;
Új Köztemetõ cemetery 99, 105,
108, 195; Új Színház 169–70;
Ukrainians 189; Üllõi út 99,
193, 194; Unger House 63–4;
unification with Buda 33, 54;
urban changes 44; Úri utca 65;
Váci utca 153, 154; Vajdahunyad
Castle (copy) 179; Vámház körút
190, 191, 192; Városház utca
155; Városligeti fasor 75, 174–5;
Városmajor utca 155; Vasvári
Pál utca 186; Vécsey utca 162;
Veres Pálné utca 156; Veterinary
Hospital 188; Vigadó tér/utca
151, 152; Vörösmarty tér 43, 152,
153, 168, 173; Wekerle estate 194;
Wesselényi utca 185; Western
Station 107, 172; Winter Garden
151; Zrínyi utca 56, 159; *see also*
Andrássy út; bridges; cafés;
churches; Deák tér; Heroes'
Square; hotels; Lipótváros;
museums; restaurants; Turkish
baths; Városliget
Pest Courier 170
Pester Lloyd 67, 68
Péterffy, Baron János 150
Petőfi, Sándor 59–60, 62, 83, 105,
133, 158, 161; Café Pilvax
association 58, 154, 155, 157
Petőfi Writers' Circle 95
Petschacher, Gusztáv 174
Piaf, Edith 192
Picasso, Pablo 124
picnickers 143
Pilvax, Károly 155
Pippo Spano, *see* Scolari (Filippo)
'Plague Column' of the Holy Trinity
115
Plato 16–17
Pliny 17
poetry/poets 160; avante-garde 135;
love/romantic 83, 158; lyrical 88;
populist 131; socialist 82;
symbolist 87; *see also* Arany;
Babits; Baudelaire; Fühmann;
Illyés; József; Kosztolányi; Petőfi
Poggio Bracciolini, Giovanni
Francesco 13
Poland 8, 9, 11, 90; Jagiello dynasty
14; reform policies 96; royal court
10
police 95, 96; *see also* AVO
Politburo 96, 105
politics 70, 93, 94; democratic
elections 106; heated discussions
157; prospect of change 105;
radical 83, 99

restaurants (*cont.*):
Postakocsiház 192; Wampetics
178; see also *kisvendéglõs*
Richter, Hans 169
Richter, Leonard 121
Rimanóczy, Gyula 145
Rippl-Rónai, József 47, 78, 171, 176
Ritz, César 45
Római Strandfürdõ 137
Romania 85, 99, 107; Hungarians in
3; *see also* Lippa/Lipova;
Nagybánya/Baia Mare;
Nagyvárad/ Oradea;
Segesvár/Sighişoara;
Temesvár/Timişoara
Romanians 66, 146, 189, 194
Romans 25, 133, 134; bathing
practices/baths 27, 137; ruins 127;
settlements 4–5
romanticism 57, 61, 63
Rome 14–15, 62, 80, 173
Roosevelt, Theodore 190
Róth, Miksa 154, 159, 175, 188–9
Rousseau, Henri ('le Douanier') 80
Royal Committee for Embellishment
56
Royal Palace (Buda) 7–12 *passim*, 16,
23, 121; architect 46; baroque
grandeur 71–2; first Jewish
quarter almost on threshold
of 118; Hungarian National
Gallery 123; main
approach/gateway 115, 122;
remodelling/reconstruction 17–18,
54, 122–3; Second World War
damage 21, 92, 122
Rózsavölgyi (music publisher) 154
Rudas Baths (Buda) 24, 27, 28, 31,
35–6
Rumbach, Sebastian 31
Russia 63, 90; Bolsheviks 85; *see also*
Alexander II; Soviet Union

Sacher, Edward 44, 45
St Imre Colony 86
St Margaret Island 5, 25, 31, 127,
129; Casino (social club) 43, 130;
Dominican convent 6; German
soldiers billeted at Hotel Palatinus
90; no one from Pest allowed on
130; Palatinus swimming-pool 33,
130; Premonstratensian chapel 6,
130; sanatorium hotel (rebuilt as
Ramada Grand) 130–1
St Petersburg 42
San Diego, California 94
sanatoria 130–1, 144
sanitary requirements 51
Santa Maria del Carmine (Brancacci
Chapel) 13
saunas 26, 35
sausages 38, 41, 44, 48
Saxlener, András 168
Scandinavia 74, 75
Schams, Francis 30
Schmahl, Henrik 154
Schmidl, Sándor 195
Schmidt, Maximilian 133
schnitzel 41, 44
schrammel 41
Schulek, Frigyes 116, 117, 143, 176
Schwabl, Franz 121
scientific inventions 65
Scolari, Andrea, bishop of Nagyvárad
12–13
Scolari, Filippo (Pippo Spano) 13, 14
Scotland 61; *see also* Clark; Szabados;
Watt
Secessionist movement 75, 142, 154,
186
Second World War 4, 7, 8, 50,
90–2, 145; caves and passages used
for defence 121; damage 21, 92,
116, 122, 150, 151, 155, 158, 164,